ART FOR ALL

ART FOR ALL

Art Appreciation as Related to Dress, Home, School, and Work

FRANCIS GRANT BARTLETT

Los Angeles Secondary Schools

and

CLAUDE C. CRAWFORD

University of Southern California

Edited by

RAY FAULKNER

Teachers College, Columbia University

New York   *London*

HARPER & BROTHERS PUBLISHERS

Drawings by
OSCAR OGG

Contents

~~~~~~

Preface   xi

Acknowledgments   xiii

I. *ARE YOU READY? Learning how to study art appreciation*   I

PART I. DRESS

II. *ENSEMBLE. Planning your total costume*   9
  1. CLOTHES MAKE THE MAN. Dressing to Improve Your Personality   10
  2. UPKEEP. Utilizing Neatness and Cleanliness   14
  3. THE TOTAL EFFECT. Planning a Costume so That the Parts Are Harmonious   17
  4. AT HOME ANYWHERE. Choosing Clothes Appropriate for the Occasion   19

III. *FINE POINTS. Choosing specific articles of costume*   22
  1. DESIGN AND MATERIAL. Choosing a Dress or Suit   23
  2. TRIPLE A. Choosing Shoes   27
  3. TOPPING IT OFF. Choosing Hats   29
  4. TRIMMINGS. Choosing Accessories   33
  5. HELPING NATURE. Choosing and Applying Make-up and Nail Polish   37

IV. *THE SHAPE YOU ARE IN. Dressing according to shape and size*   40
  1. DANGEROUS CURVES. Minimizing the Appearance of Overweight   41
  2. THE SHORTEST DISTANCE. Adding Curves to the Straight Figure   46
  3. THE LONG AND SHORT OF IT. Stressing and Minimizing Height   48
  4. TAILOR MADE. Counteracting Figure Defects   51
  5. HUMAN CLAY. Minimizing Facial Defects   55
  6. BATHING BEAUTIES AND LIFEGUARDS. Dressing the Normal Figure   59

v

CONTENTS

V. YOUR HARMONY. *Selecting and combining colors* — 62
  1. JOSEPH'S COAT. Choosing Your Total Color Scheme — 64
  2. THE HAIR WAVES. Flattering the Hair — 67
  3. THE EYES HAVE IT. Flattering Your Eyes — 70
  4. THAT RUDDY GLOW. Choosing Colors to Counteract a Sallow Complexion — 71
  5. LIKE A RED, RED ROSE. Choosing Colors to Counteract a Florid Complexion — 73
  6. PEACHES AND CREAM. Displaying to Best Advantage the Normal Toned Skin — 74
  7. SUN TAN AND BRONZE. Choosing Colors Becoming to the Sun-tanned Skin — 75
  8. FROZEN NORTH. Choosing Colors for Cool Color Types — 77
  9. SOUTHERN SUN. Choosing Colors for Warm Color Types — 79
  10. BETWIXT AND BETWEEN. Choosing Colors for Intermediate Color Types — 82
  11. CINNAMON, SILVER, AND PLATINUM. Choosing Colors for Gray and White-haired Types — 83

PART II. HOME

VI. HOMESTEAD. *Planning your home as a whole* — 89
  1. VIEW FROM YOUR WINDOWS. Choosing Your Neighborhood — 91
  2. NEIGHBOR'S-EYE VIEW. Designing the Setting for Your Home — 94
  3. FOUR WALLS AND A ROOF. Aiming at Functional Design — 99

VII. AREAS OF ACTION. *Planning the different rooms in your home* — 105
  1. SANCTUARY. Designing Your Bedroom — 106
  2. ALL THINGS TO ALL MEN. Designing Your Guest Room — 109
  3. HOT AND COLD. Designing Your Bathroom — 112
  4. FAMILY PERSONALITY. Designing Your Living Room — 115
  5. DINNER IS SERVED. Planning Your Dining Room — 122
  6. BRIGHT AND EARLY. Designing Your Breakfast Room — 126
  7. NEAT AND CLEAN. Designing Your Kitchen — 129
  8. ROYAL ROAD TO LEARNING. Designing Your Study — 132
  9. LET JOY BE UNCONFINED. Designing Your Recreation Room — 135
  10. SUN TAN. Designing Your Sun Room — 139
  11. CONNECTING RODS. Planning Your Halls — 141
  12. THE WORKS. Designing Storage and Workrooms — 142

CONTENTS

VIII. *COMFORT AND BEAUTY. Furnishing the home*   144
  1. SOLD ON THE OLD. Choosing Good Lines in Period Pieces   144
  2. THE SPIRIT OF TODAY. Choosing Good Modern Furniture   153
  3. STAYING PUT. Choosing and Placing Rugs   156
  4. SETTING THE STAGE. Choosing and Placing Furniture   159
  5. WALLS AND WINDOWS. Choosing and Arranging Draperies, Textiles, and Mirrors   164
  6. LANDSCAPE, STILL LIFE, OR PORTRAIT. Choosing and Hanging Pictures   167
  7. EXTRAS. Choosing and Arranging Art Objects and Flowers   172

PART III. SCHOOL

IX. *BEAUTY AND BRAINS. Using art in school activities*   181
  1. EVERYBODY COME. Making School Posters   181
  2. THE PLAY'S THE THING. Putting on Dramatic Entertainments   185
  3. "LIFE GOES TO A PARTY." Decorating for School Social Events   189
  4. TEMPLE OF LEARNING. Beautifying School Buildings and Grounds   193
  5. LABORATORIES FOR LEARNING. Making Classrooms Attractive   198
  6. THE DAY'S WORK. Doing Assigned Work in Good Taste   204

PART IV. WORK

X. *ART ON THE JOB. Using art principles in the workaday world*   215
  1. MODERN MERCHANDISE. Turning Out Attractive Products   216
  2. FOR ALL TO SEE. Displaying Merchandise for Sale   219
  3. WITH A SHINGLE OUTSIDE. Setting Up a Place of Business   223
  4. TELLING THE WORLD. Advertising Your Business   227
  5. MAN TO MAN. Selling Your Wares   231

PART V. SUMMARY

XI. *THE ROUND-UP. Summarizing art elements and principles*   239
  1. ART ELEMENTS. Line, Form, Dark and Light, Color, and Texture   240
    Line   240
    Form   243

CONTENTS

Dark-and-light   245
Color hue   247
Color value   248
Color intensity   250
Texture   252
2. PRINCIPLES. Developing Your Art Judgment   253
Visual satisfaction   254
Originality   255
Unity   256
Rhythm   258
Balance   261
Harmony   263
Fitness   265

INDEX   269

List of Illustrations

Bedroom in Chintz and Maple   *Frontispiece*

                                                        FACING PAGE

Effects of Colored Lights on Colored Pigments   66

Motion Picture Artists and Costume   78

Harmonizing Natural Coloring and Costumes   79

Modern Furniture in Sunroom   110

Modern Furniture in Dining Room   110

Convenience in Living Quarters   111

Utilizing Attic Space   111

School Room   188

Exhibit of School Posters   188

School Banquet   189

School Breakfast   189

Re-designed and Old Style Vise   216

Re-designed and Old Style Saw   216

Re-designed and Old Style Kitchen Equipment   217

Piano Window Display   220

Record Window Display   220

Christmas Present Window Display   221

Glass Case Linen Display   221

Store Fronts   224

Lamp Floor Display   225

China Floor Display   225

ix

Preface

Art is important today. It is important in everything we do because making this world of ours an attractive place to live is one of man's greatest interests.

Making ourselves attractive comes first. Millions of dollars are spent each year for clothes, cosmetics and beauty treatments, for ornaments and accessories to make us look our best. But how much of this money is wisely spent? How often do we select clothes that will give good service and be good looking until they are worn out? We all want to be as handsome as possible, but not all of us know how.

Then come our homes. Each one of us lives some place—in rented apartments or rooms, in our own homes, on farms. Very few of these quarters are just the way we would like to have them *but they can all be made attractive.* This does not mean spending a great deal of money. It means making the most of what we have. Rearranging furniture, painting walls a new color, dyeing old draperies or buying new ones, arranging flowers and plants can make our surroundings brighter. This is the basic point: make whatever you have as good to live with as possible.

Once our schools were all painted cream and "school-room brown." But today teachers and pupils together are making their classrooms gay and cheerful. How? Many suggestions are offered in the chapter on Schools.

Business men know that beauty pays. The automobiles, kitchen stoves, plumbing fixtures, furniture, lamps, and textiles they make and sell are in many cases, but not always, well designed. Can you tell a good design from a poor one?

With art playing a vital role in every one of our daily activities, it behooves each of us to learn as much as he can about it. This book *Art for All* will help you enjoy art more deeply and to solve your art problems more satisfactorily.

Some people think that everything in art is merely a matter of personal opinion, that we either like things or we do not, that there are no principles or standards. These people have not studied art. They have not given the same thought to art that they have to history, English, and arithmetic. They have failed to learn that there are many principles which are useful in improving one's sense of discrimination. To be sure, there are no rules of what is "right" and what is "wrong." But there are helpful suggestions.

This book has been planned to show how these guiding principles work in your daily life. It is developed around problems and situations which you have already met and which you will meet in the future. As you think of ways to solve these problems—better ways to select and wear your clothes, better means of making your home beautiful—you will gain a new understanding of the fundamentals of art. You may not have time to participate in all of the activities suggested, but you will undoubtedly think of others which apply to your own situation. From each you will learn something. The more you participate, the more questions you ask, and the more problems you solve, the more you will learn.

And remember that this course is only a beginning. It should lead to a lifetime of study and enjoyment of art.

RAY FAULKNER

Washington, D. C.
August 24, 1942

Acknowledgments

Many persons generously gave their time, ideas, and critical abilities for the betterment of this book. Among them were large numbers of teachers and graduate students who examined parts of the work in manuscript form in education classes at the University of Southern California and the University of Oregon. Thanks are also due to hundreds of students in high school art classes to whom these materials were taught in various stages of their development.

Most helpful of all were those in the following list, each of whom either contributed written reactions, criticisms, or suggestions based on a critical reading of one or more chapters of the mimeographed experimental edition which preceded the present publication or helped in some other significant way to improve the work:

Abbott, Mary Beth, Head of Art Department, Glendale High School, Glendale, Calif.; Aikin, R. B., Art Department, Tamalpais High School, Mill Valley, Calif.; Alexander, Mary M., Art Instructor, Placer Union High School and Junior College, Auburn, Calif.; Allen, Marion G., Assistant Professor of Art, Illinois State Normal University, Normal, Ill.; Arbuckle, Mabel, Supervisor of Art Education, Detroit Public Schools, Associate Professor, Wayne University, Detroit, Mich.; Blevins, C. M., Department of Industrial Education, Senior High School, Fort Smith, Ark.; Bowne, William, Art Instructor, Los Angeles, Calif.; Bradley, Charles B., Professor of Art Education and Head of the Department, State Teachers College, Buffalo, N. Y.; Bray, Ethel, Head of Art Department, E. V. Brown School, Washington, D. C.; Brown, Wm. B., Director of Secondary Curriculum, Los Angeles City Schools, Los Angeles, Calif.; Brueckner, L. J., Professor of Education, University of Minnesota, Minneapolis, Minn.; Buttles, Virginia Walsh, Teacher, Edison Technical High School, Fresno, Calif.; Carpenter, Lottie B., Director of Art, Pawtucket, R. I.; Cleaves, Helen E., Director of Manual Arts, City Schools, Boston, Mass.; Cocking, Gretta, Head of Art Department, Black Hills Teachers College, Spearfish, S. D.; Couchman, Victoria, Los Angeles, Calif.; Czurles, Stanley A., Instructor in Art, State Teachers College, Buffalo, N. Y.; DeWitt, Verna M., Chairman, Art Department, Fremont High School, Oakland, Calif.; Donlevy, Harry A., Head of Art Department, Oakland High School, Oakland, Calif.; Ellyson, Hermione, Head of Art Department, Redondo Beach, Calif.; Elrick, Thomas K., Art Teacher, Napa Union High School, Napa, Calif.; Emerson, R. H., Head of Art Department, Kern County Union High School, Bakersfield, Calif.; Fillmore, Marie Leonard, Head of Art Department, Yuba City High School, Yuba City, Calif.; Ford, Eugene, Shafter High School, Shafter, Calif.; Foster, Bertha Knox, Head of Art Department, Hoover High School, Glendale, Calif.; Gifford, Myrtie, Art Department Chairman, Berkeley High School, Berkeley, Calif.; Grant, Forest, Former Head of Art Department, New York City Schools; Hadley, Gertrude M., Chairman, Art Education Department, School of the Art Institute of Chicago, Chicago, Ill.; Harman, Maud, Supervisor of Art in Salt Lake City Schools, Salt Lake City, Utah; Harris, Pickens E., Associate Professor of Education and Philosophy, University of Pittsburgh, Pa.; Hastings, Elsie, Santa Barbara, Calif.; Heath, Pearl B., Assistant Professor of Art, Oregon College of Education, Monmouth, Ore.; Hillerich, Lena, Supervisor of Drawing, Louisville Public Schools, Louisville, Ky.; Huston, Agnes, Art Teacher, Charleston Senior High School, Charleston, W. Va.; Ingle, Mary, Art Supervisor, Junior High School, Whiting, Ind.; Kersey, Vierling, Superintendent of Schools, Los Angeles, Calif.; Kitt, Katherin F., Head of Art Department, University of Arizona, Tucson, Ariz.; Knouff, C. W., Vice-president, American Crayon Co., Sandusky, Ohio; Lambert, Rosa A., Art Teacher in Senior High School, Aberdeen, S. Dak.; Lecklider, Mary O., Teacher of Art, Niagara Falls High School,

Niagara Falls, N. Y.; Logan, Robert Fulton, Chairman, Department of Fine Arts, Connecticut College, New London, Conn.; Lowe, Edith W., Art Teacher, Excelsior Union High School, Norwalk, Calif.; Lueders, F., Head of Art Department, Compton Junior College, Compton, Calif.; Mather, Bess Foster, Art Supervisor, Minneapolis Public Schools, Minneapolis, Minn.; McKee, Katherine, Art Instructor, Andrews School, Willoughby, Ohio; McKibbin, Mary Adeline, Art Instructor, Fifth Avenue High School, Pittsburgh, Pa.; Mitchell, L. C., Director, School of Painting and Allied Arts, Ohio University, Athens, Ohio; Muller, Melanie Martha, New London, N. H.; Murdock, Mary, Assistant Professor of Art Education, Carnegie Institute of Technology, Pittsburgh, Pa.; Nathans, Annabel J., Director of Art, New Orleans Public School System, New Orleans, La.; Newton, Francis, Art Instructor, Lewiston State Normal, Lewiston, Idaho; Parker, Virginia, Head of Art Department, Knoxville, Tenn.; Patton, Charles E., Assistant Professor of Art, West Virginia University, Morgantown, W. Va.; Penny, Laura, Art Instructor, Citrus Union High School and Junior College, Azusa, Calif.; Pepper, Stephen C., Chairman, Department of Art, University of California, Berkeley, Calif.; Perkins, Cordelia M., Head, Allied Arts Department, Phoenix Union High School, Phoenix, Ariz.; Raymond, Ruth, Professor of Art Education, University of Minnesota, Minneapolis, Minn.; Reel, Grant A., Santa Fe, N. M.; Reitzel, Marques E., Head of Art Department, San Jose State College, San Jose, Calif.; Rivers, Georgie T., Director of Art, Huntingdon College, Montgomery, Ala.; Rooney, E. E., Supervisor of Art, Sacramento Senior High School, Sacramento, Calif.; Salisbury, Cornelius, Head of Art Department, West High School, Salt Lake City, Utah; Schlicher, Karl, Art Instructor, Senior High School, Beloit, Wis.; Schwankovsky, Frederick J., Chairman of Art Department, Manual Arts High School, Los Angeles, Calif.; Scott, Clare, Teacher and Head of Art Department, Lodi Union High School, Lodi, Calif.; Searcy, Creola, Fort Worth, Texas; Severino, D. Alexander, Director of Art Education, Rhode Island College of Education, Providence, R. I.; Sherwood, Mary Clare,

All Saints' College, Vicksburg, Miss.; Sibell, Muriel V., Professor of Fine Arts and Head of Department, University of Colorado, Boulder, Colo.; Theil, Marcella, Teacher of French and Art, Roosevelt High School, Oakland, Calif.; Varnum, William H., Chairman, Department of Art Education, University of Wisconsin, Madison, Wis.; Watters, Ethel Reed, Director of Home Economics, Bessie Tift College, Forsyth, Ga.; Weber, Edith M., Union High School, Anaheim, Calif.; Weyl, Lillian, Director of Art, Public Schools, Kansas City, Mo.; Whitacre, Gertrude, Covina Union High School, Covina, Calif.; Winebrenner, D. Kenneth, Instructor in Art, State Teachers College, Buffalo, N. Y.; Winslow, Leon L., Director of Art Education, Department of Education, Baltimore, Md.; Winstersteen, Marjory, Art Teacher, New Mexico State Teachers College, Silver City, N. M.; Yeck, Ralph R., Art Instructor, Central High School, Sioux City, Iowa.

ART FOR ALL

I. Are You Ready?

Learning how to study art appreciation

Art, many people think, is for the few. It is for those who have special creative talent, or for those who have money to buy masterpieces or the leisure to enjoy them. Many young people think that art appreciation means looking at famous paintings in museums. To them art is a thing apart from normal everyday life. If you hold any of these misconceptions, this book is especially for you. It has been prepared in order to open up the world of art to those students who feel that art appreciation is not for them. It is also planned for those who, having taken a brief survey course in art theory or appreciation, have failed to apply the knowledge in daily life. If you are one of these, you are missing much that is enjoyable and interesting, experiences that might change your whole pattern of living and open your eyes to things in daily existence of which you have never dreamed.

Art is by no means confined within the walls of museums. It is all around you. Art is in the clothes you wear, in the rooms you live in, in the way you comb your hair or choose your shoes. It is a living thing, closely connected with every action. Your reaction to any color combination—on the stage, in the furnishings in your room, or in the tie of a friend—is an experience in art appreciation.

The important thing for students to know, however, is not only that such experiences are in the realm of art appreciation but why their reactions are what they are—why one color is appealing or seems appropriate in a given setting, why the stripe in a dress or suit is becoming or unbecoming, why one picture looks well on the wall and another does not. When one becomes aware of such reactions, the first step in art appreciation has been taken. But it is only a beginning.

Merely to see a work of art as such is not enough, satisfying and worth-while though it may be. You should gain from it some insight or inspiration, so that not only art but life itself will take on new meaning. An appreciation of art must be an active rather than a passive experience. Therefore, this course must not be considered as mere entertainment. Merely looking at lantern slides might be pleasant, but the true value of art can come only when you begin to judge, choose, select, and plan the arrangement of things for yourself. To help you to do that is the aim of this book.

Lines, forms, patterns, colors, textures—all should stimulate you, either to admiration or distaste or something in between. Learn to translate what you see into acts or deeds, or at least be able to define it in terms of your own inner reactions. If you remain completely indifferent, if you get no inner response from what you see, you might as well be made of stone. For after all, aesthetic experience lies in *you*, not in the picture or design or fabric or color. If you fail to react to the world around you, you are depriving yourself of a great deal of enjoyment and satisfaction. You are not actively stimulated if you do not recognize a lack of order in yourself and your surroundings and react to create harmony out of that disorder. You are not making the most of yourself or of the environment in which you live. Not only should you recognize art all around you; it is equally important to judge the appropriateness of art. A fine painting may be tremendously effective and valuable in one situation, yet completely out of place in another, just as a costume which is appropriate and in good taste for an evening party is completely out of place in a classroom.

In this course you must learn by doing. An art-appreciation classroom is a laboratory. It is a place where you learn to do things by doing them, to make things by making them, to arrange by arranging, and to improve your judgment by passing judgments and having those judgments checked and verified. If time is very limited for your course, you may not have much opportunity for drawing, painting, and construction; but, even so, you will have a chance for vigorous personal participation in the making of decisions, choices, and judgments. The kinds of laboratory work you do will depend upon the skills you are trying to develop. To become a discriminating buyer of costumes you do not need to design costumes or operate a sewing machine, but you do need to try on different dresses, coats, suits, or ties and compare the effects.

The units of instruction in the art-appreciation course which you are about to take consist of problems which people face in the choice and arrangement of forms, substances, and articles. The chapters are organized around these problems and difficulties rather than around historical periods, art concepts, or art principles. This organization is not due to mere accident. In daily life we do not practice art in such units as "The arts in primitive life," "The art of the Greeks," or "The art of the Romans," but rather we use our knowledge of design to solve problems in the art of dress, of the home, of the school, and of the job. In solving these real art problems in your course or afterwards you naturally need to draw on fact, history, science, and art theory, but these are means rather than ends in themselves.

You will be encouraged to study the finished works of others in order to find why each one gives its unique effect. You will find out the principles back of good design in clothes or furniture by comparing several different designs, so that you can embody these principles in your own future creations. You will experiment with different arrangements to see which one gives the best effect, and then try to find out why. Such work is more profitable than using all of your time on the construction of one or two designs. Valuable as creative work is, you can learn much more about design by comparing and judging many different designs constructed by others. Naturally, it will be more helpful if you can go beyond the comparative type of activity and develop your own creative skill, but analysis and understanding are first necessities.

Don't ignore art knowledge, art theory, and art history. You cannot do much with art if you do not know much about it. The mere process of arranging a bouquet of flowers requires thought, judgment, and knowledge. Your choice of pictures for your living room depends upon your knowledge and understanding of line, pattern, form, color, and texture, as well as on information about the great artists, their works, and the times in which they lived. Information about art theory and history is not worth much unless it is applied to the problems and activities of everyday life; but acquired in this way and for this purpose, it is permanently valuable in enlarging your understanding of the things about you.

Show due respect for prevailing standards of taste. Art is social, not purely personal. To say "I like what I like, and the rest of the world may say what it will" is a form of narrowness. In the first place you seldom "like what you like." You like those things which you understand and to which you have become accustomed. There may be a new world of visual forms of which you are ignorant and toward which you are therefore antagonistic. It is a natural reaction for you to defend the tastes to which you have unconsciously been trained. Just as others have been responsible for your development, it is your responsibility to improve the visual world for others and to attain a wider philosophy and a deeper understanding that will influence those who come to depend upon your judgments. Times change, and the world moves on. A willingness to change and an ability to understand and appreciate new phases of development in the visual world are necessary for happiness. These changes have come about through the leadership of men and women who have spent their lives in adding to our heritage. Slowly the best of their work is accepted as a larger number of people come to understand and appreciate it. In this way the standards of taste of an ever larger proportion of the population may reach a continuously higher level. Critical judgment and ability to make fine choices have too often been confined to the wealthy or the leisure class who could afford the time and money to make of them a life's work. Just as the ability to read has come to be considered a necessity for everyone, so is the ability to create a satisfying environment important to everyone. You have a definite personal social duty to perform in this field.

Be as creative as your time and talents permit. Talent and opportunity for inventive or creative work are sometimes limited. Most of us will have to be content to make full use of what the more talented create for us. Our creative faculties, however, have full play in the combination and arrangement of our choices. Art is nothing more than "choice," the choosing and arranging of lines, forms, colors, and textures whether in an original painting or in a costume or in a room ensemble. Every time you choose and combine forms, your emotional reactions or feelings should first be allowed full play; then your

4

critical judgment may be used as a check to perfect your composition. Each of us has some creative ability and energy. It is our privilege and responsibility to develop and utilize this energy.

Problems and activities. (1) Explain why it is better to have a little training in art than none at all. (2) Debate: "It is better to survey the whole field of art briefly than to spend your time developing skill in a few specialties." (3) Compare experiences with your classmates to show that art appreciation involves some kind of reaction either in feeling or in behavior. Describe some of your own inner reactions of this kind. (4) Test yourself by ranking three pictures which your teacher will show you according to their real merits as pieces of art. Compare your rankings and your reasons for them with those of your classmates, and see if you can decide why you agree or disagree. (5) Make a similar evaluation of the three pictures as possible decorations for the front of your classroom. Compare reasons again. How does the presence of a definite *use* for the pictures affect your rating of them? (6) Three of the many uses of art are (a) to give a feeling of exaltation, (b) to communicate a feeling of power, (c) to induce a feeling of peace. Name several types of art that would be effective for each of these three purposes, and explain why each gets the desired effect. (7) Make a blackboard list, compiled by the entire class, of the life situations in which you feel embarrassed or handicapped by your lack of skill in selecting good lines, colors, or designs. (8) Let some class member volunteer to allow the class to judge how appropriately some article of his or her clothing has been chosen, and discuss the reasons. What questions growing out of this experience do you want to have answered during the remainder of this course? (9) Name the kinds of knowledge of art history or art theory which you think you would need in order to choose pictures for the school library; to select furniture for your living room. (10) Report to the class things which you have known other persons to do that made you think they were artistically "out of line" but which they seemed to think were "creative."

Part I
DRESS

II. Ensemble

Planning your total costume

How important is one's personal appearance? How often do you judge people by their looks and by the clothes they wear? You may insist that you like or dislike others for what they are and that you are not influenced by appearances. But is that entirely true? Until a person speaks or acts, you are compelled, consciously or unconsciously, to judge him by his looks. And whether you like it or not, others are judging you in the same way.

The color of what you wear, the lines, the texture, the way you carry yourself—all have a great deal to do with the impression you give to the world. The first impression may not be the same as later ones. What you say and do are in the end more important than the way you look. But your appearance every day is a part of that total impression. Does your appearance express the best of you? Do you know how to plan and choose clothes which reveal the finer aspects of your personality?

The principles of art should be your guide in these practical everyday matters. Color, line, and texture are as definitely a part of clothing and of personal appearance as they are of painting. Comparatively few persons ever create great paintings, but everyone has the opportunity of making himself and his surroundings harmonious and pleasing. Everyone can learn to apply the principles of art to his own appearance.

It is not sufficient, of course, to know that this or that costume of today is good. You must go far enough in your study to know *why*. Styles, fabrics, and conditions of living change from month to month. If you are willing to master the underlying principles of art in dress, you will then be in a position to solve any problems about clothes and your appearance which the future may bring. No one need ever say of you, "Yes, that girl has excellent abilities, but you'd never know it by looking at her," or, "I had heard so much about his achievements, but I was so disappointed when I first saw him."

1. Clothes Make the Man

Dressing to Improve Your Personality

Your clothes are important not only because of their effect on others but because of their effect on you. You know how much better you feel in some costumes than in others. Is it because certain colors definitely give a lift to your spirits? Is it because you are conscious of being admired when you wear that blue evening dress or that well-cut tweed suit? Is it that your favorite costume expresses the kind of person you are or the kind you are striving to be? For any or all of these reasons some clothes give you satisfaction, and that satisfaction is reflected in your behavior. It helps to give you self-respect and poise. A part of real poise is self-forgetfulness. When you are conscious of looking your best, you are able to forget yourself and devote your time and energy to your work and to making others comfortable and happy. That way lies the road to popularity, well-being, and happiness.

On the other hand, you have doubtless had the experience of feeling ill-at-ease in certain clothes. This feeling, in turn, had its effect on your behavior. It probably made you self-conscious, perhaps aloof and unapproachable, perhaps disagreeable and envious of others. These are not desirable qualities and do not in their turn help your appearance.

Are you constantly discouraged about this problem of clothes? Do you go about with a hang-dog air because you think you haven't enough clothes in your wardrobe or because they aren't expensive ones? If so, you had better change your mind and your behavior at once. Quantity of clothes and high cost do not of themselves guarantee a good appearance. Many a person with a small budget makes a better appearance than those with unlimited means. It is exactly at this point that the principles of art can be of help to you. A knowledge of line and color and texture are free to you as to everyone. You can apply them to your wardrobe no matter what your resources may be. And had you ever thought of this? Perhaps it is not your clothes which are at fault but your way of wearing them.

One word of warning is in order. Do not be deceived into thinking that clothes are *all* important. Clothes merely *express* what you *are*. Too much attention to your clothes may leave too little time for becoming the person you wish to be. Clothes cannot, when all is done, hide a shallow mind.

How do soft curves or diagonals change personality?

On the other hand, it is foolish to go through life thinking that people will like you no matter how you look. Careless personal appearance is not a compliment to others. If you take no pains to look your best, you simply raise a barrier which you yourself must overleap by brilliant achievements. It is easier and far pleasanter to study and apply the principles of art to your appearance.

Line as a factor in costume. Knowledge of the effect of lines is most helpful in planning clothes which will enhance your personality rather than detract from it. Lines, like words, tell us something. They affect our feelings, depending chiefly on their direction. Their character is also important; some are straight, some curved, some irregular.

We think of straight vertical lines as strong, dignified, and stately. They are upward reaching and give an effect of added tallness. Think, for example, of a tall and sturdy pine tree holding its head high in the air. It is the true expression of a strong, poised personality.

Straight horizontal lines are formal and dignified but less strong and active. They hold the eye down and shorten the total effect. They also suggest poise, repose, and stability, just as the great pine, felled at last and lying on the ground, relieves us of any fear that it might fall.

Curved lines suggest feelings of gaiety, sprightliness, or graceful softness. They may thus be youthful or softly feminine.

Diagonals and pointed lines give a restless, animated feeling because they have neither the strength of vertical lines nor the stability of horizontal lines. This impression of activity and energy is called "dynamic." A scheme based on dynamic lines is more difficult to carry out successfully than one based on straight horizontals or on verticals or on curves. If diagonals are well used, the effect may be sophisticated and striking. If used poorly, there is an impression of too great restlessness. This type of line scheme is best suited to an active, energetic person.

What line scheme of those just described seems best suited to your own personality? Do not be disappointed if you cannot give an answer at once. This problem of the impressions made by lines will be constantly coming up throughout your study of art in daily life. But do not pass by the problem of line with a mere wave of the hand. The effect of your costume always depends in part on its line scheme.

Colors and textures as factors in costume. The colors you choose and the coarseness or fineness of the textures in your clothing are important factors in suggesting your personality. Whether you wear red or green will depend upon your complexion, figure, hair, and eyes. But there are many kinds of reds and greens. Some are bright, others are dull. Some are dark, others are light. How can you learn to choose those which are best for you?

Each color has three characteristics. First is *hue*, which refers to the name of the color, such as red, green, blue, orange, yellow, or violet. Second is *value*, which refers to the lightness or darkness of the color. Reds can be dark as in apples and sweet cherries, or they can be very light and pale as in apple and cherry blossoms. The third characteristic of color is *intensity*, which refers to its brightness or neutrality. For example, some reds are very bright and clear like the red in the flag, while other reds are grayed, neutral, or dull. Bright and intense colors are best suited to the personality that is strong or vivacious enough not to be submerged by them. If you are a quiet, reserved person, you will do well to use less intense coloring so that your clothes will remain subordinate and you will still be in evidence as a person. Your clothes should never be more forceful than your personality; otherwise the real you may be overlooked and ignored, and your friends will merely get an impression of a striking costume coming down the street.

The textures that you choose also enhance or hinder the effectiveness of your personality. Rough, medium, and smooth weaves produce various effects. Stiff or soft fabrics, glossy or dull ones should be chosen for definite reasons. The relation of fabrics and textures to your total clothing problem will be developed more fully as you study later sections of this book.

Problems and activities. (1) Think of a time when you have completely misjudged a person because of his appearance. Perhaps you were favorably impressed by his looks and later found his personality less pleasing, or you may have disliked his appearance and learned to like him as a person. Try to analyze what it was in his appearance which misled you in your first opinion of him. (2) Consider how you have selected your clothes in the past. Decide what kind of impression you have been trying, consciously or unconsciously, to make and whether you have succeeded in your attempt. (3) If you do not mind being frank in the presence of your classmates, tell them what type of personality you are trying to maintain, and get their suggestions as to the clothes you might wear to achieve that effect. (4) Volunteer to be an "Exhibit A" before your classmates while they decide whether your present costume is based on lines that are vertical, horizontal, diagonal, or curved. Get them to tell you which lines they think would be most appropriate for you. (5) Look around the room, note the costumes of your classmates, and decide which have chosen colors that are not striking enough to support their personalities. (5) Ask several of your friends and classmates what colors they think are most becoming to you and why. See how well they agree.

13

DRESS

2. UPKEEP

Maintaining Neatness and Cleanliness

Many persons who would otherwise be smartly dressed fail to keep their clothes in good condition. Neatness and cleanliness take time, effort, and energy. It is easy to grow careless about details, but if you really take pride in your appearance, you will develop high standards of personal cleanliness and neatness. Do not misunderstand what is meant by such standards and get the idea that you must avoid all work which might soil your clothes and hands or disarrange your hair. Many kinds of work cannot be done without your getting dirty or mussed. If you are afraid to get dirt under your fingernails or on your sleeve, you will not last long in some jobs. An efficient worker wears the kind of clothes that are suited to his work, keeps them in as good condition as possible, and has strict habits of personal cleanliness. The daily bath is one of the foundations of good appearance as well as good health.

Work clothes as well as dressed-up clothes should be cleaned, repaired, and kept in good condition. No costume, however beautiful in lines or handsome in material, is attractive when badly soiled. Many young people who complain about having too little money for clothes could expand their budgets by taking proper care of the clothes they have. Are you the girl who says to herself, "Oh, well, why clean the spot on that dress? It will be out of style next season, so I'll be wearing it only a few times more"? Remember that the impression you make during those few times may be more important than the impression you make next season.

Mending, cleaning, and protecting clothes. Before buying your clothes, decide on what kind of wear is expected of them. Even perishable types of clothing should have firm weave and adequate seams, and should be able to stand some sort of cleansing. Repair small rips and runs when they first appear. This type of care will lengthen the life of fine garments. Silks should be pressed on the wrong side while damp. Acetates and woolens should always be protected by a cloth between the iron and the fabric. Velvets should be steamed. All garments should be thoroughly aired and dried before being hung in the clothes closet or folded away in drawers. Keep delicate-colored fabrics away from the bleaching rays of the sun.

Shoes and kid gloves should not be worn too many consecutive days, since continuous dampness from the body will rot the leather.

At the end of a season all clothes should be thoroughly cleaned before storing. Closets and drawers should be regularly fumigated for moths, and woolens and furs should be stored in moth-proof bags or boxes. A closet carefully planned for clothes storage and also adequately lighted will help to simplify your clothing upkeep.

Removing spots. Stains in your clothes may be set, or made permanent, if you do not follow the correct method of removing them. The safest course is to leave the work to an experienced cleaner, but in case of emergency it is well to know some of the rules. However, unless you have had considerable experience with different fabrics, you had better play safe by testing a small piece of the material to see whether it will stand water or cleansing fluids. Usually you can cut a tiny strip from a seam or the under side of the hem. If this is not possible, test a part of the garment which is least conspicuous.

Perspiration should be soaked in cold water before washing; hot water will set it permanently. If set, it may possibly be removed by a strong borax soap solution and a sun bath. Blood and milk or cream should be soaked out with cold water before washing. These are animal matter and would be cooked into the textile by hot water. Fruit-stained material should be stretched tightly and have boiling water poured through it provided the fabric will stand such treatment. This method is usually good for fruit punch stains. Cold water is likely to set a fruit stain. Ink, if set, may be soaked in sour milk and washed out. Grease spots should be dissolved by gasoline, alcohol, ether, or chloroform. Mildew yields to lemon juice and a sun bath. Scorch may be bleached out by a sun bath. Surface-burns in materials may be removed by a gentle rubbing.

Wearing your clothes well. Tucked-in blouses and shirts, snug belts, well-fitted shoulder seams, smooth necklines, and smooth-fitting socks or stockings with straight seams are a few of the points that denote the carefully dressed person. Neatness with cleanliness is more important than "classiness." Many a three-year-old suit looks better than the newest model merely because the owner is an expert in the art of wearing clothes well. Are you guilty of clothing slouchiness?

Does it matter how you carry yourself and how you wear your clothes?

Posture. With many persons it is slouchiness of posture rather than of clothes which spoils the effect. Stand tall with a straight line through the center arch of your foot, your hip bone, your shoulder, and your ear. The habit of dropping the chest and allowing either the abdomen or buttocks to protrude is a common fault. A simple way to test your own laxness in this matter is by standing with your back to a straight wall. Press your heels, buttocks, waistline, shoulders, and head into one straight line. Place a book on your head, and walk away holding this position. How many of your acquaintances maintain such a posture?

Do you? Sports, correct exercises, and fresh air help to keep the muscles toned up so that good posture becomes natural.

Problems and activities. (1) Have a class discussion in which boys may discuss points of neatness commonly disregarded by girls and vice versa. Of course, you will not be personal in any of your remarks. If you prefer, you may write your comment in a letter and deposit it in a box without signing your name. Then appoint a committee to assemble the data and report on the important points brought out by boys and by girls. (2) Check over your own clothing at home, note the places that are spotted or soiled or in need of mending, and set about putting the garments into proper condition. (3) Bring to the class some garment that has spots and stains, and demonstrate to the students your best techniques for cleaning or removing these stains. Get criticisms based on the experience of others. (4) Talk to someone in a cleaning and dyeing establishment, asking all the questions you can, and report to the class what information you get about how to keep clothing in good condition. (5) If you don't mind being a little conspicuous, wear to class some of your more run-down clothing, and ask your classmates for suggestions and techniques for rejuvenating the different pieces.

3. THE TOTAL EFFECT

Planning a Costume so That the Parts Are Harmonious

All together, not piece by piece, is the way your costume strikes others when they first see you. Your face and figure, your line scheme, and your texture and color relationships should form a single picture which is unified, harmonious, and interesting.

Ensemble contour. Have you ever bought a hat that was becoming to your face and then discovered that it did not suit your figure? Have you bought shoes and found that they were either too dainty or too heavy for the rest of your costume? The size of your hat in relation to your feet, the proportions of your shoulders in relation to your feet and to your hips, the outline of the upper parts of the body in relation to the lower parts—these are all problems of ensemble contour. When you buy any garment, you should put it on and study it in a full-length mirror in relation to the rest of your silhouette.

Inner line scheme. The skeleton of a body, the veins of a leaf, or the trunk and branches of a tree are "inner line schemes." They give the object its basic structure. They combine with the silhouette, or outer contour lines, to create the pattern of directions. The hat, suit, shoes, and accessories have inner lines and contours which are vertical, horizontal, circular, or diagonal. You can use each of these in creating a perpendicular dignified line scheme, a horizontal effect, a curved youthful ensemble, or a diagonal sophisticated costume. In any ensemble one of these line schemes should be dominant, with the others subordinate. What type of line scheme is most becoming to you? Although one

Can you find main centers, subordinate centers, or
lack of centers of interest here?

may be more becoming than the others, you may want to change from time to time for the sake of variety.

Texture relationships. Fabrics differ in their effects on your sense of touch. They range from smooth to rough, warm to cold, hard to soft, and from narrow-meshed to wide-meshed. These differences of surface produce different textures. Textiles also differ in other ways. They may be transparent, translucent, or opaque. A combination of fabrics too much alike is sometimes tiresome, while too great contrasts are also unpleasant. Satin, for example, combines better with other smooth-surfaced materials than with rough materials, while linen or raw silk goes well with somewhat rougher surfaces. If a costume is divided above and below the center, as are coat and trousers or coat and skirt, similar textures are advisable even though the patterns may differ.

Center of interest. Sometimes a costume, otherwise attractive, gives a wrong effect because it lacks unity. The eye is pulled from place to place by competing interests. There should be but one center of interest in a costume. This is preferably near the face, but it may be at the waist or on the shoulders or sleeves. This center of interest may be embroidery, a tie, a scarf, a brooch, a clip, a necklace, a belt, or some other interesting accessory. It should generally form the sharpest contrast in hue, value, or intensity among all the articles in the ensemble. All other interest notes should be more closely related in color, in darkness or lightness, and in intensity to the basic costume color, or they should be subordinated.

Problems and activities. (1) Get the members of your own family to check you over when you are dressed up in what you consider your best total outfit, and have them make suggestions for further improvement. (2) Wear one of your favorite combinations to class, and ask your classmates to criticize it and make suggestions regarding contour, line scheme, textures, and unity. (3) In your classroom do a little trading of coats, sweaters, or other articles, and see how a different combination can be made to improve or to spoil an ensemble. (4) Have one student after another stand before the class to have his costume judged in terms of inner line scheme: whether it is built on perpendiculars, horizontals, curves, or diagonals. (5) Look over your own costume, decide what you consider its center of interest, then stand before the class and see how well others agree with you. (6) Get your classmates to judge also how well you have built up subordinate centers of interest in your costume and how appropriately these relate to the main center of interest.

4. AT HOME ANYWHERE

Choosing Clothes Appropriate for the Occasion

Have you ever been completely miserable because you were wearing the wrong kind of clothes for the occasion? Perhaps the invitation for a party was not clear. You thought it was an informal out-of-door affair, and it turned out to be formal and indoors. Or perhaps the weather changed abruptly and you sweltered through a day in a scratchy sweater or shivered in a fresh summer print. Some mistakes of this sort are unavoidable, but most of the time you should be able to dress to suit the time, the place, and the event.

Your wardrobe should contain costumes suitable to your various activities. If you are in school or working in an office, the major part of your clothing should consist of outfits suited to school or work. One of the commonest mistakes that girls make is to spend too much of their clothes allowance for sports or party dresses and accessories and too little for everyday requirements. As a result, the school or work dresses get shabby with too much use. Then the girls are tempted to wear old party dresses or gay sports clothes at times when they are quite inappropriate.

It should be remembered, however, that the code of correctness varies greatly in different sections of the country. Clothes which might be entirely suited to a party in New York City might be quite out of place at a social affair in a small town. Climate, too, makes a difference. In Tahiti cotton may be popular for all day wear while in Boston it would look odd and be quite inappropriate for most of the year. Today sensible persons are more likely to consider what will be comfortable and attractive than to hold to any hard and fast rules of fashion. Common sense is one of the best guides.

Suitable styles. School or business clothes should be dignified and simple, but they need not be drab and severe. Frilly accessories, for instance, may improve a very simple dress, provided they are clean and fresh-looking. A rich sequence of colors and combinations of patterned and plain material may be used effectively. In men's clothes color is usually confined to ties, scarves, handkerchiefs, shirts, socks, and sweaters. However, there is a definite trend toward more color in boys' and men's attire, especially in sports clothes.

Freedom of movement, comfort, and protection are the chief requirements of sports clothes. They should be designed and fitted to allow for any strains that the particular sport demands. Seams should be sewed with unusual care to prevent their pulling out during rough wear. If loud patterns and bright colors suit you, sports clothes offer the opportunity for indulging in them.

The test of suitability should be applied to all details of the costume—shoes, hats, and gloves—as well as to dresses and suits. High-heeled pumps, for instance, cannot be worn with comfort in hiking through the woods or over rough ground. Therefore, they are not suitable in a costume planned for active sports.

Suitable textures and patterns. For house clothes you usually want light-weight, soft materials that are fresh-looking, easily cleaned, and comfortable. For downtown wear it is wise to choose materials that will be smart looking but will also stand up under hard treatment, and will not be ruined by bad weather. Street and office clothes should be kept in condition for outside wear, and should not generally be worn at home. Very fine or sheer materials are most suitable for dress occasions. Finely woven, smooth-textured serges, worsteds, and other similar materials are appropriate for boys' party clothes; satin, taffeta, net, lace, and chiffon are generally worn by girls. Since dancing is fatiguing and warming, clothes light in weight, well-ventilated, and soft in texture are most suitable.

There is a trend toward the use of cottons and synthetic textiles for many purposes, because they are inexpensive and serviceable. Various textures become suitable according to popular use.

Problems and activities. (1) Cut out of newspapers or magazines several advertisements of articles of clothing, show these to the class, and get reactions as to places or situations in which each would be most appropriate. (2) Stand on a street corner watching people go by, and note the costumes which you think are particularly appropriate or inappropriate to the situation. Be sure to consider the time, the weather, and the place. Report your observations to the class. (3) Tell the class what kind of costume you think is best for the person who has to get along with a very limited wardrobe by using the same articles in many different situations. Get class reactions to your ideas. (4) From your mother's sewing room or from other sources bring quite a number of samples of different fabrics, and have your classmates judge their appropriateness for sports wear, street wear, and party wear respectively. See how well they all agree.

III. Fine Points

Choosing specific articles of costume

One of the most important principles to remember in choosing your clothes and accessories is that the whole of a costume is greater than the sum of its parts. Each article is seen not by itself, but in relation to all the others. The effectiveness of each thing you wear depends upon how well it fits into the whole combination. The world's most beautiful hat is not a good hat for you if it is not in harmony with your personality and your costume. The most "stunning" pair of shoes in the world, if out of harmony with the rest of your ensemble, will attract too much attention to themselves. Who wants to be thought of as the unnoticed wearer of the much-noticed shoes?

You have made a beginning by studying some of the general problems of costume design. Now it is time to consider some of the more specific problems of suit and dress patterns, shoes, hats, accessories, and make-up.

As you face these problems thoughtfully, you will realize that your own good common sense is of great importance. Clothes which are not sensible are seldom good. But dressing in a distinguished manner takes a little more than just common sense. It takes an understanding of such art elements as line, form, dark and light, color, and texture. It also takes an understanding of unity, rhythm, balance, harmony, and fitness. As you solve your costume problems, you will learn a great deal about art in a very natural way. You will come to understand some of the principles and techniques which artists use in fields other than clothing. You might be introduced to these principles and techniques as abstract ideas, but you will undoubtedly prefer to learn about them in connection with problems which have immediate and obvious value to you.

22

CHOOSING SPECIFIC ARTICLES OF COSTUME

I. DESIGN AND MATERIAL

Choosing a Dress or Suit

Two important things to think about in choosing every garment are its design, or cut, and the material from which it is made. A good garment is made from a suitable material and cut in a pleasing design. Both need to be carefully considered, not separately as though they had nothing to do with each other, but as closely related parts of the same problem. A moment's thought will show why this is true. Each textile from which clothes are made has its own special qualities which suggest that it be used in certain ways. Tweeds and other heavy woolens are generally used for clothes which are cut somewhat loosely; satins and serges, on the other hand, suggest clothes which are more carefully fitted. Dresses of velvet are not cut in the same patterns as dresses of linen, nor are corduroy garments patterned the same as those of lace. These differences are not accidental, but come from a study of how each textile may be used to best advantage. Coarse, loosely woven, rough-textured goods need a different treatment from fine, tightly woven, smooth-textured cloths. In general, the finer the weave and the smoother the texture, the more refined and subtle will be the pattern.

The general lines of the design and the material are decided on first. All trimmings and adornments should be secondary considerations. They are good only if they supplement and enrich the main lines. Fussy details clamoring for attention are the mark of poorly designed garments. To be well-dressed, avoid such excesses and wear simple clothes that depend on good material and good design.

Natural divisions. The real basis for the design of a suit or dress is the human body which it will cover. Important points or areas of the body which need to be considered are the shoulders, chest, waist, and hips. Frequently, to improve the proportions or to get a special effect, the designer deliberately changes the appearance of these natural divisions. Thus, the height of the shoulders may be apparently raised or lowered by careful design, and the same holds true for the waist and hips. The waistline, in particular, is often raised or lowered for special effects. Sometimes the natural divisions of the body are ignored in the interests of fashion. When this is carried to an extreme, as with the excessively low waistlines which were popular some years ago, the results are unpleasant. Intelligent changes in the natural divisions, however, are a justifiable use of art for the sake of greater beauty.

Natural widths. Natural widths, like natural vertical divisions, also furnish interesting proportions on which to base clothing design. Shoulders, chest, waist, and hips have a rhythmic variation in width. In general, it is wise to respect these natural dimensions, and plan garments accordingly. But there are many times when art may be called in to produce different effects. If you wish to make shoulders, chest, waist, or hips appear narrower than they are, use some kind of contrasting ornament in the center of the garment. This will attract attention from the edges to the center. If, on the other hand, you wish to increase the apparent widths, contrasting accents should be placed at extreme edges. The general principle is that ornament in the center tends to make an object look narrower, while ornament at the edges tends to make it look wider.

The use of horizontal lines is another means at the disposal of the costume designer. Horizontal lines, whether they are used on a dress, a package, or a building, tend to make objects look wider. The use of horizontal lines on one part of the body can make it seem wider in relation to the other parts. But again we must remember that the parts are never seen separately. If one part of the body is made to appear wider, other parts are also affected. Thus, wide shoulders create the impression of smaller hips. A small waist enlarges the apparent size of the chest, but also enlarges the apparent size of the hips. By intelligent use of all these means, every figure can be altered and improved in its appearance.

Considered space divisions. In a good costume design you seldom find equal space divisions, because two areas of exactly the same size are likely to be less interesting than two of different size. Transitions from large to small or groupings of various widths are more pleasing than a monotonous repetition of equal proportions. Equal horizontal divisions in a costume are always unpleasant; since neither top nor bottom is dominant, the wearer is likely to look as if he or she were cut in two. On the other hand, small space divisions, such as occur in pleats, stripes, or plaids, are very satisfying, for in these there are enough repetitions to set a pattern or rhythm. In all clothing, equal vertical divisions are fairly common. Most men's clothes—suits, jackets, and shirts— are designed in this way, and many women's dresses and coats also have a divi-

A   B   C

How could you improve balance in these costumes?
A. Which way would this girl fall if you let her go?
B. How could you improve this balance without
making it symmetrical? C. How does this costume
balance from top to bottom?

sion in the middle. This seldom strikes us as being unpleasant or even uninteresting because the body itself is divided in this way, and such clothes merely emphasize the underlying structure.

Since a jacket divides the costume in two nearly equal parts horizontally, how might you change it? How can a belt be helpful? How can you proportion other parts of the costume, such as pleats, tucks, or pockets, to avoid monotonously equal space divisions?

Balance. A costume balances in two ways: from top to bottom and from side to side. In order to give a feeling of vertical equilibrium, the heavier weights

25

and greater widths are usually placed low, just as they are in a building or a piece of furniture. Equilibrium from side to side is maintained through balancing weights on either side of the center. This balance may be symmetrical or asymmetrical. Symmetrical balance means a repetition of like shapes on either side of the middle line. Asymmetrical balance is the weighting of unlike interests at unequal distances from the middle. This must be done carefully so that lopsidedness is avoided. Thus, a strong interest near the center may be balanced by a lesser interest farther away from the midpoint on the opposite side. Have you seen costumes that seemed lopsided because pockets or accessories were all on one side with no counter-balance on the other side? How might this error have been corrected?

Textile design. A dress or suit design depends partly on the design of the material from which it is made. Some of the most beautiful materials are plain and depend on surface textures and color for their effectiveness, but many others have some kind of pattern. Most of what has been said about costume design in general applies to textile design. Striped material is often more interesting when the stripes vary in width. Plaids which form rectangles have more variety than those which give the effect of squares. Checks, if small, create a sparkling effect, but if large, they may be monotonous. Abstract patterns or conventionalized designs are likely to be more appropriate than naturalistic pictures on dress or suit material. In selecting a textile design, it is well to keep three things in mind: the motifs, or dominant shapes, should form a unified pattern, the sizes should be interestingly varied, and the background shapes as well as the motifs should be pleasing in effect. In combining two or more materials, you will generally find that two patterned materials are less effective than a pattern offset by a plain surface.

Problems and activities. (1) Borrow a book of suit samples from the tailor, bring it to class, and spend some time deciding which patterns would be most appropriate for particular members of the group. (2) Ask the tailor how he helps people who are not well proportioned to look better through his understanding of lines and proportions. Report your findings to the class. (3) Have several girls stand before the class so that you can compare the different ways in which their costumes achieve vertical balance. (4) Do the same thing with reference to balance from side to side. (5) From costumes found in the class pick out a number that achieve symmetrical balance and others that achieve asymmetrical balance. Study them carefully for effectiveness of balance and for the reasons why they balance. (6) Tell the class about costumes you have seen in which pockets or other trimmings failed to balance, and indicate how this could have been corrected. (7) Let several boys in the class trade coats and stand before the group to show how different patterns of coats and trousers harmonize or fail to harmonize with each other. Note particularly whether a patterned coat with unpatterned trousers or a plain coat with patterned trousers is better than an unmatched combination of patterned coat and trousers.

2. TRIPLE A

Choosing Shoes

Triple A may be a shoe size of which to be proud, but only if it is adequate to balance your body. Your foot is, after all, the base upon which you rest. It is as inconsistent for a large person to have extremely small feet as it would be

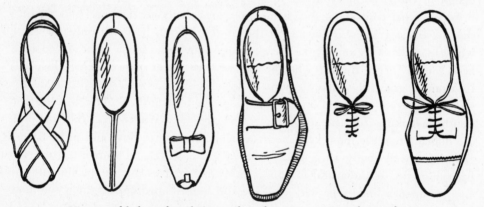

How would these shoe designs affect the apparent size of your feet?

for an elephant to have the tiny hoofs of a deer. Your shoes are part of your whole costume design; as such, they should be a consistent part of a line, form, color, and value scheme. Shoes should be chosen for their suitability for the occasion and the costume.

Suitability. What type of shoe should you like to have with your favorite school costume? What type of shoe do you prefer for dress wear? Dress shoes with sports clothes, and sports or walking shoes with dress clothes have ruined

27

many a costume. Strong sturdy lines and rough textures belong with sports clothes. Have you ever seen a man wear brogues with a dress suit? Fine textures and more delicate lines belong with dress clothes. Can you remember having seen shoes that were too dressy with a street costume?

Line. Streamlining is as appropriate for modern feet as for modern automobiles. Heavy cross bands, intricate cross lines, and all divisions that stop the eye on its journey from toe to heel are as poor for shoes as they would be for a car. All lines should have a continuous unarrested movement from toe to heel. If the foot is extremely long and narrow, cross lines may be used to make it appear shorter. A stubby look should be avoided, except by the small person with small feet. It is surprising how few shoe models achieve this smoothness, and how many, even in the more expensive groups, seem choppy and clumsy in effect. How many shoes have you seen this season that have the perfection of design of the latest streamlined automobiles?

Form. What contour of shoe is most becoming to you? The heel and toe of a shoe have the greatest influence on the contour. High heels are only for those who can walk easily on them. The overplump girl who looks unsteady on high heels should forego the extra height and wear the kind of heels which help her to attain a graceful walk. Medium or low heels are always in good taste for sports and street wear and are most appropriate for youth. Stubby toes are also youthful-looking for the small foot. An extremely stubby toe and low heel are difficult to wear, however, even for slender, graceful boys and girls. Before choosing them, study their effect with your ensemble. The pointed toe has been discarded as unnatural in appearance, since it does not fit the lines of the foot. A smooth-lined shoe with oval toe and heel of medium height is the most becoming footwear for most people.

Color. Black shoes go well with all colors, but with blue costumes, blue shoes of the same value or darker may look even better. With beige or brown clothes, brown shoes are nearly always more successful than black. Brown also combines well with green. Shoes should harmonize with the general color of the costume or should match the purse, gloves, and hat. Gaily colored shoes are often used to repeat the color of the accessories against a white, gray, or black costume, but they may also be used with the more neutral colors. White shoes may be worn most successfully with white or very pale pastels, since they are light in value.

Value. What color of shoes do you prefer for a blue suit? A brown suit? A rose-beige dress? A white dress? It is often said that shoes should never be of lighter value than the rest of the costume. This rule arises from the fact that the feet are the base for the ensemble and a light value is an unsubstantial base for darker values; it is likely to create a top-heavy effect. If you follow this rule, white shoes should never be worn with darker costumes. But we have all seen both men and women wearing white shoes very effectively with colored suits and dresses, proving that the rule does not always hold true. However, matching or darker values are good with any costume, and black seems to be the most consistently suitable color for footwear. In selecting shoes, always study the total effect of your costume rather than rely on any hard and fast rules.

Problems and activities. (1) Let some class members line up where the others can see their feet, and let everybody pick out examples of unusually good shoe design. (2) While these students are lined up for shoe inspection, let the class decide what improvements in ensembles might be achieved if certain pairs of students in the line were to exchange shoes. (Ignore the problem of fit.) (3) In a similar way decide what shoes would be especially appropriate for particular colors and textures of clothing worn by students in the class. (4) Arrange a loan from a shoe store of about a dozen designs in men's shoes and another dozen in women's shoes. Study them with reference to design and suitability to different persons and different types of costumes. (Be sure to take good care of them and return them in good order.)

3. Topping It Off

Choosing Hats

Hats play an important part in the total effect of the costume. Because of being near the face, the hat is conspicuous and therefore occupies a strategic place in the ensemble. Its very nearness to the eyes, however, often leads us into error. We study its relation to the face and forget its relation to the whole figure and to the rest of the costume. The hat should complement the other clothes, the face, and the figure. To make it achieve this three-fold purpose, one needs special knowledge of line, form, dark and light, color, and texture.

Suitability. No young man would think of wearing a cap with a tuxedo or a fedora with a baseball suit, but the dividing line between dress and sports clothes in girls' apparel is not so easily drawn. There are, however, differences which should be kept clearly in mind. Fine textures and dressed-up effects are for dress clothes. Velvet and ribbons do not combine well with rough tweeds; lace and flowers and picture-hat brims do not usually suit casual cotton wash dresses. However, there are no hard and fast rules, for styles in fabrics change

What kind of hat will do most for your face?

and new materials are constantly being introduced. The expert costumer with a fine sense of color and texture may produce interesting effects which seem to violate ordinary rules of suitability.

Accentuating good lines and ignoring poor ones. If you have a beautiful chin or fascinating eyebrows, you may accent them by repeating the good line in the line of your hat. Every facial or body line that you repeat is made a prominent part of your physical design. If you have lines which you wish people to ignore, such as a saggy expression, a double chin, or angular cheekbones, be careful not to repeat them in your hat lines. On the other hand, a direct opposition, such as a severely straight line contrasted with a definite curve makes each type of line more noticeable. If you have angles which you wish to minimize, choose soft curves, since they will neither repeat nor oppose

30

those angles. Small hats display perfect features, but they overdisplay features which are large, irregular, or too prominent. Have you seen errors of this type in hat choices?

Lengthening face and figure. Your hat can be used to add apparent height to your figure. Diagonals, points, and upward rising lines carry the eye up and give greater apparent length, but this is only one way of achieving that effect.

What kind of hat will do most for your face?

Another is using close harmony of color and texture with the rest of the costume to create an uninterrupted rising movement. A dash of interest, high and just off center, completes the effect. Flat, wide brims and hats of contrasting color should be avoided by short persons for they tend to shorten the figure.

These same rules may be applied to men's hats, although they have less variety in shape and color. Narrow brims and high crowns, as a rule, tend to heighten the figure. The way in which the crown is creased and the way the brim is rolled affect the apparent length of both face and figure.

Shortening the face and figure. To make the face or figure seem shorter we try to stop upward, uninterrupted movement. Thus, straight-across lines for brim and crown stop the eye and apparently shorten the length of the form

31

supporting them. If the face and figure are well formed, this severe type of hat may be used, but if the jaw is too square or if face and figure are too angular, the line of the hat should be softly dipped. Another way to decrease too great height is to select a hat which contrasts in texture or color with the rest of the costume. On a man's hat, a hat band of contrasting color or darker value helps to shorten the figure.

Increasing the width of face and figure. When you shorten face and figure, you also increase their apparent width. A wide brim, or one that droops on both sides, or a flat, straight crown all cut off the length apparently and make the figure appear wider in proportion to its height. A small turban, as well as a straight crown, increases the apparent width of the face. A wide effect can also be achieved by a center division in form or trimming, because the break into two equal parts gives breadth. Is a small turban always suitable to tall, thin girls? What less severe lines can you suggest that will at the same time add to the apparent width of the figure?

The hat as a part of the ensemble. Besides height, other problems of contour should be kept in mind. Is the head large or small, the neck long or short? Are the shoulders square or sloping? The hat should be studied in its relation to all of these lines. Too many persons, both men and women, buy hats without having considered the whole body picture. When choosing a hat, always stand before a full-length mirror and examine all views, back, side, and front. Remember: for the too tall, slender figure, lines, hues, and values which cut off or stop the eye should be used. For the wide, heavy figure, uplifting lines and closely related hues and values are essential, since they draw the eye continuously upward and give apparent length. Small, close-fitting hats display a perfect head and features, but soft, medium-full lines should be used by those with irregular features. A very small hat enlarges the apparent size of the feet. A medium-small, soft-lined hat with diagonal lines and asymmetrical trimming is best for the average person.

Problems and activities. (1) Whether or not you ordinarily wear a hat to school, bring one to class for the day's study, and let your classmates judge its appropriateness to your face and figure. (2) Let class members exchange hats and study the effectiveness of the various combinations. (You will probably get some humorous effects, but do not be diverted from the purpose of the experiment.) (3) Arrange with local stores to get a loan of a number of men's hats and a number of women's hats of different designs and sizes. Try them on various members of the class, and let the group decide which ones are appropriate to which students. (4) From the collection of hats brought by the class, or borrowed from the store, experiment with ways of lengthening or widening the appearance of your face and figure, and get your classmates' judgment as to which hats are best for you. (5) Have the same student try on a number of different hats in the presence of the class to see which ones bring out good facial lines and which ones do not. (6) Try the same hat on several different students, and judge its appropriateness to the different textures and types of clothing with which it is combined.

4. TRIMMINGS

Choosing Accessories

In choosing accessories, too many people behave as if the human body were a Christmas tree to be decorated with tinsel and ornaments. Even when trimming a tree, a thoughtful person considers its size and shape, and tries to emphasize its beauty instead of hiding it. How much more important it is to make intelligent use of the principles of design when adding decorations to a costume! A good rule to follow is: Do not add anything to your costume unless it is actually needed.

Jewelry is only for the purpose of adding color and brilliance. Flowers may add interest through color, form, and fragrance. Furs are soft and flattering in texture. Each of these is good in itself, but if too many are used together, the effect is confusing. One thing too many is the error of many girls. How many accessories do the best-dressed persons you know wear at one time? Learn to exploit and emphasize one piece of jewelry, a flower, or some other single accessory. Eliminate everything else that detracts from its beauty. Keep in mind that unity usually develops from emphasis on one thing, with all others subordinated or eliminated.

It is true that the term *accessories* is often used for certain essentials of clothing as well as for ornaments. For example, men's ties, socks, handkerchiefs, and scarfs are usually thought of as accessories, largely because they may be used to give color and contrast to the costume. Their hues and textures have decorative value.

With what kinds of costumes should you use patterned accessories?

Pattern versus plain areas. The relation of plain to patterned surfaces should always be considered in good costuming. Each pattern is generally most effective when offset by a plain area. Patterned socks and ties go well with plain suits; plain ties, handkerchiefs, and socks are good with patterned suits. In dresses, decorated or flowered material should be left unadorned as far as possible, and will seem most beautiful against unpatterned areas. Lace, embroidery, and appliqué should not be obscured by too lively a background. Many persons fail to realize how important plain areas are and consequently make a number of mistakes. They use lace collars on decorated material, patterned handkerchiefs with plaid or striped suits, elaborate corsages on flowered dresses, and patterned clips against sparkling weaves. What fine choices of decorative design and unpatterned areas have you seen in dress design? How many ensembles have you seen today that overused pattern?

Colors. Accessories may harmonize with the color of the costume or contrast with it. Brilliant green and dull green-gold are striking against a dress of reddish or orange color because they contrast. Amber and topaz on the same costume might be good because they would create a close harmony. Red-violet against mustard is striking but no less beautiful. Some accessories, of course, may duplicate the color of the costume, giving the opportunity to spotlight a single piece by contrast.

For further information about selecting and combining colors, refer to pages 62-85.

The problem of color in sports accessories should receive special study. Since the costume itself is often colorful, take care not to ruin its effect by too many or the wrong accessories.

What accessories might you wear with a yellow sports dress? A white formal dress? A flame-colored formal? What colors in tie and handkerchief do you like with a blue suit? A suit of brownish tweed? Why are black and white rather than colors the traditional style for men's formal dress? Does the matter of contrast with the bright or delicate colors in women's evening dresses have something to do with the question?

Sizes. In choosing accessories as in choosing shoes and hat, the whole figure should be considered. What reasons can you think of for a large person's not wearing dainty ornaments? Large, bold accessories are for the medium-sized and well-formed figure; dainty ones are definitely for the small. Too large ornaments on a large, heavy girl will only emphasize her size, and a dainty figure is overpowered by bold ornaments. Therefore, in selecting costume jewelry, bear in mind the size of the person who is to wear it and do not be caught by a fad of the moment.

Shapes. Triangles, squares, rectangles, circles, ovals, and many-sided figures are basic geometric shapes used in art. In addition to these, many irregular shapes inspired by nature are used in accessories. Each shape may be considered individually for its interest, the beauty of its proportions, and its charm of contour. You can ask yourself before purchasing any ornament, "Is the shape really good-looking?" Then: "Does it harmonize with the costume for which I have chosen it? Does it repeat the lines of other accessories which I will wear?"

A good principle to remember is that it is difficult to combine many varieties of shapes. In other words, repetition of like forms is a safe method of securing unity. A single striking ornament will be most effective when offset by simple forms and plain surfaces, although repeating the same shape in small sizes will also emphasize it. What was the most attractive combination of costume and accessories you have seen recently? Why was it attractive? Have you

Why can't small or large people wear massive
accessories?

seen people who seemed to be wearing every shape imaginable? What was your impulse on seeing them?

Problems and activities. (1) Arrange for each member of the class to bring several different costume ornaments or accessories and to try different ones or combinations of these in the presence of the class for criticisms and suggested improvements. (2) By trading accessories from student to student, see what good and bad effects you can get and what mistakes you should try to avoid. (3) Display several different accessory articles of clothing apart from any ensemble for the moment, and judge each one as to its appropriateness of design in and of itself. (4) Lay a dozen or more different kinds of accessories on the table, and let a committee of the class choose the ones that would be particularly appropriate for a given student. Repeat the process to make selections for other students. (5) Do this same kind of experiment with the attention centered primarily upon color harmonies and contrasts. (6) Choose several accessory articles which would be appropriate to a given individual, and add them one at a time until you feel the point has been reached at which any others would do more harm than good by overloading.

5. HELPING NATURE

Choosing and Applying Make-up and Nail Polish

Various kinds of make-up are an accepted part of today's costuming for women and can be used to enhance natural beauty. They can also obscure nat-

How can your rouge change the apparent shape of your face? The faces above are identical.

ural beauty if used in excess or without care. A natural effect is still the ultimate aim of the beauty expert, but an effect somewhat different from that admired by former generations. Color may be used for either harmony or contrast or both. The skin may be brought into tone with the general costume ensemble and the mouth, cheeks, and nails may serve as color repeats or accents.

Always bear in mind that the make-up is a part of the general costume effect. Make-up suitable for a party when you are wearing a sophisticated frock is likely to be quite out of place with your tweed suit at a football game.

Powder base and powder. Before powder is applied, the pores of the skin should be thoroughly cleansed and then protected with a good powder base.

37

Powder should be lightly patted on and dusted with a powder puff. It should never be rubbed into the skin. The powder should be chosen to match the underlying color of the skin, but may be slightly warmer, darker, or lighter, according to the effect desired. If it is very different from the skin color, it will show for what it is—a surface application. For sallow skin a slightly orange tone is advisable in the powder. If your skin is too pale, a slightly darker shade may give it a more healthy effect. Sun-tan powders should be used in seasons when they match the healthy outdoor look. Too light a powder over a warm tan is very noticeable and may be even ludicrous.

Rouge and lipstick. Purplish make-up is for the skin with the underlying purplish tone, and the more orange, pure red, or brownish shades for the orange-toned and sallow skins. Paste or liquid rouge of the same color may be applied to both the lips and cheeks, or lipstick and powdered rouge may be used. When applying rouge for daylight wear, always do so under a strong light, or by a window in flooding sunlight. A subdued light is a harmonizer that deserts you when you step into the daylight. Allow for the most revealing light possible in the place where your make-up is to be seen, whether it is daylight or artificial. For an oval face the rouge may follow the natural line. If the face is thin, apply the rouge at the edges; if it is round and plump, be careful not to stress the edges. The chin and the tips of the ears may be given a slight color if this improves your facial design. For the small mouth apply lipstick evenly to the edges; for the large mouth, accent the center of the lips and blend toward the edges. For the thin mouth, accent the upper lip.

Eye make-up. When skillfully applied, eyeshade is useful for theatrical effects, but sensible girls will not strive for such effects in everyday life. Languishing looks may be suitable on a tropical isle in a movie scene, but they are not for school or business office. A light penciling of subdued or very pale eyebrows is sometimes needed. Eyelashes may be slightly darkened with mascara if they are thick enough to allow accenting in this way. The eyelashes should match the eyebrows in color. However, any eye make-up must be very skillfully used, else it will give the face a highly artificial look.

Nails and nail polish. Nails which make the hands look like claws violate all principles of art. Nails should never be so long that they make the hands look as if they could do none of the things for which hands are intended. No one can play the piano or use the typewriter or do even light work efficiently with inch-long nails. And very few persons have hands of sufficient natural beauty so that they can bear the spotlighting which brilliant color gives. Hands were made for use, and hands that look useful and capable have a kind of beauty which is not improved by strong color accent.

A moderately long nail with a rounded point is always in good taste, and a polish of flesh pink or slightly deeper tone is becoming to all hands. Brighter color to repeat the accent of rouge and lipstick may be suitable for some persons and occasions.

How many boys really like to see a girl's nails inch-long, sharply pointed, and covered with scarlet, cerise, or deep red polish? It is one of the puzzles of modern life that so many women follow this fashion even though the majority of men seem to object to it.

Problems and activities. (1) Arrange beforehand for the girls to come to class made up as best they know how so that their taste and skill may be judged and evaluated by the other girls and by the boys in the class. (2) Arrange for a capable beauty expert to do the same girl's face in several different designs or styles, and let the class judge the effectiveness of each. (3) Demonstrate before the class how the placing of lipstick or rouge can have the effect of increasing or decreasing the size of the mouth, the width of the face, or achieving other proportions. (4) Using actual cases of make-up on girls in the class, get a comparative judgment of their effectiveness as rated by the boys and as rated by the girls to see how well the standards of boys and of girls agree. (5) Let the boys of the class express themselves, anonymously if they prefer, regarding the use of eye make-up or nail polish.

IV. The Shape You Are In

Dressing according to shape and size

Human beings are not machine made, and few are blessed with perfect figures. In fact, the perfect figure, like the so-called average man, is a myth. The matter of perfection is largely a matter of proportions, and not all persons agree as to the perfect proportions. Slenderness in the feminine figure seems to be the ideal of the day, probably because it suggests youth, but the fuller, more mature figure has been in vogue in the past and has many admirers today. In America the tall, rather lean, broad-shouldered man is usually admired as having the ideal figure, but among other peoples different standards prevail. The important thing to remember is that beauty of figure is largely a matter of proportions and that you can improve the apparent proportions of your own figure by applying the principles of art in planning your clothes.

What kind of figure have you? Are you round and plump or thin and angular? Are you too tall or too short? Have you figure defects, such as too wide hips or too thin arms? Turn to the section in this chapter that fits your case and find what artistic wizardry may be performed with lines, shapes, and colors. If you are overweight, turn to "Dangerous Curves." If you are thin and angular, read the section entitled "The Shortest Distance." If you are too tall and heavy, or too short and thin, you have a conflicting problem which is dealt with in the section called "The Long and Short of It." If you find fault with the original construction job done on your chassis, try being "Tailor Made" and your figure defects will melt away. If you are well built for your height, you need not envy "Bathing Beauties and Life Guards," but even you must dress carefully or you may submerge your charms. In the section by that title you will find helpful suggestions.

40

DRESSING ACCORDING TO SHAPE AND SIZE

What shape is your face? A perfect oval, round, or long and thin? Are you satisfied with your reflection in the mirror, or do you wish to do something about it? Is your head large or small in relation to your body? Does your neck appear to be too long or too short? Do you wish to change the apparent contour? Have you a facial feature you would like to remodel, such as a large or a turned-up nose, an aggressive or a receding chin, a too prominent or too low forehead, a droopy expression, or a bad skin? In the section entitled "Human Clay" you will learn how to subordinate these limitations by reshaping the head and neck contour so as to take attention away from them.

Creating a beautiful body is as much an art problem as any other development of form. In a very real sense it is the most important art problem you have. Using clothes to aid you, in addition to diet and exercise, is only common sense, since all artists use line, form, dark and light, texture, and color to create illusions or to express their feelings. Your costuming, if it is possible for you to choose or create your own clothes, is an expression of the way you feel about yourself. Pride in yourself will make itself known by presenting to your fellows the best-proportioned figure possible.

1. Dangerous Curves

Minimizing the Appearance of Overweight

Dangerous curves are those that are dangerous for your happiness, but do not be foolishly sensitive if you are somewhat overweight. Some persons are naturally heavier than others, because of a heavier bony structure, more muscle, or greater amounts of fatty tissue. It may be perfectly natural for you to weigh more than the person of the same height living next door to you. Even if we all ate identical foods there would be considerable variation in weight because of our differing glandular, nervous, and emotional make-ups. It is advisable, however, to be as near normal as is comfortably possible. Rest, exercise, adequate liquids, and carefully chosen foods are essential in regulating your body. Warm cleansing baths and stinging cold showers clean your pores and stimulate the blood flow, thus helping to improve your health and make your flesh firm. Understimulated glands may be accelerated by medicines prescribed by a physician, but unprescribed faddist diets or tricks are dangerous, and may permanently undermine your health. Get the advice of an expert before undertaking any drastic reducing program.

However, there are several things that you yourself may do about the problem of overweight. First, do not feel self-conscious about it; second, remember that no flesh is added to the body except by way of the mouth; and third, select your clothing to minimize your size.

Silhouette. Contour lines are the outline of the figure as it silhouettes itself against the background. Black and very dark colors create precise well-defined edges, and therefore should be avoided by those with excessive curves. Medium values, neither too dark nor too light, will melt most easily into any surroundings and give a certain indefiniteness to the silhouette. Garments and hats that are neither too loose nor too tight, with upward reaching lines, lend height and reduce apparent width. As a rule normal divisions of the body should be followed for belt and shoulders. Neck lines should be smoothly fitting. Tight collars and excessive frills should be avoided. Tight or very full sleeves and kimono sleeves are bad for the large figure, since each adds to the appearance of bulk. Flowing sleeves also stress width, particularly when they end at the widest part of the hips. A smooth-fitting set-in sleeve beginning at the normal point of the shoulder gives a satisfactory silhouette.

In men's clothes similar rules apply. Double-breasted coats and raglan sleeves add to the look of bulkiness. A very loose-fitting overcoat enlarges the silhouette, but one too tightly fitted emphasizes curves.

Moderation should be followed in the cut of trousers or skirt. They should be neither too skimpy and curve-revealing, nor too full and bulky. A medium-length skirt is better than one that is long or short, because the long skirt creates too large a bulky area and the short skirt increases the apparent width by contrast.

Shoes and hats that are neither too small in scale for the body nor too wide and flat are most effective in the ensemble design of a heavy person. Both slender high heels and thin high hat trimmings emphasize by contrast the large proportions of the figure. Hair should be smoothly and softly dressed, since the head should appear neither too small nor too large.

DRESSING ACCORDING TO SHAPE AND SIZE

Space divisions. Everything that tends to divide the length of the overweight figure should be avoided. Suits and overcoats without belts are best. Full length coats are better than those of three-quarter length for both men and women with broad figures. Separate waists and skirts or unmatched coats and trousers,

How many causes can you pick out that explain the apparent differences in size between these identical pairs?

overskirts, broad sashes, wide collars and cuffs, all divide the body into shorter parts instead of creating a streamlined whole.

Moderation in sizes of trimming, jewelry, and all accessories is best for the overweight person. Very small accessories are out of scale; massive ones add to the appearance of weight.

Line. Upward reaching lines, of course, tend to lengthen the body and to narrow it proportionately. Center lines, including narrow panels, divide the figure into two equal parts, however, and this division always tends to widen it. Very wide central panels also lead the eye across and thus stress the width. A double-breasted coat gives the same squaring effect as a wide panel. Off-center lines, long, smooth, draped curves, and diagonals are most lengthening, since they stress height and avoid the widening effect of equal divisions. Of these, the diagonal line is most effective. A costume with a long line topped off by a hat with a slanted brim and high off-center trimming will have a surprisingly slenderizing effect. A turban, not too closely fitted, may also be becoming, especially if the fold is diagonal so that it extends the upward linear effect of the costume.

Do not make the common mistake of thinking that lengthwise stripes, pleats, and tucks always emphasize length. A closely spaced repetition of perpendicular lines pulls the eye across the body and stresses its width. Stripes, pleats, and tucks are becoming only when designed in varied widths or in well proportioned panels. Severely straight surface lines in the design or material only emphasize contour curves. On the other hand, circular repeats emphasize roundness. Large smooth curves are the most satisfying lines for the stout figure. If patterned material is used, the repeat motifs should be longer than they are wide.

In men's suits, lines have similar effects. Stout men should avoid loud checks and decided stripes. Pin stripes or very inconspicuous wider stripes usually help to give an effect of height. A chevron pattern or weave, because of the diagonal lines, is good for breaking the width of the figure.

Dark and light. Very dark colors throw the silhouette sharply into relief against most backgrounds. Medium values are more becoming to the stout figure because they are less revealing. Pastels and softened grayish colors camouflage the contours. Neutral browns and grays are good for men's suits. Light-colored forms seem emphatically lighter in weight than dark ones. The light color is most successful if slightly softened or grayed. Contrasting values may be introduced in an accessory, particularly near the face, but should not be used on the belt or hips. White cuffs on a dark dress accent the width of the figure usually at the widest part. Strong dark and light patterned materials are not usually advisable for the overweight person.

Color. The effect of colors on apparent size is important. Colors are sometimes divided into "warm" and "cool" hues. The bluish colors are cool, and the reddish, orange, or yellowish ones are warm. Such common phrases as "blue with cold" and "red-hot" illustrate this difference. Observation shows that cool colors tend to recede into the distance, and to appear farther away than they really are. Because they seem to recede and to shrink, cool colors make things seem smaller than they are. Warm colors are just the opposite. They seem to advance into the foreground, and to demand attention for the entire surface they cover. Because warm colors are advancing and demand attention, they make areas that they cover seem larger.

You may have noticed another fact about color which is important in clothing selection: color in the distance appears lighter (in value) and grayer (in intensity) than the same color in the foreground. For example, trees in the distance are a lighter, duller, and cooler green than those nearby. Therefore, we say that warm, bright colors stay in the foreground or advance toward you, and that cool, grayed (or less intense) and light colors recede or go away into the distance.

If you do not want to call too much attention to your figure, therefore, you will wear the cooler, less intense colors. That is, girls will be likely to select grayed greens, blues, and dull violets, and boys will choose neutral tans, browns, grayed blues, and grays. You will not select bright red or orange or even very bright blue. Pure warm colors in large areas are taboo for the overweight person, but they may be worn for accessories or for small areas of contrast. If a person's general coloring demands warm hues, they should be subdued or grayed for the large portions of the costume. But, as a general rule, grayed intensities of the bluish hues are best for the large person because they are soft and retiring.

Texture. Texture is the result of several factors: the nature of the material from which the fabric is made, the type of weave or construction, and the applied surface pattern. The material may be shiny and pliable like silk, medium shiny like linen, or dull and lusterless like tweed. In addition, it may be closely woven or wide-meshed and soft or rather stiff. The applied pattern may be bold or dainty, of strongly contrasted or closely related values and hues, and with perpendicular, horizontal, or diagonal feeling. The stout person should choose dull nonreflecting surfaces and avoid shiny materials that would highlight and reveal bulk. Likewise, the medium soft and soft weaves are best. Stiff woolens, piqués, and taffetas should be avoided, since they stand away from the figure, and add to one's size. Transparent materials, in whatever color they are used, should be of the same value as the surface they cover; otherwise they accentuate size. Plain material, as a rule, is more becoming to the stout person, but patterned and plain materials may be combined to cut the figure becomingly. In this case the pattern should be on a larger scale than if it were for a small person, and it should not be too contrasting in hue and value. Plaids are not good, since the straight lines contrast too strongly with the curves of the figure. Also a boy who is very short and heavy set should avoid rough tweeds which tend to thicken the figure and should choose softer, smoother materials of plain or all-over pattern.

Problems and activities. (See end of chapter for learning activities which apply to the various types of figures.)

2. THE SHORTEST DISTANCE

Adding Curves to the Straight Figure

The boy or girl who is underweight, like his too heavy neighbor, should remember that certain variations are normal. If you are too far below the normal, or if you should lose weight suddenly and rapidly, by all means seek the advice of a physician. Slenderness is usually attractive, especially in youth, but a starved-looking body is not the ideal figure. Usually proper rest, food, and exercise can work wonders toward correcting that too angular look, as well as toward improving health. If you are in excellent health and still naturally thin and angular, you can do much by means of costume design to improve your appearance.

As you know, the shortest distance between two points is a straight line. Therefore, in clothing the angular figure, everything should be done to arrest the speeding eye. It should be led the longest way around, with many stops and starts. Contours, division lines, hues, and textures should be utilized for this purpose, so that angles are disguised and a more rounded figure is suggested.

Contours and division lines. Tight, angle-revealing clothes should be avoided by the slim person. Central division lines, very narrow panels, and very wide panels give a widening effect. These should be in softened lines, if possible, since all severely straight lines or angular effects add to the angularity of the figure. Short jackets and short wide sleeves have a widening effect. Three-quarter length coats with flared or "swagger" lines are widening and shortening. Slender boys and girls can wear belted coats well. The Norfolk or the half-belted jacket is excellent for concealing angles. Hats of average size and irregular lines with low crowns and drooping brims arrest the eye and shorten the apparent height of the figure. High, pointed hats should be avoided.

Hues, values, and intensities. The major problem for the too-thin person in selecting colors is to find something which will camouflage rather than emphasize thinness. Because the thin girl does not want to call attention to bony angles and flat chest lines, she should not use colors which stress contours and outlines. Warm colors, intense colors, and dark values define edges sharply. Therefore, dark, intense, warm colors, such as pure red, are the worst possible choice for the thin person. Cool colors, on the other hand, tend to recede, and therefore blur edges. If they are slightly grayed and light in value, they are excellent choices for the too-thin figure. Warm colors, if grayed and light in value, may also be worn, since the grayness and medium lightness do not emphasize the edges, and lightness expands apparent size. Light values, although technically supposed to add to size, have the more important asset of making contours indefinite unless used against a very dark background. A medium value background is the usual one in life situations.

Textures. If the aim is to make a person seem larger, it is logical to select materials which will stand away from the figure, rather than those which cling to it. Furthermore, it is sensible to select opaque rather than transparent textiles, and these may be starched if the starching does not make them seem too stiff and angular. Shiny materials highlight and call attention to angles, and are therefore not as good choices as soft and dull weaves. Anyone with an

47

angular figure, either boy or girl, can wear tweeds and similar rough woolens with good effect.

3. THE LONG AND SHORT OF IT

Stressing and Minimizing Height

The long and the short of it is that in most cases tall people should be proud of their height and short people should capitalize on individuality. It is the contour of the figure and the proportion of its width to its height that needs at-

What do these costumes on the same figure suggest about how to look tall or short?

tention. A figure that is too tall in relation to its width needs to be widened and thereby shortened; a figure that is too short in proportion to its width should be heightened and thereby narrowed. The person who is both heavy and tall has the double problem of contracting in both directions. The short

48

person who is too thin needs to add bulk without reducing apparent height. In any case, it is a problem of using lines, values, and textures in such a way as to cause the illusion of perfect proportions.

The long of it. If you are tall and too thin, your problem is comparatively easy, because in trying to correct the look of thinness you ˙ ill use lines to widen the figure, and thus you reduce the apparent height. If your body is tall but perfectly proportioned, smart, square-cut tailored lines are excellent. In addition, use contrasts in value in horizontals of varying widths. If you are tall and too bulky, you will wish to contract both downward and inward. In order to achieve this contraction it will be necessary to plan well spaced vertical lines offset by horizontals. Since an unbroken costume surface emphasizes size, you will seek some kind of pattern to minimize both height and width. You already know that horizontal lines used alone stress width, and perpendiculars usually stress height. Therefore, the only possible solution is a balance of upward reaching lines (to reduce width) which are neatly checked by cross lines (to minimize height). By such opposition of verticals and horizontals the desired effect of contraction can be obtained. Naturally, extremes should be avoided. The patterns should be neither too large nor too small, nor should they have too much contrast.

Proper colors are also important. Cool colors of medium or weak intensity and of medium or light value are generally best for the angular figure, because these colors camouflage contours. Warm colors, if grayed in intensity and light or medium in value, may also be worn to good advantage. Soft, dull textures are better than shiny ones.

Accessories should be carefully chosen. Experiment with the type of heel that is most becoming to your figure. You will find that contrasting hats, shoes, ties, scarfs, and jewelry usually tend to reduce too great height.

The short of it. If you are short and too wide, you have the problem of making yourself appear taller and thereby more slender. You will strive to minimize your width and emphasize your height in ways which have already been explained. If you are short but well-proportioned, you have some latitude of choice in the effect you aim at. You may dress in such a way as to create either a dainty or a sophisticated appearance. Wide, circular lines, ruffles, and bows will stress the dainty, youthful quality which many small women possess. On the other hand, smooth tailoring with youthful box-cut effects, plus diagonal lines and ornaments, gives distinction and dignity. However, both boys and girls who are under average size should take care not to go to extremes in their desire to look taller and more dignified. They can afford to capitalize on their youthful figures.

For the person who is both too short and too thin, the problem is to expand both upward and outward. Long diagonal lines will give the maximum illusion of height. If these long, upward-reaching diagonals are offset by crossing diagonals at their upper extremity, both height and width are apparently increased. An unbroken costume surface is usually too dignified and sober for the small person, and in the case of the angular figure it is too revealing. The dainty thin girl should use frills, ruffles, and ornaments of proper scale. The short, slight young man should beware of clothes that make him look like a pocket edition of his elders. Moderately rough textures and diagonal lines are most helpful.

The short person has a wider range of colors from which to select than do most types. Either warm or cool colors of medium or light values may be used, and the colors may be strong or weak in intensity. Warm colors and strong intensities enlarge the apparent size of the figure, and are very flattering if a person's contours allow her to wear them. Dark values should be avoided; although they accentuate contours, they also make the wearer seem smaller. The matter of suitable scale of textures needs also to be considered. Thus, finely-woven, supple fabrics and flat furs are in scale with a girl's small figure. For boys salt-and-pepper textures or small, all-over patterns of contrasting hues or values add to both height and width without being cumbersome. Shoes and accessories should not contrast too strongly with the costume, but should be of the same hue, or at least the same value, as the suit or dress. Since the short person is trying to appear taller, interest should never be concentrated at the belt line, but rather at the neck line, hair line, or hat.

Checking up on your knowledge. Try now to answer the following questions about the use of line and color in costumes for special shapes and sizes:

Why are diagonal lines good for the short person?

Where should you place the center of interest for the too tall person? For the too short person?

Do vertical lines always make the figure look taller?

Which colors are expanding? Which are contracting?

For which type of person should you suggest shiny, reflecting surfaces? Which type should avoid these?

Which type of person may best wear warm colors of strong intensity? Which type may wear these colors least well?

The facts about colors and lines which you have been learning apply not only to costumes but to all fields of art. Later you will apply the same general principles to home, school, and business.

4. TAILOR MADE

Counteracting Figure Defects

If you feel that you are handicapped by round or sloping shoulders, large hips or upper arms, too long or too short a waist, do not be discouraged. Sometimes a person with a real defect of figure achieves a better appearance than one with perfect proportions just because he has to strive to attain it.

First of all, try to improve your posture. Round shoulders, flat chest, protruding abdomen, and a sway-back line can be partly cured by good posture.

Other defects can be counteracted or camouflaged by an adjustment of lines and spaces and by careful use of dark and light, hue, and texture. You can learn how to achieve the effect of a well-proportioned figure by using all that you are learning about the principles of art.

All figure defects. Grayed and cool colors, medium and light values, and dull (nonreflecting) textures help to camouflage figure defects. Intense and warm colors, very dark values, and shiny textures accentuate shapes and contours. Clinging materials, such as chiffon, jersey, and soft knitted fabrics, reveal the lines of the figure. These general rules alone should help you solve many of your problems.

Round shoulders. Materials that are of sufficient body but not too stiff may be cut in such a way as to lessen a bad outside shoulder curve. Set-in sleeves should be used and raglan sleeves avoided. Armhole seams should be set slightly back of the normal line to minimize the width of the shoulder silhouette. Take care not to let the shoulder seam slant forward, thus repeating and emphasizing the rounded line of the back. If possible, get the help of a good tailor or dress-maker to correct any tendency a garment may have to shrug up into a fold

What can a skillful tailor do for you if you have round shoulders?

across the back of the shoulders. A round-shouldered girl should avoid any heavy ornament that tends to pull down the front of the blouse. Soft collars are better than collarless sweaters or blouses. Triangular lines or long ovals in pat-terned material are better than circular lines which accentuate round shoulders by repeating them, or squares which emphasize them by opposition.

Sloping shoulders. Built-out shoulders and puffed sleeves counteract the weak effect of a sloping shoulder line. Lines in the costume which parallel the downward slope and those which run directly into it should be avoided, since either repetition or opposition will stress the weak line.

Protruding abdomen. Your abdominal muscles should never be allowed to sag. Put effort into strengthening them so that they will do their work properly.

52

A correctly fitted girdle will help, but posture is important. Press the top of your head up into the sun and lift your chest proudly. Any bulge which you cannot control should be camouflaged by correct lines of dress or suit. Have your dress, especially the skirt, fitted smoothly but not too tightly, with a semilow belt line. A belt that is too low emphasizes the wrong lines. A suit coat or cardigan with straight lines helps to camouflage curves. A tucked-in blouse, shirt, or sweater with a tightly belted skirt reveals poor lines. A ruffled or draped blouse for a girl or a full four-in-hand tie for a boy helps to balance the lines by giving fullness above. Fancy belts and sashes, watch chains, and fobs which attract attention to the waistline should be avoided.

Large hips. Your hips can be made to look smaller by enlarging the apparent size of the rest of the body, and by forcing attention to some other area than the hip line. Triangular lines, ovals, and diagonals which direct the eye to the shoulder or waistline are good. Wide-shouldered garments and puffed sleeves make hips seem smaller by comparison. If you wear short sleeves, have them short enough to end above the widest part of the hips. On long sleeves do not wear white cuffs, because when the arms hang at the side, white attracts attention to the hip line. Have long sleeves fitted at the wrist so that they will not accentuate the width. In the costume as a whole, avoid horizontal lines and stress instead well-spaced perpendicular lines. Since evenly spaced stripes and pleats draw the eye crosswise, avoid them at the hips. Circular skirts, with the flare beginning just above the widest part of the hips, are excellent. Belts should be of medium width and of the same color and value as the costume. Wide belts which contrast in color and value should be avoided. Skirts should be long or of medium length. Hats should be large and designed on diagonal lines.

Large upper arms. Well-designed sleeves made of carefully chosen fabrics help to conceal large upper arms. Transparent fabrics reveal the arms; therefore semiopaque materials are a better choice. Shiny fabrics highlight the curves; therefore nonlustrous fabrics are preferable. A plain material, or one that has a perpendicular pattern, is better than one which stresses width by horizontal lines. If lines are a part of the texture of the material, they should be arranged lengthwise rather than crosswise on the arms. Sleeveless dresses and tightly fitting sleeves should be avoided. Set-in sleeves, with the shoulder seam running to the extreme outer edge of the shoulder, are helpful. These should be set into a semifitted or loosely fitted waist. Horizontal lines in the bodice may stress its width in relation to the apparent size of the arm.

A flat chest. Push like a pouter pigeon against your chest muscles, and fill out your concave front. Your shoulders should not be allowed to fall forward, nor should they be pressed back. Either of these two positions cramps the lungs. The entire body should be pulled in and up in one plumb line from the arch of the foot through the knee, the hipbone, the shoulder, and the ear. This muscular pressure will help fill out the hollow chest.

Flat-chested boys should wear loose fitting shirts with full four-in-hand ties; girls should choose dresses or blouses with soft-gathered front draperies. Firm, semistiff materials, with enough body to stand out and create apparent bulk, are good. Very fine, soft, clinging materials should be avoided. Soft long collars give a better line than small, close-fitting ones. A blouse or shirt with a front that is tucked, gathered, or pleated into the shoulder seam creates an appearance of fullness. Double-breasted coats are better than single-breasted ones for the same reason. Horizontal lines and plaid effects in the pattern or texture of the material are good, since they expand apparent chest size.

The overdeveloped chest. A well-developed chest is a figure asset, but if the rest of the body is out of proportion in relation to it, lines and colors must be carefully arranged. Tightly fitted waistlines or skirts should be avoided. A low belt line and long ovals and triangular lines through the waist relieve the feeling of bulk. Horizontals should be avoided across the chest, but may be used to stress the apparent width of the hips if the figure will permit this shortening effect. Semiloose garments are less revealing than snugly fitted ones. Low, soft neck lines and softly falling draperies are better than fitted bodices with tight, high collars. There should be no contrast in values at the breast line because they center extra attention there and increase the apparent size. Corsages, brooches, or other accessories should be placed high, near the shoulder line.

Waists longer or shorter than normal. If your waistline is either higher or lower than you wish it to be, merely lower or raise the belt line of your costume. Wear your clothing rather loosely fitted at the waistline, and use firm materials with enough stiffness to stand away from the body. Triangular lines and diagonals will help to lengthen the part of the body which is out of proportion.

General principles. In this section you have been given a number of very specific ways of overcoming certain figure defects which might otherwise interfere with your best appearance and, consequently, with your greatest happiness. These are not laws or rules in any sense, but are guides based on observation. They should not be followed slavishly, but should be studied, interpreted, and used intelligently.

As you have seen, lines, forms, colors, and textures may be used to emphasize or minimize certain portions of the body, or certain characteristics. The important thing to remember is that these elements—like words—can be used in a number of ways. Some call attention to one thing, some call attention to another. Size up your figure again, and decide which parts you want emphasized. Then plan your clothes so that they attract attention where you want it.

Problems and activities. (1) Ask a tailor or dressmaker to describe methods by which the appearance of round shoulders and other faults of the figure can be counteracted in designing and making clothes. Perhaps you can find one who will come to your class and demonstrate these matters by fitting a coat or dress right before your eyes and showing how the lines must be altered for different figures. (2) Experiment with coats of different design and see which ones emphasize or minimize slanting shoulders or any other feature of your appearance which you wish to correct. (3) Draw on the blackboard diagrams showing particular figure defects, then add the corrective touches which you would make by your choice of clothing. (4) Select well-dressed students from the class who are about the same size but of different builds; have them exchange articles of clothing, and note the effect produced on each by the change.

5. HUMAN CLAY

Minimizing Facial Defects

No one has a perfect face. Even the top-ranking movie stars have certain facial irregularities which in reality add to your interest in them. You can readily think of actors and actresses whose noses are too large, whose ears protrude, whose chins and mouths are weak, or whose foreheads are too high or too low. If you glance at pictures of successful people in any walk of life, you will find that very few of them are really beautiful. If you find them attractive, it is usually because their faces reveal strength of character or personality, and in the long run this is vastly more important than looking like a baby doll or an advertising model.

Your face is the mirror of what you are. It reflects your thoughts, your emotions, your actions. It tells the world a great deal about *you*, and it does this far more through expression than through features. Your features came from your ancestors, but your expression is what you make it. A person who is happy and friendly looks that way. If you are constantly angry, pouting, or sad, your face takes on that look. The place to begin improving your face is with your thoughts and attitudes.

But your features are important too. Often by selecting your clothes and hats carefully, and by combing your hair intelligently, you can do a good deal toward improving your facial appearance. As with clothes, a good principle to follow is: *Never repeat or strongly oppose an unattractive line or feature.* A number of specific applications of this principle are given on the following pages. As you try to apply the principles to yourself, avoid getting self-conscious over what you have to start with.

Drooping facial lines. Drooping facial lines are one of the commonest defects, and, fortunately, one of the easiest to remedy. When you feel happy or gay, drooping lines usually disappear. The intricate facial muscles become lively and energetic. As they pull in and up, sagging lines vanish as if by magic. Cheerful thoughts will do more than cosmetics to cure drooping lines. If you have allowed sagging lines to appear, work to remove them and at the same time dress in such a way that they will seem less conspicuous. Avoid repeating the drooping lines in the brim of your hat, the edge of your hair, or the collar of your dress or suit, and also avoid lines which directly oppose them. Wear hats, hairdress, and neck lines with soft indefinite edges. Avoid hard, tailored lines.

Your skin. At times almost every person has a poor complexion. Usually this is a transitory condition, and disappears without special treatment. Keep your skin clean by using pure soap and water, and the chances are that before long your complexion will be good. If blemishes persist, however, it may be wise to consult a doctor to learn the cause and to effect a cure. If your skin is not perfect, there are several things you can do to improve its appearance. Avoid wearing materials that put your skin at a disadvantage. Do not wear shiny, smooth materials, because rougher textures will call less attention to your face. Linen is less trying to an imperfect skin than chiffon, and tweeds are better than serges. In general, woolens are more becoming than silks.

A prominent nose. If your nose seems a little too large for your other features, try to counteract its prominence by watching your actions and your voice. Avoid conspicuous mannerisms and a loud voice. Try to belong to the group you are with rather than to be out in front of it. Hairdress and hats can help to disguise a large nose. Avoid the following: (1) a hairdress with bunches at the back or sides of the head on a level with the nose; (2) tight waves in your hair; (3) turbans and small, turned-up hats; (4) hats which have trimming at the top or back. You will find that soft, full hair which is brushed forward over the forehead is best for the large-nosed face, and soft, full waves are most becoming. Hats with soft, rolling, wide, front brims are most flattering, and trimming should be at the front.

A turned-up nose. This kind of nose also deserves study. If it is your most charming feature (and it may very well be that), you will wish to emphasize it. But if it is not in keeping with your other features or your personality, you will wish to make it as inconspicuous as possible. Remember the general principle of neither repeating nor opposing an unattractive line. Avoid both a hairdress that parallels the curve of the nose and one that reverses it. Instead, try hair lines which form a soft background for the face without emphasizing the nose. The same principle can be applied to hats. A hat with a downward drooping brim emphasizes the upward tilt of the nose by opposition. An upward curving brim that repeats the line of the nose should also be avoided in favor of a fairly straight brim of medium size. A heavy hat stresses the smallness of the nose.

A prominent chin. A strong, prominent chin is nothing to be bothered about unless it detracts from the other features. If that is the case, several things can be done. In order to bring the rest of your face into proportion with your chin, the hair and hat above the ears should be widened, and any widening at the jaw level should be avoided. Your hair should be built high and wide above the ears. A large hat is better than a turban or small hat. A full, soft mass of hair or a hat brim extending over the forehead will help to neutralize the heavy chin and jaw.

A receding chin. Many a person wishes that his chin were a little more prominent than it is. Mere wishful thinking will not change it, but the right

How can you adjust your hair in order to look like a lady instead of a dictator?

thoughts can help. Discontent and fretful pouting manners merely increase and draw attention to a weak chin and sagging mouth. Cheerfulness and resolution, on the other hand, actually change the lines around the mouth and chin. If you are poised, gracious, and self-controlled, few people will notice your chin line. If there is any possibility that teeth or adenoids are deforming the facial contours, consult a doctor or dentist. In many cases the chin line can be made inconspicuous simply by avoiding an overbalance of weight on the upper part of the face. Hair, hats, or trimmings massed over the forehead stress the smallness of the chin. Irregular hat brims of medium width are best. Turbans and "beanies" should be avoided since they emphasize a receding chin by repeating the same type of line. A small knot of hair at the neck, or short hair with a soft medium-full wave, is good. A high, wide, or bushy hairdress should be avoided if the lower part of the face is weak.

A prominent or a low forehead. The forehead that is too high and bulging and the forehead that is too low and flat create opposing problems. A boy with a low forehead may add to its apparent height by a pompadour haircut. A side part is more becoming to the narrow high forehead. For a girl with a low forehead, the hair may be drawn back and arranged high off the face. Bangs or curls will cut the high forehead, and hair dressed wide over the ears will widen and shorten it. Softly waving lines are usually more flattering than straight ones.

6. BATHING BEAUTIES AND LIFEGUARDS

Dressing the Normal Figure

Bathing beauties and lifeguards have no figure difficulties. Their problem is to make the most of their assets and dress their perfect figures to the best advantage. They may wear the hues, values, and textures that are most becoming to their eyes and hair, but when several choices are possible for the color ensemble, it is only sensible to choose those that will emphasize good proportions. If you are one of the persons whose figure is an asset, you may learn to use tailoring, hues, values, and textures to good advantage.

Colors that reveal contours. Warm colors in the red and orange range reveal edges sharply. Greens and blues containing yellow are next most effective. Blue, blue-violet, and violet are not your best choices since they have the effect of blurring contours. Strong, intense, vivid colors will reveal your proportions and lines more distinctly than grayed intensities. If you wear red, it may be slightly grayed, but if you choose blue-green or blue, use it pure and clear, provided your complexion will allow it.

If you are a boy with a fine figure, you may indulge your liking for color in sports clothes. You are the type to wear vivid sweaters or striped blazers with gray or white trousers as well as the softer colors now popular for men's informal suits.

Girls should remember that very dark values create distinct, precise edges.

Black will give the impression of greater slenderness than bright, pure colors, while at the same time it reveals your good lines. Medium values in pure colors are good. Light values may be worn whenever they are suitable, but they will not enhance your silhouette. Dark and light patterns are possible for you, but should be chosen to emphasize your good lines rather than to camouflage them.

Lines. Well-built persons should not hide their light under a bushel basket nor their good lines under a tent. They should avoid ruffles and frills. If you

If you are well built,
why hide your perfec-
tions?

are tall and slender, make the most of your good proportions by smooth tailoring. Small hats and turbans do more for a good figure than do wide brims, because they allow the eye to continue upward without stopping. A person with a well-proportioned figure may wear evenly spaced horizontal stripes, since they give the effect of expanding the figure both upward and outward. Long diagonals offset by short ones are also good, particularly for a small person. Perpendicular lines, such as tucks or stitched pleats, follow and reveal contours. Plaids are better on the good figure than on any other type. Boys should take pains to have school or business clothes well tailored if they wish to show off excellent natural lines.

Problems and activities. (1) If you feel the need of aid in planning your clothes and are willing to accept suggestions, see how well you and your classmates can apply what you have learned. Have several tall and several short persons exchange coats or hats or other articles of clothing in a series of experiments to see which types of costume best solve their particular problems. (2) Experiment with the effects produced by changing from a snug sweater to a full coat as a means of correcting a too angular impression. (3) Try on several sweaters or coats of different colors, and see if your classmates can notice any difference in your apparent slimness because of the differences in color. (4) Change from a sweater of very fine weave to one of very coarse weave, and let your classmates judge what this does to your appearance. (5) Experiment with the different effects produced by short, three-quarter, or full-length coats on your apparent height and weight. (6) If possible, try on two coats of the same hue but of different values to see what these do to your figure. (7) Decide which hues are best for you to wear, which poorest. Do the same with values and intensities. Also with textures and weaves. In each case be sure that you know the reason behind your decision. (8) Try several different hats to see which type is best suited to your size, figure contour, and face. (9) Draw several figure silhouettes on the blackboard all of the same size and shape; then demonstrate how different uses of horizontal, vertical, and diagonal lines can create apparent differences in the lengths of the figures as well as in the widths. Try this with average, short, tall, heavy, and slender figures. (10) Bring to class some photographs or drawings from magazines or newspapers showing well-dressed people, and tell why they are well dressed. Could you suggest any improvements? (11) If possible, get some photographs of the clothes worn ten, twenty, or thirty years ago, and compare them with those being worn today. What are the differences? Can you explain them? (12) Through photographs or drawings compare the clothes which we wear with those worn by people in other parts of the world: Eskimos, native Africans, Chinese, Japanese, French peasants, and the like. Try to find in each some effective use of line, color value, and texture.

V. Your Harmony

Selecting and combining colors

You are a color scheme. Every color in your costume must work for you or it will work against you. Therefore, it is only sensible to plan the total costume so that the colors will harmonize with one another and also with your skin, hair, and eye colors. At the same time you must consider what colors will favor rather than detract from your figure and facial contours. As you study the problems presented in this chapter, keep in mind constantly what you have been learning about roundness, thinness, and other characteristics of the figure.

First, you will need to get a clear conception of the total problem of color combination, and of the general principles that underlie the use of color in all fields of art. Next, you will study ways of adapting colors to particular kinds of skin coloring, because colors worn near your skin may modify or alter the skin's apparent hue.

Since your colors must be planned with regard to skin, hair, and eyes, and not with regard to any single one of these, it is convenient to classify people into "color types" and to consider the unique color problems of each type. What is your color type? Are you cool, warm, betwixt and between, or neutral?

Blue is the coolest color. It makes one think of water, the ocean, or even of ice. Green is a little less cool, suggesting grass, gardens, or leafy dells in the shade of protecting trees. A person of cool type has bluish eyes and either blonde, neutral blonde, or blue-black hair. If you belong to this type, and are interested in completing your color harmony, study the suggestions in the section entitled "Frozen North."

The warm colors are orange and red. They remind one of the flames in the fireplace, the live, glowing bed of coals, or perhaps of forest fires, or flaming sunsets, where an abundance of heat is the cause of the color. Actually the light rays for red and orange are much nearer to heat rays in wave length than are the light rays for blue and green. If you go down the color series from blue to red and continue far enough, you cease to have color at all and merely have heat, sometimes spoken of as infra-red light.

Persons of true warm type have red, copper, auburn, or blackish-brown hair with warm glints. The eyes of this type may be either brown or blue if the hair is very rich in color. In order to be classified as a warm type a person must have eyes of warm color if the hair is not a rich color. If you belong to this type, the material in the section entitled "Southern Sun" will help you to complete your color ensemble.

It is obvious that if you combine a forest fire with a cool, damp, leafy dell you have an unhappy combination, unless the combination is so skillfully done that one becomes a retreat, as it were, from the fury of the other. Likewise, there are many other ways in which you may make your colors "fight" if you are not careful to analyze what each one does or tends to make the observer do.

Boys need not get the idea that this problem of color is largely a girls' problem. It is true that the range of colors used in men's suit materials is not so wide as that used in women's clothes, but it is no less important. Since the color effects are often more subtle, they need more careful study. Besides the color of the suit, there is the problem of shirt, tie, and accessories, especially in relation to the color of skin, hair, and eyes.

The task of combining colors, although by no means simple, can be great fun if done with enthusiasm and taste. But there are many things to remember. Because of the way in which the eye reacts to color, some seemingly strange things happen. Thus, if you stare steadily at a square of green paper for a few seconds, and then quickly look at a sheet of white paper, you will see a reddish square on the paper. This is known as a "negative after-image," and helps explain why colors affect each other as they do. If you know how to take advantage of such facts, you may make a florid complexion seem less ruddy or a pale complexion appear to have more color and life.

63

Another interesting factor is that of reflection. Hold a red book next to your white sleeve in the sunlight and you will see a pink or reddish area on the sleeve, because the brilliant light of the sun causes reflection of color. Applying this knowledge directly to clothing problems will make you remember that a blue hat may reflect a few blue tones on the face of the wearer while a green dress may reflect some green tones.

Then there is the fact that some colors make others seem more intense than they really are. Thus, a piece of red cloth will look even redder if placed against a green background, and a piece of yellow will look brighter if seen against violet. The best way to become familiar with all this is to observe constantly the things around you. Try changing them and see what happens. Put the same color against different backgrounds, hold books of different colors together, try several hats with your coat. Gradually—not suddenly—you will come to understand how colors play together. This question of color will be taken up again in Chapter XI, but start observing now.

1. Joseph's Coat

Choosing Your Total Color Scheme

Joseph's coat of many colors may have been beautiful, but if so, it was not because of the variety of colors but because of the way in which they were chosen and combined. A carefully chosen and arranged color scheme can, through emphasis, subordination, and transitions, be harmonious in spite of variety. The sensation of a single hue will dominate, though there may be minor notes of contrast. In choosing an ensemble color scheme it is possible to avoid both a jumbled effect and drabness by learning to combine colors effectively. Remember that negative tastes are as inadequate as negative good manners or negative goodness. You deserve no credit for them; they are yours because you don't *dare*. Learn how to be daring with colors so that you may combine them vividly or softly as you wish.

As a start, consider three major ways of creating your color ensemble. The first is by choosing a complete harmony. The second is by contrasts with an opposite or an opposing harmony. The third is by choosing a basic neutral color, such as white, gray, black, blue, or brown, and playing a group of harmonizing or contrasting colors against it.

Harmonies. Close harmonies are composed of neighbors on the color circle or rainbow, such as the hues from green-yellow to green, from green to blue, from blue to red-violet, or from red to orange-yellow. In each case a single hue predominates; a greenish, bluish, purplish, reddish, or orange sensation prevails. In such a harmony, variety may be obtained through different values and intensities. But such changes must be handled with care. Rhythmic transitions from light to dark may be effective in stripes, plaids, or in larger areas of the costume; for example, the skirt might be dark bluish-green, the blouse a lighter green, and the hat still lighter in value and more yellowish. Or harmonies may be found in printed or woven materials. In color schemes of this sort, it is always more interesting to have some change in value and intensity as well as in hue. Close harmonies are useful in sports, business, and dress clothes. What harmony might you use in a man's sport outfit? In a girl's sport costume? In a girl's formal dress?

Contrasts. Contrast is the opposite of harmony. Contrasts may be clashing, dissonant, exciting, or stimulating, and they are produced when opposite colors are combined. We usually think of contrasts in terms of hue; green opposes red-violet, yellow opposes violet-blue, orange opposes blue, and red opposes blue-green. In each of these pairs one color belongs to the warm group, the other to the cool. In a scheme based on contrast, a group of either warm or cool colors is usually chosen as the basis, and the opposite is introduced in smaller quantities. These minor amounts of contrast may be either at strategic points or distributed throughout the pattern. Contrasts in weave and pattern create sparkle. Boys should study the problem of color contrast in choosing ties. Look carefully at the color scheme of the next five costumes you see, either men's or women's. Notice the dominating hues and the manner in which contrasts are used.

Budget color schemes. If you are budgeting, as most people are, you will do well to choose one basic color for the more substantial articles in your wardrobe. White, cream, gray, black, blue, or brown is good for your basic color.

White and black are neither warm nor cool, since white is the presence of all colors and black the absence of all colors. Either of them is a perfect background for showing off warm or cool colors. Cream is warm and combines most harmoniously with warm colors. Gray may be either cool blue-gray or green-gray, or warm yellow-gray or rose-gray. Warm gray usually combines best with warm colors and cool gray with cool ones.

Blue as a costume base is usually dark and medium in intensity. It is the coolest of all colors; any color containing yellow or red is warm by comparison. It is, then, a cool dark background for any of the greens, yellows, oranges, reds, or violets. It may also be combined with lighter blues and with white or gray. Cool rather than warm gray is usually preferred with blue, but there are exceptions to this. Black does not always combine well with blue, except for footwear, in which it forms a darker base. Brown is grayed yellow, grayed orange, or grayed red. It usually combines best with tints and tones which are closely related in hue, such as cream, yellow, yellow-beige, flesh color, orange, orange-beige, rose-flesh, or gold. Opposites, such as blue or blue-green, in order to be successfully combined with brown, may be employed as enlivening accents in a great variety of ways. The smartly dressed man or woman usually uses one or more of the basic colors in the wardrobe and varies the color combinations with them. What basic color do you prefer for your wardrobe? Whether your budget is large or small, you cannot afford to overlook the possibilities offered by using basic colors varied by means of harmony and contrast. If you can wear both warm and cool colors well, plan your costumes around a warm basic color for fall and winter and around a cool basic color for spring and summer.

Color in relation to personal coloring. You have learned that a color is emphasized by repetition or by direct contrast. Therefore, colors that you wish to bring out in your personal make-up should be either repeated or opposed in your costume scheme. If you wish to emphasize warm orange tones in your skin, you may select clothes in browns or tans for repetition, or you may select pale green blues for contrast. On the other hand, if your skin is sallow (that is, yellowish), you will make it less noticeable if this color is neither repeated nor opposed. What color schemes might you use to avoid this repetition and direct

COLORS OF LIGHT

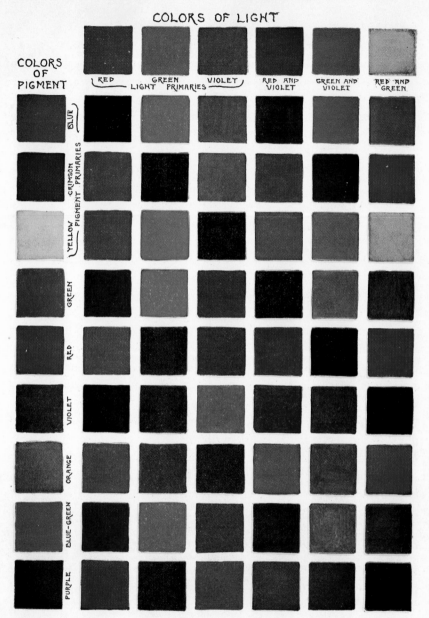

From *Art of Play Production* by *John Dolman, Jr.*

Choose materials in relation to the lights under which they will be used.
The approximate effects upon nine typical colors of materials can be found
if you run the pigment rows across to the proper light columns.

contrast? Which colors in your own make-up do you wish to emphasize and which do you want to make less noticeable?

The effect of light on your color scheme. The color of artificial light merges with the hues of your clothing and changes them. Have you ever noticed the drab nighttime appearance of a dress that was a lovely pale orchid color in the daylight? The yellow of ordinary electric light tends to gray all violets; to make oranges and reds more yellowish; and to make blues take on a greenish cast. Colors, therefore, should be tested with the type of light under which they will ordinarily be worn.

Problems and activities. (1) From your mother's sewing basket or scrap bag bring a number of samples of cloth of various colors. Make a class collection of colors for experiments to be carried out while you are studying this chapter. (2) Holding actual pieces of material where everyone can see, practice identifying colors so that you can promptly distinguish between the different hues and also between different values and intensities of those hues. (3) By using actual samples, show the class what is meant by color harmonies and color contrasts. (4) From samples, choose three different background colors which you could use as a costume base, and arrange with each the costume colors which you think could be appropriately worn with it. (5) Experiment with samples of color under sunlight and under electric light to see what the yellow of the electric light does to the apparent color. (6) See *Webster's Unabridged Dictionary* for an accepted list of color names under the word *color.*

2. THE HAIR WAVES

Flattering the Hair

Hair makes more difference in the human face than most people realize. Have you ever failed to recognize a friend at the beauty parlor because her head was tightly wrapped in a towel following a shampoo? Whether your hair is naturally fine or coarse, straight or curly, limp or crisp, dull or glossy, it is an extremely important item in your general appearance, and this statement holds true for boys as well as for girls. You may be a person with only passable features and an indifferent figure, but with a glorious head of hair. If so, make the most of it.

So-called permanent waves and other artificial curling methods have made it possible for most women to imitate the more desirable qualities in hair, but the problem does not end with having a permanent wave. The hair may still look drab and dull or wild and unkempt unless it is properly cared for. At their best, hair waves can sparkle and glow and send forth iridescent colors. And the hair can make an interesting frame for the face, if you decide upon a good design and exercise patience in keeping it in that design. It's your problem. If you want to make the most of your hair, first keep it clean and glossy, second, design a way of wearing it becomingly, and third, choose costume

What are some good ways of flattering the hair?

colors that will bring out the color of the hair. These methods are much surer and safer than any bleaching, dyeing, or tinting processes ever invented.

Clean and glossy. A massage and a steaming with oil, followed by a shampoo will remove any clinging dirt and the dulling effect it gives. A rinse with lemon juice or vinegar in the water cuts the grease and has a chemical reaction which produces luster and adds vitality. Massage also adds vitality to the hair. How often do you massage your scalp? Do you use a vinegar or lemon rinse? Cleanliness and gloss are just as important for boys' hair as for girls'.

Becoming design. The shape of your hair dress should be decided upon after a careful study of the suggestions about face design (Chap. IV, Sec. 5). Remember that, in general, soft curves and graceful, circular lines are youthful, straight lines are dignified, and diagonals are dynamic and sophisticated. Your hair

68

design is thus one method of presenting your personality. In addition, it has its place in ensemble design. The size and contour of your head in relation to the rest of your body must be considered. Does your contour as a whole call for fullness, medium fullness, or slick-tight smoothness of hair design? In case of doubt, choose a medium design.

Boys and men have less chance for variety in hair dress than women have, but that is no excuse for not choosing a haircut that suits the face and figure. A part in the middle is trying to most faces. It emphasizes any irregularity of the features, but it may be used to broaden a face that is extremely long and narrow. The side part suits most faces. A pompadour, if neatly kept, helps to lengthen a broad face. Cropped haircuts are severe but suit some heads very well. If the hair is hard to keep in place, try wearing it fairly short rather than using too much oil or pomade in your effort to keep it smooth.

Emphasizing or subduing color. Your hair may be light or dark. Actually it is yellow, orange-yellow, orange-red, bluish silver, brownish-black, or black with bluish lights. A repetition of the color in the hair in a weaker intensity, or the use of an opposite in relation to it, will enhance the hidden lights. Violet-blue opposes yellow. Greenish blue opposes orange and red-orange. Warm colors, such as grayed orange, red-orange, and red, oppose cool hair with bluish lights. Repeating in the costume the underlying color in your hair in a stronger intensity harmonizes with the hair but subdues its color. What is the underlying color in your hair? What colors oppose and enhance it? What colors subdue it?

Problems and activities. (1) View yourself in a full length mirror, decide whether your hair should be shaped full, medium, or tight, and whether softly curved, round, straight, or diagonal. Tell the class what you decide, and see how well they agree with you. (2) Practice judging hair color by observing the hair of your classmates and deciding through group discussions which person's hair is yellow, yellow-orange, orange, red, brown, black, or possessed of a bluish light. (3) Using the samples of cloth assembled in the previous lesson, pick out colors which harmonize with your own hair and other colors which enhance its hidden lights through opposition. Check your decisions by getting the reactions of your classmates. (4) Experiment by using harmonizing and contrasting colors one after another next to your hair to decide whether you get better effects by repetition or by opposition.

69

3. THE EYES HAVE IT

Flattering Your Eyes

The eyes have it, whether they are blue, brown, gray, or green. What you are or wish to be is communicated in great part through them. Whenever possible, their color and brilliance should be enhanced, but it is not true that their color should be the dominating factor in choosing your color ensemble. Your skin is the most important color and texture influence; second is your hair, and third, your eyes. But when the hues that bring out your eye color are also becoming to your complexion and hair, they serve a double purpose.

Intensifying eye color. There are two ways to strengthen the apparent richness of your eye color, just as there were two ways of enhancing hair color. One is to repeat their color in your costume in a grayed intensity; the other is to exercise the law of contrast. Thus the color of blue, brown, or violet eyes is strengthened when their owner wears the same color, and flecks of amber, green, or violet in the eyes can be brought out by the use of like colors in suit, dress, or accessories. In thus repeating the eye color you may use it in the same intensity in small areas, but in larger areas it should be grayed. What variety can you achieve in your eye color by repeats? Do you know anyone who could make his eyes more attractive by repeating in the costume an eye color which now goes unnoticed?

The eye color may also be intensified by use of its opposite. Flecks of orange are apparently intensified by blue, and blue eyes appear more blue when contrasted with dull orange. Green eyes seem more intensely green when offset by violet-red or reddish colors, and violet eyes are intensified by green-yellow or yellow. What colors can you find in your eyes? What opposing colors can you use to intensify them? Boys especially should consider the eye color when choosing suits, hats, shirts, and ties, because for them the color of the eyes is just as important as the color of the hair, perhaps more so.

Eyebrow shaping. Unless your eyebrows are very bushy or excessively thin and pale, it is just as well to let them alone except for brushing and smoothing them and plucking the few hairs which go awry. A natural appearing eyebrow, neither too thin nor too bushy, is the aim of the well-groomed person. In shaping the brows in any way, the shape of the mouth should be considered, since a repetition of line may be good or bad. If the mouth droops, take care not to accentuate that poor line by repeating or directly opposing it in the eyebrows. Try to form habits of thinking which will mold a happier mouth line for the brows to follow. What shape of brow would repeat the line of half of your upper lip? Would this be becoming to you?

Relaxing the eyes. The eyes seem to benefit by stretching no less than do feet released from the confinement of shoes. To relieve tight eye muscles, strain your eyes to see objects far in the distance and alternate with focusing on fine writing held close at hand. Close your eyes, and strain to see into the distance, then open them and relax. Move your eyeballs in circles so that you see as far up, down, and to the side as possible. When your eyes are thoroughly stretched, splash them with cold water, and then rest for a few moments with your head back and eyes closed. Give nature and good health a chance; they can usually do more for your eye appearance than any amount of make-up can do. Clear, bright eyes, whether in girl or boy, need no artificial beautifying.

Problems and activities. (1) Practice the identification of eye color by observing your classmates' eyes and comparing impressions as to which colors are represented in them. (2) Stand before the class where your eyes can be seen, and let your classmates decide what costume colors could be used best to bring out your eye color by repetition or by contrast. (3) Have several students stand at the front of the room while you analyze the shape of each one's eyebrows with reference to other lines of the face. (4) If you have occasion to consult an oculist, ask him to give you instructions for relieving eye fatigue and strain, and report his advice to the class.

4. THAT RUDDY GLOW

Choosing Colors to Counteract a Sallow Complexion

If your skin is sallow, you can improve it to some extent by proper diet and exercise. Drink plenty of water—eight glasses daily—and eat plenty of fresh vegetables and fruits. These will help give a healthy glow to your skin. Regular exercise outdoors, facial steams, and cold rubs will speed up the circulation and pump more blood into the face. But art may also be called in to aid nature. To neutralize the yellowish hue of the skin and accentuate the warm blood color, recall what you have learned about repetition and contrast.

Accentuation by contrast and repetition. Color is caused by light rays registering on the retina of the eye. Any color vibration spreads about it an afterglow of its opposite. In this way any two opposites tend to intensify each other. Violet-blue is directly opposite yellow in the color chart. Avoid it, therefore, if you are inclined to be sallow, since it will spread a glow of yellow over your skin. Green-blue, however, is opposite to red on the color circle; it will spread that slightly warmer glow over the complexion which many persons need. This green-blue will be more becoming if it is slightly grayed rather than of full intensity. As you know, the repeating of color calls attention to it. Since you do not wish to stress the yellow underlying your skin, you should avoid wearing any kind of yellow—green-yellow or orange-yellow—in any value or intensity except in small amounts well away from your face.

Reduction by use of neighboring hues. Neighboring colors tend to neutralize each other. Yellow-green and green, yellow-orange, orange, and red-orange are all neighbors of yellow in the color chart. In slightly grayed intensities they should be becoming to a pallid complexion. What colors in suit, sweater, shirt, and tie can you suggest for a boy with a sallow skin?

Adding color by reflection. Purplish reds should be avoided, since they have a tendency to call up the yellow in your skin by contrast. Orange-reds, however, side-step this danger and have the added value of reflecting warmth in your complexion. This includes all of the orange-reds, ranging in value and intensity from slightly grayed apricot to henna or brick red. Another way of utilizing reflection is to take advantage of the light from light or high values. Pale warm flesh colors and pale grayed rose will, by reflection, throw color into your skin. Black absorbs all light and therefore has a tendency to drain color from surrounding areas. It is a poor choice for the sallow-skinned person. If you like the neatness or sophistication of black and it suits your figure, what accessories might you add to a black dress or suit to counteract its bad effect on a sallow skin?

Problems and activities. (1) Join other classmates who are of this color type at the front of the room, and get the rest of the class to judge how well or poorly you have

72

chosen your colors to help you overcome the sallow appearance. (2) Try samples of different colors of fabrics near the faces of different students who have this same problem, and see which ones bring out the desired color effects best through simultaneous contrast. (3) Likewise try samples of color to see which ones produce bad effects through repetition of the already too dominant yellow color. (4) Try different color samples to see which ones would be good neighbors to your yellow skin and would be good to reduce the apparent yellowness if used in grayed intensities. (5) See what effect you can get by the use of orange-reds and other red colors to reflect more coloring into your skin.

5. "LIKE A RED, RED ROSE"

Choosing Colors to Counteract a Florid Complexion

Just as some persons have too little of the red tone in their complexions, others have too much. Then the problem becomes one of lessening the orange-red in the skin and the violet-red which may predominate in cheeks and lips. Wearing very much orange-red or violet-red will emphasize those colors in the face through repetition, and wearing greens and blue-greens will force reds and oranges into the complexion by contrast—the very thing the florid person wants to avoid. Remember that if you wish to minimize a color, you will neither repeat nor directly oppose it.

Reduction by means of neighboring hues. Red-violet and violet contain enough red to be neighbors of your complexion colors, but not enough to accentuate your floridness. They will have a tendency to neutralize your high color. If you wear grays, they should be warm ones, lavender gray or pinkish gray.

Lessening color by absorption. Black absorbs light rays, and therefore tends to minimize color in areas against which it is used. It is, therefore, an excellent color for the person with florid complexion to wear. White should be avoided in areas surrounding your face, since it reflects light and thus adds color to surrounding areas. For the same reason, shades or dark rich colors are better for you than tints or weak light colors. Dark shades of colors with a purplish hue are better than shades of green. Intense reddish hues should be avoided, since they will reflect red on the skin. What range of colors in ties should the boy with red hair and florid skin consider?

Problems and activities. (1) Join your red-faced classmates at the front of the room, and get suggestions from the rest of the class as to ways in which you could improve your present costume to counteract excessive floridness. (2) Try different samples of color to determine how yellow-greens, orange-reds, violet-reds, and violets respectively increase or decrease your apparent redness of complexion. (3) Experiment to see whether you can get a better effect by draining color away by absorption than you can by reducing it by means of neighboring hues.

6. PEACHES AND CREAM

Displaying to Best Advantage the Normal Toned Skin

Peaches and cream complexions are unusual in these days of outdoor activity. Protective care is necessary to preserve them, but the hard work involved is more than compensated for by the wide range of hues, intensities, values, and textures that are becoming to such skins. If you have a clear pink and white complexion, you may wear almost any colors becomingly. Nevertheless, certain hues and textures will stage-set your unusual possession more dramatically than others. Learn to accentuate your good skin by means of contrast or repetition.

Accentuation by contrast. Creamy orange, grayed pink, and soft violet-red are the underlying colors of your complexion. If you wish to accentuate the rosy glow of your lips and cheeks, you will wear the cool colors directly across the color circle from your complexion colors. Green, blue-green, turquoise-blue, and pure blue create your strongest contrasts. These may be worn in any tint or shade, that is, in any value from light to dark, and in any intensity from pale or weak up to full saturation. You are the type on which navy blue is better than on any other. Or try a suit in pale cool gray accented with blue in hat and accessories. If your skin is smooth and satiny in texture, it may also be shown up by contrast against wide-meshed weaves, provided they are not too heavy. Black is exceedingly good on you, since it contrasts becomingly with the paleness of your skin. The fact that black drains color from surrounding areas is no drawback to you, since your color is warm enough and clear enough to offset this handicap.

Accentuation through repetition. Pale flesh, shell pink, and ashes of roses in fine smooth textures call attention to your skin through repetition. You are the girl who can wear pink satin and get away with it. You may also wear shiny, light-reflecting textures unless your size prevents. The grayed warm colors in the orange range, including taupe and brown, will do nothing for you unless they repeat the color of your eyes or hair. It is best not to repeat your complexion colors in their fullest intensity, nor even in dark, grayed shades, but rather in delicate tints. Of course, warm colors of any intensity or value may be worn in your accessories if your costume calls for them.

Problems and activities. (1) Join other "peaches and cream" students at the front of the room, and let the rest of the class decide what colors your type should wear and what improvement you could make in your present costume to suit your coloring. (2) Experiment with actual color samples to see how much difference is made in your appearance when you change from the warm to the cool colors near your face. (3) Test the effects of black near your face, and see whether your coloring is warm enough to bear the amount of absorption of light which results from it. (4) Pick out the colors which would best accentuate your peaches-and-cream complexion through repetition, and see how well your classmates agree with your selection.

7. SUN TAN AND BRONZE

Choosing Colors Becoming to the Sun-tanned Skin

"Outdoor complexions," if the tanning process is successful, are beautiful rich browns, that is, shades or dark grayed intensities of yellow-orange or orange. This rich, dark, subdued, warm skin may be displayed to advantage in two different ways. You may emphasize its importance as a successful achievement by wearing clothes which contrast; or you may include it as a part of a closely harmonized, rich color scheme. Whether you contrast or harmonize, you will achieve distinction.

Emphasizing by means of contrast. Since your sun-tanned skin is dark, light values will contrast with it. Pure white will be the strongest contrast possible, and will therefore emphasize your skin in the most startling manner. All cool colors will stress the warmth of your skin. Pale jade green, pale green-blue, and pale blue, will most strikingly contrast with it. Black will do nothing for you except as sharp spots of contrast in small areas of your costume. Pink and pale apricot will make your skin look dirty. Intense warm colors, strong cool colors, and black and white may, of course, be used in small areas for accessories, or as a pattern on a white or cool field. Values or intensities which approach the color of the skin should be avoided, else your appearance will be mediocre. Whether you are a boy or a girl, if you are spending the summer out-of-doors, what colors shall you choose for sports clothes and for autumn wear to emphasize that warm tan or healthy bronze?

Harmony by means of neighboring hues. Warm, subdued colors ranging in value from rich cream to brownish black will make you into the color scheme of a Rembrandt painting. The colors that harmonize with your underlying skin color are those ranging from orange-red through orange and yellow to green-yellow. Any of these hues, if used in too strong intensities, will subdue your skin and make it look muddy. In grayed intensities they will create a warm, rich color ensemble. Men's and women's fall suits are often keyed to this effect. Mustard, henna, various browns and tans, wine, and burgundy may be used in small areas for costume contrast. All light values that you choose should be warm and creamy in order to achieve this type of harmony. You should avoid dead blacks or cold dark navy blues. All dark values which you use in large areas should be rich in color. Gold jewelry, rather than platinum or silver, should be your choice. Use cream-colored pearls rather than white ones, and topaz, garnets, and rubies rather than sapphires, diamonds, or the other cold-colored stones. Cold, contrasting hues, particularly in the greens or violets, may be used, however, in small areas in your ensemble.

Problems and activities. Planning your color scheme can be great fun if you enter into it with a spirit of adventure. The principles and rules which have been given may be helpful in getting you started in the right direction, but they should not inhibit you too much when it comes to planning your clothes. *Try everything for yourself before you accept it.* There are many exceptions, and you should look for them. You may be startled at what you find. Look around with open eyes. As an additional help, find and read the section in the following pages which applies to your particular type. (1) Join several of your classmates at the front of the room and see, by the advice you receive, how much others have learned about choosing colors. Exchange articles of clothing as other students direct, to see which ones do the best things for your personal coloring. (2) Try samples of different-colored textiles near the faces of other students who have problems similar to yours, and see which ones bring out the desired color effects best.

(3) Get your friends to help you decide whether you should give more thought to your hair or to your skin in choosing colors to be worn near your face. (4) Experiment with different colors to see which ones help your appearance through contrast and which aid through harmony. (5) Try several samples of the same hue—red, for example—which vary in value and intensity. Which ones are best for you? Why?

8. FROZEN NORTH

Choosing Colors for Cool Color Types

Frozen north types are most easily recognized when you learn to see bluishness or coolness in colors. Blue is the coldest color, since it makes you think of ice and deep water. With the addition of yellow it forms the entire range of greens and green-blues. With the addition of red it creates the range of violet-reds and violets. These are the colors, plus cooled or grayed yellow, that are found in cool color types. Their eyes are gray, bluish gray, greenish gray, green-blue, blue, or violet. Their underlying skin color is usually violet-red which contains blue, rather than the warmer orange or yellow-orange. Their hair may be blue-black, ash blonde, golden blonde, or neutral blonde. Cool types are usually classified by their hair. If you belong in this category, study the following material and discover how to make the most of your possibilities.

Vivid blondes. Sparkling golden hair, pale cool skin, red-violet lips and cheeks, and cool eyes designate the vivid blonde. If you answer to this description, you may stress any of your natural colors; either use its opposite or repeat it in more grayed intensity. Strong yellows and oranges, being the stronger intensity of the same hue as your hair, will make it appear dull; therefore, it is wise to avoid them. Yellows which are pale or slightly more grayed than your hair will set it off to advantage. Green-yellow and yellow-green are more cool than your hair; if not too intense, they should be becoming. Cool colors are opposite on the spectrum to your hair, and, if not of full saturation, should intensify your golden hair.

Try planning an outfit built on harmonies of yellow-green or green-blue or violet-blue. Warm colors of the reddish groups, if slightly grayed, should be becoming. Light values and weak intensities, such as pale rose, apricot, and peach, should be good, and you may wear medium and dark values if the intensity is weak. The fact is, the whole range of values from off-white through pale, medium, and dark colors, including black, is good on you if the intensities are weakened or grayed. Taupe grays, however, will do nothing for you; if you choose a gray for your ensemble background, it should be distinctly coolish or blue-gray.

Ash blondes. Pale, silvery-golden hair is the feature that distinguishes the ash blonde from the golden blonde. Because there is less orange in your hair, you classify as a decidedly cool type. Your hair, cheeks, lips, and eyes are all cool. Very dark and very light values are good on you. Pale, slightly grayed tints are excellent, but all drab colors should be avoided. Try a suit or dress of dark green, dark blue, or black to dramatize your pale coolness. Sharp contrasts of hue and value in your accessories should be good. What should you plan, for instance, with green in the way of accessories?

Neutral blondes. If you belong to this type, your color ensemble is not so dramatic as that of the vivid blonde. Your hair is soft yellow or orange yellow. Your skin is slightly yellowish, your lips and cheeks have a pale violet flush, and your eyes are bluish, greenish, or grayish.

This neutral scheme can profit from enlivening and brightening effects. Since there are no eye-arresting contrasts or accents in your person, these must be achieved in your costume. After choosing your basic costume color, try a dark accent near the face, as it is the natural center of interest in the personality design. Avoid large areas of neutral colors since they create a drab effect. Hues slightly brighter than those in your personal coloring should enrich without eclipsing your face and hair. Pale, light, clear colors may make you look grayish by contrast. Intense hues containing yellow will make your hair look drab. Do not choose a bright orange-yellow sweater. Light, slightly grayed, cool colors are good, particularly if they are slightly greenish or slightly reddish. They should tend to brighten up the color of your hair. This cool group, as you know, includes green, blue-green, green-blue, blue, and blue-violet. Medium dark and dark values of the same colors are also good. You may wear the warm hues, too, in either light or dark values. Colors which are too yellowish, such as green-yellow and yellow-green, will call up the yellow in your skin and should be avoided.

ANNE ROONEY   ROBERT STERLING

Motion picture artists are concerned about their costume colors. Are you?
(Photographs by courtesy of Metro-Goldwyn-Mayer Studios)

MARK DANIELS   JUDY GARLAND

A is a redhead with brown eyes and orange-red lip and cheek coloring. What kinds of red are becoming to her? B is suntanned and has blue eyes and dark brown hair. Why is his dark blue uniform, combined with his white shirt and black tie, becoming to him? C is a blue-eyed ash blonde with cream colored skin and violet-red lip and cheek coloring. What are her most becoming colors? D is cool-complexioned, blue-eyed, and has black hair. Why should she not wear brown? E is a brown-eyed suntanned golden blond. Why do his tan tweed suit, brown tie, and biscuit colored shirt create a perfect ensemble? F is a blue-eyed golden blonde with violet-red coloring. Is her cream colored sports dress appropriate for her?

(Photographs A and D by Wilson; B by Joseph Banning; C by De Freitas; E and F by Jean Daiken)

Dark-haired Nordics. Cool eyes combined with cool light skin, violet-red cheeks and lips, topped with either blue-black or brownish black hair, compose the cool brunette. If you answer to this description, you are lucky, for you have the advantage of a strong value contrast in your personal coloring. You may continue dramatically with strong value contrasts, such as black and white, in your costume. Strong color contrasts should also be good but do not choose neutrals, such as tans, grays, or unrelieved pale colors. Large areas of dark dull color will destroy you. Medium-intense cool colors, including the range from green, through blue, to red-violet, should enhance your dramatic possibilities and play up your cool coloring. The warm colors from yellow-orange through orange and red to violet-red should be good if not too strong nor too grayed. Magenta, cerise, green-yellow, and yellow-green are difficult colors for anyone to wear. They are apt to do nothing for you, and if you wish them in your color ensemble test them carefully before you decide to include them.

Problems and activities. (1) If you are one of the cool-colored types, get your classmates to analyze your particular coloring and help you decide which colors you should wear. (2) Have your friends decide and advise you as to whether you should give more thought to your hair or to your skin in choosing colors to be worn near your head. (3) Experiment with different colors to see which ones help your appearance through contrast and which aid you more through harmony. (4) From the class collection of sample fabrics make selections which are best for you, and keep a few small squares of these colors as guides for your future buying.

9. SOUTHERN SUN

Choosing Colors for Warm Color Types

The southern sun is a fitting symbol for the warm type whose golden and reddish hues can cheer the dullest day. Although the general effect of this color type is warm, one feature may be cool, as in the case of blue-green eyes or cool skin with a "carrot top," or dark blue eyes with auburn hair or warm dark hair.

Recognition of warmth in colors helps in picking warm types. Reddish-gold, golden-brown, auburn, or dark hair with colorful lights and hazel, brown, or dark brown eyes are warm. Creamy, golden, olive, and sun-tanned skins are warm. Lips and cheeks of warm types are orange-red or red, rather than violet-red. Sometimes, however, if the skin is cream, the cheek coloring is cooler. If you are of this type, your problems differ, depending upon the intensity of your hair coloring. Find your definite classification in the following material, and test the suggestions which are offered.

Red-haired type. If you are a "red-head," you can have plenty of fun with color. Voltaire once said, "Life means to transform into light and flame all that we are or meet with." You carry the flame with you; it is your own fault if you do not have a good time. Begin by not believing everything you are told about what you should wear. Make a few tests and discover your possibilities for yourself. Pure red in any value, light, medium, or dark, probably will not do much for you, but don't take anyone's word for this; try it out. Your skin may be of the shell pink variety that will harmonize with pink or grayed rose. If so, take advantage of the fact; you will be eye-arresting. Orange, ranging from orange-yellow to red-orange is your color. Apricot is a tint of orange-red, and peach is a tint of red-orange. Wear them brighter than your hair if you want to tone it down or slightly more grayed if you wish to intensify it. Yellow is also good. It may be lemon yellow, pure yellow, or orange-yellow, either a tint or slightly grayed. Discover which is best for you. Because browns are medium or dark values of yellow, orange, or orange-red, they are all good for you. Blue, green-blue, blue-green, and green contrast with your orange hair. Since your color is bright enough without a strong contrast, grayed intensities of those colors are best for you. For summer sports clothes, pongee or cream color may be better on you than white. Black is good. Gray is questionable, but test it. Cool blue-gray or green-gray should be the best. Cerise, magenta, and red-violet are purplish reds and are difficult for you. Violet verging on the red side is not so good, but violet-blue is permissible. How many of these colors do you wear? How many have you tested to see whether they are becoming?

Auburn-haired type. Lustrous dark orange-red hair is a rich beginning for an ensemble. If you are of this type, you have warm skin, orange-red coloring, and either brown or blue eyes. Experiment to find colors that are most flattering to you. Don't take anything on faith, but here is a list of possibilities with which

80

you may experiment. (Remember that your job is to play up the orange-red and red-orange in your cheeks and hair.)

Tints, if very light and pale, make your coloring look heavy. Avoid them. All shades ranging from red to orange are good on you. Dark creams, light browns, and dark browns are good because they are grayed intensities of your own coloring. Violet-red, red-violet, and violet are tricky for you. If your hair is quite orange, beware of these colors; if it is mahogany color, give them a trial. Green, blue-green, green-blue, and blue may be worn if intense and dark. Pale tints are too delicate for you. Black is good, but try lustrous black if your figure permits it. Blue-gray is out of key; warm gray may be worn. White is not as good for you as cream unless your skin is very sun-tanned and you wish to create a startling effect. In that case, try a vivid color pattern on white.

Dark-haired oriental type. If you are the warm dark type, your skin is dark but not ruddy, and your eyes and hair are a rich dark brown. You are a symphony in browns with a subdued red-orange flush on your lips and cheeks. Your coloring is not so brilliant as that of other warm types, but is rich and subdued. It is obvious that either tints or pure colors will make you look heavy and muddy.

If you wish to obtain the best total color effect possible for you, test the following suggestions. Think of yourself as a brown statue, and try to find colors that harmonize with brown. Omit pale colors. Omit colors of full saturation. Omit blues. Greens ranging from green-yellow to blue-green should be acceptable if not too intense or too light. All reds in dark shades, ranging from grayed orange-red to grayed magenta or violet-red should be good. All orange shades ranging from grayed orange yellow to grayed red-orange should be excellent. All browns are good for you. Try to plan a costume using deep cream, beige, or yellow-brown as the basic color with accents of darker value or intensity from orange-brown to dark rich chocolate brown. If you wear black it should have a hint of warmth in its depth, and blue-black should be avoided. White should be creamy. Gray should be warm.

Problems and activities. (1) Join with others of your same warm color type, and get class reactions and criticisms of your present costume and suggestions for its improvement. (2) Experiment with color samples to see how the same color produces different effects on different members of your warm-colored group, according to whether they are red-haired, auburn-haired, or dark-haired. (3) Test one color after another upon yourself, and get your classmates to judge which ones have the best effect. Then keep samples of these pieces of material as guides to future buying.

10. BETWIXT AND BETWEEN

Choosing Colors for Intermediate Color Types

Betwixt and between the coolness of the blonde and the warmth of the red-head is the cool-skinned type with either fair or brown hair, cool violet-red coloring, and either brown or blue eyes. Brown-eyed blondes, blue-eyed brown-haired people, and brown-haired brown-eyed people with cool skins belong to this group. If you possess one of these color combinations and wish to know all of your costume color possibilities, find your type below and test the suggestions offered.

Brown-eyed blondes. If your hair is fair, your eyes brown, and your skin warm, you are a warm type; but cool skin throws the balance of the scales from warm to "betwixt and between." Since your eyes are brown instead of blue, blues will not do much for you, because there is nothing in your color ensemble that they repeat. Your best plan is to play up the warmth of your eyes and hair or the violet-red of your cheeks and lips.

Consider the following suggestions: All yellows, including orange-yellow and green-yellow, are good if not more intense than your hair. Yellow-orange, orange, and red-orange are good if somewhat subdued. Orange-red, red, or violet-red in either tints or shades may be worn. If you have ever tried red-violet and violet in light or dark values, see what effect they may have for you. Violet-blue and blue should be grayed if they are worn, else the contrast will be too harsh. Greens are better than blues, because they harmonize more closely with yellow. They are best when slightly grayed. Yellow-green is acceptable. Try playing up your color with yellow-brown, orange-brown, or red-brown darker than your hair.

Blue-eyed brown-haired type. If your hair is brown and your eyes are cool, you rate as "betwixt and between." The colors in your personal ensemble are grayed orange or red-orange, some type of blue, and soft reddish purple. These colors are your starting place. Orange and red-orange will pick up the color of your hair. They are best if slightly grayed, but should be avoided if too dull. Not-too-pure violet-red, red-violet, and violet play up your skin color. Green and blue-green are excellent; blue and violet-blue are very good. Use all of these freely in creating harmonies or in accessories for contrast. Red is difficult for you to wear, because it picks up no hue in your personal color. A grayed light value is wearable, as is orange-yellow, if slightly grayed.

Brown-haired brown-eyed type. Cool instead of warm skin accompanying brown hair and eyes keeps this type from being warm and places it in the "betwixt and between" group. Your personal color ensemble is composed of grayed orange or orange-red and violet-red. Orange-yellow and orange are good if slightly grayed, but darker colors are better. Shades of red-orange, orange-red, red, and violet-red are very good. Try creating your costume in warm tan, taupe, or brown, with rich dark shades for accent. Violet is wearable, and shades of violet-blue, blue, and green-blue are very good except in strong intensities or in tints. Dark greens and dark blue-greens are good as are blackish browns. Egg-shell white and cream are better than pure white.

Problems and activities. (1) If you are one of the types that is neither definitely warm nor cool in coloring, join others of your kind in getting your classmates to analyze your particular color notes and to make suggestions concerning what you should wear. (2) Try samples of different colors near your face and hair to see which ones are becoming to you, and have your classmates check your judgment of their suitability. (3) Try the same sample of cloth on different intermediate color types to see what different effects are produced, and decide which colors go with which types. (4) Since some of your coloring is warm and some cool, get your classmates to decide which parts should be the dominant factors in determining your particular choices. Your figure and your personality may be deciding factors in "betwixt and between" types.

11. CINNAMON, SILVER, AND PLATINUM

Choosing Colors for Gray and White-haired Types

As young people you have very little need to know about colors that are suitable with gray hair. However, this information will round out the picture and you may use it very profitably in helping some older persons in your family.

Cinnamon, silver, and platinum are neutral colors. Cinnamon designates hair of neutral brown sprinkled with a warm gray. White, silver, and platinum are cooler grays. The skin accompanying any of these colors may be sallow, neutral, or florid. The eyes may be blue, gray, or brown. Thus, the problem of this neutral type is exceedingly complex.

All colors worn by this type should be definitely grayed. Yellows, including green-yellow and orange-yellow, are to be avoided if the skin is sallow, particularly if the hair is cinnamon, since they call up the yellow tones of the skin. Cool colors ranging from green through green-blue, blue, blue-violet, and violet, are good if grayed, particularly if the eyes are blue. These should be dark for cinnamon hair; light, medium, or dark for gray hair; and grayed pastels, medium, or dark values for white hair. The warm colors, ranging from red-orange through red to red-violet, are becoming in all values if sufficiently grayed.

For white hair, the light grayed warm colors are exceptionally good. Cream is more harmonious than blue-white with cinnamon hair. Cold gray or silver is good with silver. Pastel tints are excellent with white hair. White is to be avoided; pale off-white hues should be worn instead. Tans and browns are not usually good with gray or cinnamon hair, but dark brown may be used for accent. Black accents are good with white hair, but should be avoided by those with gray or cinnamon hair.

Problems and activities. (1) Invite mothers of class members who have cinnamon, silver, or platinum coloring to come to class and act as models while you exchange views and recommendations as to costume choices appropriate for each. (2) Practice the matching of actual samples of coloring to the skin and hair of members of your group, and decide which colors are appropriate to which. (3) Out of the colors selected as being most appropriate, let your guests choose a few samples which they may take with them as guides for future buying.

If you feel a little bewildered by the many specific suggestions for color in costume given in this chapter, remember only those which apply specifically to your type—for those are the most important to you. But also remember the general principles: that colors are emphasized by contrast or repetition. Select those colors which you think are most desirable in your complexion, hair, and eyes, and then plan carefully so that they become dominant. Get into the habit of noticing colors everywhere. Above all, *plan your costumes*. Do not buy hit or miss because some dress or suit appeals to you at the moment or because it is on sale. Buy or make clothes which will give lasting satisfaction and will fill a real need in your wardrobe.

Part II
HOME

VI. Homestead

Planning your home as a whole

Do the surroundings in which you work, play, eat, and sleep make a difference in your life? "Of course they do," you answer. "What a foolish question!" Yet many young people never face that question squarely. They simply take their homes and the rest of their environment for granted. Do you? It is natural and probably right to do so during your childhood. If your home and your neighborhood are attractive and comfortable, nothing impels you to ask questions about them. You should, however, learn to appreciate and be thankful for them. On the other hand, if they are not exactly what you would like, perhaps you are letting them make you more unhappy than they should. Perhaps, instead of trying to change them, you are trying to escape from them.

If you long for a shady terrace in the midst of a lawn and garden where you might entertain your friends, and you have not even a window box at your house, what are you doing about it? Do you simply dream all day of the house and garden of your own which you mean to have some time when you marry a millionaire or sit on a board of directors? Or do you go off to the movies to see a picture about people who live in mansions surrounded by beautiful gardens? There is nothing wrong with doing either of these things. Every boy and girl should dream about an ideal home, and you can sometimes get ideas about home decoration from the movies, along with the entertainment offered. But there is something still better that you might do. You might make and plant some window boxes or a bit of garden at your present home.

You may answer, "It's no use doing that. The neighborhood is impossible. I didn't choose to live in a flat over a garage. What's the use of trying to do anything to make it attractive?"

HOME

No doubt many neighborhoods are discouraging, but if everyone takes your attitude, will they be any better? A window box full of bright geraniums or petunias might inspire your neighbor to clean up his backyard and plant a garden. Many big community improvements have had such slight beginnings.

Have you ever stopped to think that very few of us live exactly where we should most like to live? We are limited by the nature and location of our work, by income, by health, by family considerations, by dozens of other factors. But all of us can do something to improve our home surroundings, no matter what they are like. A knowledge of what is desirable and good is the first step toward such improvement. Just as money without good taste will not buy a perfect wardrobe, so wealth alone will not create a charming and perfect home. Many persons of modest income but with a knowledge of or an instinctive feeling for the fundamental principles of art have developed homes of real beauty.

Perhaps you feel that while you are living in your parents' home there is little you can do about changing it to suit your tastes. You have tried, you say, and your father and mother objected. It is true that the older and younger generation do not always see eye to eye in home decoration. You may like streamlined modern furniture while your mother prefers Victorian walnut or elaborately decorated golden oak. Your father may insist on keeping his comfortable shabby old armchair even though you think it ruins the effect of the living room. Are these good reasons for stopping every effort to make your home attractive? After all, it is your parents' home. They have probably worked hard to attain it. Some day you will be in their place and your daughter may look askance at the wall paper you chose. Try to think of ways of co-operating with your parents in their plans. You may find that your likes are not so different from theirs as you had thought. And one day your mother may surprise you by letting you rearrange the living room exactly as you'd like it.

A home, besides being a family co-operative enterprise, is usually a part of a community. Farmers may have no close neighbors, but for almost everyone else, the home, whether it be a house, an apartment, or a single room, is a part of a neighborhood. No one lives unto himself alone. The neighbor's-eye-view of your home and your view of your neighbor's home should work for mutual admiration and respect. Does your home or the one you dream about radiate friendly consideration for others?

1. View from Your Windows

Choosing Your Neighborhood

The view from your windows is for you either a constant source of pleasure or a continuous irritation. As you turn into your street on the way home, you unconsciously walk a little taller, breathe deeply with satisfaction, and experience an inner glow, or you drag a little and wonder if there is not somewhere else you can spend the evening. What do you think makes one neighborhood attractive and another just passable? What are some of the things you should consider when you have a chance to choose the site of your own home? Rents or cost of lot and building will narrow your choice. Convenience to work and to school are two determining factors in most families. But such matters usually still leave you some choice as to neighborhood. What are some fundamental problems to consider?

Health. Sunlight and reasonably clean air are necessary to health. It is better to sacrifice many luxuries of interior decoration, if necessary, to secure these two fundamental things. An apartment flooded with sunlight in a reasonably good neighborhood is preferable to a dark north exposure at a fashionable address. The problem of smoke-polluted air is one which many American cities have not yet solved, but usually some sections have purer air than others. If various considerations do not limit your choice too much, by all means choose a neighborhood with clean air.

Noise is also a health hazard to be considered in the present day. Traffic noises of various kinds make many neighborhoods less desirable than others. The ideal, of course, is to live in quiet surroundings, yet within reach of good transportation facilities.

Scale. A mixture of bungalows, large homes, apartment houses, and hotels presents too great a variety of size or scale for one block or for one neighborhood. Although it is not necessary for any group of houses to be of exactly the same size, there should be a feeling of unity among them. Small and medium-sized houses appear well together. Medium-sized and fairly large houses also combine well. Very large buildings, however, seem to dwarf very small ones and rob them of their charm. Apartment houses and hotels are usually most attractive in blocks by themselves, or with dwelling houses which

Which neighborhood would you prefer for your home?

are built more nearly on the same scale. Cottages or bungalows are most charming when grouped with houses of their own kind. So select a neighborhood which is built up on a pleasing scale, and then try to maintain that effect or improve it, if you build a house there.

Style. In the United States we have borrowed and adapted many architectural styles for residences. Along the Atlantic seaboard there are still standing many old houses of the pure colonial types, such as Cape Cod cottages, square Georgian mansions, houses with saltbox roofs, stone houses of Dutch colonial style, and southern plantation homes with high-pillared porticos. In the Southwest there are old houses from the Spanish era, and that style has been adapted to many new homes. In most other sections of the country architectural styles are decidedly mixed. You have only to walk along a typical street to realize the enormous variety which may often be found in a single block. In certain sections of the country you can even find houses which are adaptations of Greek temples showing rows of Greek columns and adorned with Greek details. The modern trend is toward greater simplicity and functionalism, and most examples of modern architecture show simple rectangular forms with very little or no decoration.

Architectural styles of too great variety do not combine well along a street any more than do too many shapes in your costume. Therefore, a house should be planned with thought for its setting. Perhaps you should choose a neighborhood in which houses of the type you have in mind already exist. There is, to be sure, some danger of monotony if the houses on a street are too nearly alike. In some real-estate developments whole streets of identical houses are built. These are worse than the haphazard combinations which result from a total lack of community planning. Real harmony results where houses are similar in feeling but different in plan and details.

Setting. Houses or apartments built on the street line do not combine well with homes deep-set in green lawns. A combination of this sort gives a choppy appearance to the street. Buildings that are set forward shut off the long view of pleasant front gardens, and the deep-set homes are sometimes shut in by the unattractive side walls of the buildings on the street line. Set-backs from the street need not be absolutely uniform, but the variation of depth should be considered in relation to the various views from the street and from the windows of each home.

Neatness and orderliness are also important factors in relation to the beauty of your home. A tidy yard, neat lawn, well-cared-for shrubs, and a clean house with shining windows will create a good impression, even though your home

93

may be small and inexpensive. Your home should tell everyone that you are a person with well-established habits of personal cleanliness.

Problems and activities. (1) Walk around the town, pick out blocks or neighborhoods that are especially attractive, and study the reasons for their attractiveness. (2) Pick out rows of houses that seem too uniform or monotonous, and decide on possible variations that could be introduced to relieve the monotony. (3) Compare four or five residence blocks, selected at random from the region near your school, and rank them from most to least desirable as blocks in which to rent a home, leaving out of consideration everything except health and external appearance, as treated in this section. (4) If possible, visit some other town, and make similar comparisons without the danger of having your judgments colored by personal associations or local experiences. (5) From a booklet of house designs or real-estate advertisements of homes for sale, try to select houses that would combine well on the same street and other houses that would not. Give reasons.

2. Neighbor's-Eye View

Designing the Setting for Your Home

Will your neighbor's view of your home and yard cause him to smile with satisfaction because he is lucky enough to live near you, or will it cause him to hope that someone will move into your house who will take better care of it? If you were to walk across the street from your own home, could you, by studying the exterior, decide what kind of family lives at your address? Should you like to know yourself if you were your neighbor? If there are no grounds around your own home, study the grounds of some other building in the light of the following facts.

Style. In general, there are two styles of landscape gardening: the formal and the natural. Symmetrical designs with many straight lines, garden plots in geometric shape, clipped shrubs, and formal details mark the formal style. Gardens of this type were popular in the seventeenth and eighteenth centuries. They reached their highest development in France under Louis XIV and his two successors. English gardens have usually been shining examples of the more natural style, with curved lawns following the natural slope of the ground, irregular borders of shrubbery and flowers, and beautifully clustered trees.

Which type of landscaping does your yard represent? Perhaps it is somewhat mixed. Many persons who prefer the natural style like to have a small garden of rather formal design. The house, the size of the lot, and the neighborhood should all be considered in planning the grounds. Elaborate landscaping is out of the question for most family budgets, but a little planning and work at regular intervals can do much to improve the most discouraging yard and can create a simple natural setting for the house.

If there are well-grown trees on the lot, the sensible thing is to use them as the keynote of your design. Trees cannot be grown in a day. Moving them costs a considerable amount of money. By all means use what you have and be thankful for them. Nothing adds more to the charm of a house than a beautiful shade tree. In some parts of New England there was a tradition that a young couple, starting life in their new home, should plant a maple on either side of the door. These "bride-and-groom trees" still add charm to many old homesteads.

A good rule for the amateur to follow in planning the grounds is to use, as far as possible, trees, shrubs, and plants native to the region where he lives. Later he may find it desirable to introduce novelties, but at first the native growth is more likely to suit the landscape and to help the house fit into its background, as all good houses should do.

Of course you have noticed the unfinished, restless look of new houses with no trees or shrubs around them. Even some old houses have this uncomfortable look because the owners have never succeeded in tying them to the ground. Shrubbery and trees can do wonders for a house even if it has rather poor lines. Bushes and low trees can be used to conceal too-high foundations. They help to give an air of solidity to the structure. On the other hand, if the house is very low or set close to the ground, too much shrubbery will tend to smother it.

Shape harmony. Trees and shrubs grow in various shapes. The most conspicuously outstanding of these are the triangle-shaped, Christmas-tree type and the brush-topped palm trees with column-like trunks. Other trees and shrubs are more oval in form. Some of these are long slender ovals like the poplar, while others are wide irregular ovals like maples or elms. Shrubs, if clipped, may form either rounded or rectangular shapes. Garden walks may be variations of rectangles or curves. Some amateur gardeners combine these triangles, circles, ovals, rectangles, and irregular shapes promiscuously. The expert garden designer, however, considers the fundamental shape of each tree, shrub, garden plot, and walk. In planning groups he chooses shapes that have a certain amount of likeness. Unity is attained by combining like shapes, while variety of sizes adds interest and prevents monotony. Have you examined your own shrubs and trees for their shape harmony? Have you thought of unity in planning garden beds, walks or paths, and playtime spots?

Grouping. Hit-or-miss planting of flowers, shrubs, and trees that one happens to have or to like is seldom satisfactory—any more than a hit-or-miss costume

What differences do you notice in these two settings?

is. One of the first principles to remember is that plants almost always look better when in groups. Thus, five shrubs of one kind usually look better than five different kinds, and flowers gain greatly in effectiveness from being planted in fair-sized groups. It is not only important to group them, but also to see that each group has a good background and contrasts pleasantly with its surroundings. A flower bed at the edge of a lawn or walk is improved by having a background of suitable shrubbery low enough to be related to the flowers but high enough to provide a setting. These low shrubs, in turn, become more effective if seen against higher shrubs with trees in the background.

There should, of course, be some variety in the sizes of the groups. Some should be small, others medium, and some large. These will be arranged in a definite pattern so that each shows off to advantage. By placing groups of plants of different sizes carefully, a sense of balance is established. Care should also be taken to get equal amounts of interest on the two sides of the property. All the important shrubs or trees should not be on one side. If the house is symmetrical with the entrance in the center, trees, shrubs, and plants may also be balanced on both sides of the entrance and the yard. If the house is asymmetrical, the planting should be arranged to emphasize this quality.

Emphasis. If you wish to emphasize certain parts of your yard and to subordinate other parts, where should the emphasis be placed? As a rule, it seems logical to lead the eye toward the main entrance, which should ordinarily be near the center of the house. Attention may be focused by leading the eye up paths by means of hedges, or through vistas of trees or shrubs. Large groups of trees, although important on account of size, may be grouped away from the house if they form a framework for the whole. Bright colorful spots arrest the eye, and therefore larger masses of strong color may be grouped at the house entrance, with smaller masses repeated in the yard. Large groups of trees or shrubs placed near the entrance of the house and giving emphasis by means of size may be balanced by small groups of shrubs or trees placed farther to the side.

Another problem of emphasis is that of hiding or subordinating undesirable views. Trees and shrubs may be needed to obscure the side of the neighbor's garage or to conceal an unsightly weed-grown empty lot. A fence covered with fast-growing vines may make a temporary screen until trees and shrubs have time to mature.

Color. Color is the great glory of a garden. We are all excited by seeing a gorgeous display of tulips in bloom, or by the reds and yellows of leaves in the autumn. But we may not notice some of the more subtle—but equally beautiful—effects. Have you ever noticed how many different kinds of greens there are? Some are bright and some are dull; some are dark while others are light; some tend toward the blues and others toward the yellows. Have you observed how many colors there are in the barks of trees and in the berries on shrubs?

All of these play their part in the garden picture just as surely as pigments play their part in paintings.

To get truly beautiful effects all of these colors should be planned so that they will be seen in effective combinations. We usually think of flowers first. The most colorful ones are those on the warm side of the color circle—the reds, oranges, and yellows. If these colors are arranged in progressions as they occur on the color circle the harmonies are most satisfying. Probably the best way, or at least the easiest way, to obtain a color harmony is to have each color contain one underlying hue, such as orange, yellow, and yellow-green (all containing yellow) or blue, blue-violet, violet, and red-violet (all containing blue). If colors are organized in some such way as this, an effect of spottiness will be avoided. But there is one other important point: one color should dominate in each group and be accented and emphasized by smaller amounts of other colors. A bed of flowers may be predominantly yellow with a few accents of blue and violet; or it may be white with accents of red and orange; or it may be blue with a few notes of red. But just as in costumes, equal amounts of color are usually less interesting than harmonies in which one hue dominates.

To achieve these color effects in a garden requires patience. You will probably have to plan and work for several seasons to get satisfying results. However, you will be learning more and more about color harmonies as well as about flowers.

Garden catalogues offer an endless variety of possibilities, but you must consider which plants require sun or shade, rich or less rich soil, much moisture or little. If you have never done any gardening, begin with a small plot, and add to it from season to season. You can have fun with even a few window boxes.

The best method, of course, is to make a plan on paper for each garden bed. Then with the help of garden catalogues, choose plants which will blossom during early, middle, or late summer to bring the succession and combinations of color that you desire. For example, golden daffodils with a border of creamy and purplish-blue hyacinths may be your plan for an early spring garden. For summer you may design a bed of blue delphinium towering above pink and white phlox, with accents of violet-blue ageratum and a border of pink and lavender petunias.

The color of foliage also deserve careful consideration. Cool gray-greens are effective against rich, dark blue-greens; yellow-greens will be effective placed in front of duller foliage. There are also a few trees and shrubs on which the foliage is reddish, purplish, bluish, or almost neutral gray. These can be used to mark points of special importance, and add to the variety possible in foliage effects.

Finally, we come to the fruits, berries, and barks. All of our edible fruits— apples, cherries, peaches, oranges—are beautiful while growing and can be used as ornaments in the garden. Many shrubs have berries which, in colder climates, stay late in the fall or winter to give color and interest. The scarlet berries of a barberry hedge, for example, are vivid against the snow. Some bark colors are gray, some black or brown, others green, yellow, and red. Each is part of the total garden picture.

Problems and activities. (1) Draw on the blackboard three pairs of tree shapes: one pair of cone-shaped trees, one pair of oval-shaped trees, and one cone-shaped with an oval-shaped tree. Decide which pair is preferable, and why. (2) In the neighborhood near home or school, select two or more yards close together, and compare the effectiveness of their tree or shrub arrangements. (3) From pictures of homes advertised for sale in the newspapers, choose those that have good tree and shrub designs and those that have poor ones. Decide how much difference in price these factors should make if you were to purchase one of the homes. (4) Make a trip around the neighborhood to find especially good use of flowers to set off the houses or buildings to advantage, and decide which you could adopt for your own yard. (5) As a class project, make a recommended plan for improving the yard or approach to the home of one of the members of the class whose parents will welcome the assistance and make use of the plan when it is completed.

3. FOUR WALLS AND A ROOF

Aiming at Functional Design

If a house is truly functional in design, it suits exactly the needs of the family living in it. The number of rooms and their arrangement are determined by the family needs. Then the architect plans the interior and the exterior accordingly. If he is skillful, he uses lines and spaces so that the rooms are comfortable and pleasing to the eye and he also achieves an exterior which has good proportions and is an attractive composition.

More and more home-owners are thinking in these terms of functional design. At present, however, many of the houses in our cities and towns owe their design to quite different ideas. In the past most home building was done by the traditional, or "copycat," method. The prospective owner decided on the general style he preferred: Dutch colonial, Georgian, English Tudor, French, or Spanish. Then the architect planned the house to look as nearly as possible like the houses of the period suggested by the name. Changes were necessary of course, because of plumbing, garages, and other needs of modern life. This method, at its best, has produced many beautiful homes. At its worst it has resulted in whole streets of architectural atrocities.

The chief weakness of this method of design is that it begins with imitation. Unintelligent imitation is bad, but intelligent imitation plus originality is good. No one wants to discard all the art of the past any more than he would wish to deny that he had any ancestors. The best of our traditional designs were functional in their day. The Cape Cod cottage, for example, exactly suited the needs of the fishermen on the Massachusetts coast, and its lines suited the landscape. The great southern plantation house, such as Washington's home, Mount Vernon, suited the Virginia planter. If we choose from the traditional styles those aspects which are functional in modern life, we can develop functional designs with traditional influence which are suited to the American landscape.

But you say, "At present, I have no chance to choose any design, functional or otherwise. I live in a house which my parents chose, or in one which, like Topsy, just grew, or in one thrown together by some builder who did not know functional from traditional design."

It is true that very few of us live in houses of our own design. Many of us will never build the castles in the air which we see in dreams. Still, we have or shall have some choice when we rent or buy property; so it is wise to learn what constitutes good design in a house. And bad design in an old house can sometimes be corrected at a fairly moderate cost.

Materials. Today we have a wide choice of materials—brick, stone, timber, steel, cement stucco, glass, plastics, and various synthetic products. Supply and demand affects the cost, and the cost limits the choice for most of us. Still, we have much more of a choice than our forefathers, who usually built their homes of the materials nearest at hand. Thus, the early settlers in forested regions constructed log cabins; those on the prairie, sod houses; those in the Southwest, adobe huts. Later they used the native timber or stone or bricks made from native clay to build bigger and better homes.

Often the builders were influenced in their choice of both material and design by the traditional styles of the countries from which they came. Thus, the brick or frame houses of the later colonial period in the East show the influence of the English Georgian style, and the old ranch houses of California are definitely Spanish in their feeling.

In the interest of functional design we may well take a tip from our ancestors when choosing the material and style for our houses. Native materials help to make a house fit into its setting. An adobe house belongs in New Mexico but not in New England. New materials, such as steel, glass, and plastics, call for new design. Traditional materials, such as brick or timber, may be used in a variety of styles to suit the climate and the setting. However, a medieval castle, imitated in stone or wood, is not functional on the plains of Kansas.

Your needs. What are your needs? What do you demand of a home? It is contended today that a house is a machine—constructed for the purpose of making life pleasurable. There are still houses, however, with too much pierced scroll-work and too many wooden gimcracks, turrets, bay windows, and ornate ornamentations which do not fill any real need. The wearing of excess jewelry on your person and the sticking of too many extra ornaments on your home both arise from the desire to show the world that you possess quantities of material things in excess of your bodily needs. This does not mean that a house should have no ornament, but simply that it should not be burdened with an excess amount.

In the nineteenth century, when machine production and expanding markets created widespread wealth, ornate display became a disease. Hand-made ornaments of priceless materials, or machine-made imitations of cheap materials, cluttered the exteriors and interiors of homes. That is the heritage of the nineteenth century, in which the twentieth century had its roots. Many of these nineteenth century over-decorated houses abound in nearly every town. Unfortunately in some modern homes this practice of over-decoration has survived. Some of these houses could be greatly improved simply by removing the excess decoration.

Today you want many things that conflict with this nineteenth century over-display. You want each room that is necessary for your family's needs to be suited to those needs. You want these necessary rooms so placed that there is privacy for the kitchen, the living room, and various living quarters, without wasting hall space and wall construction. You want windows and fireplaces placed for maximum comfort in each room, plus an interesting arrangement of lines and a beautiful balance of forms. You want this balance to be apparent both inside and outside the house. These are some of the many problems in functional home planning.

The exterior of the house. Before designing your own ideal house or trying to improve an old one, study the fronts, or façades, of quite a number of houses

Do you need an architect to design your home?

in your town. Analyze the general proportions of these houses and the relationships of line, form, texture, and color. What are the dominant lines of the house and the prominent shapes in the façade? If a house has gables or peaked roofs, the peaks should not be a variety of shapes. It is better, as a rule, to have the lines of the gable edges parallel in order to give unity to the design. Variety may be obtained by a variation in the size of the gables.

On some houses, one triangle, one oval, or some other single shape dominates the front. This is sometimes successful, but is often unsatisfactory when the form or line is not repeated elsewhere. Repeating shapes is a means of creating unity. For instance, horizontal lines may be continued and repeated in order to create a horizontal feeling. There may also be a carefully considered use of triangular forms or curved arches. All horizontal, perpendicular, diagonal, and curved lines, however, should be considered as lines in a design, and hit-or-miss combinations of rectangles, triangles, and curves should be avoided, as should ornamental details which serve no purpose. Pillars which support nothing, for example, give a false note to the design.

In observing houses, note the treatment of doorways and windows. The door is usually the most important form on the house front. Doors and windows should create a definite, orderly design; they should not be of assorted shapes and sizes and placed at various levels without regard to the design they produce.

As we know, closely related colors create unified designs, and this applies to houses. Accents of contrasting colors should be only on the most important areas. Thus, the doorway is often colored differently from the rest of the house and the windows may have a similar treatment. Roofs are invariably in contrast to the sides of the house because of the difference in material. In many houses, both old and new, variations in materials serve as a substitute for different colors. It is well to remember that the windows of a house create a color pattern in themselves because of the way in which glass reflects light. Also the shadows cast by eaves which overhang, or by anything which projects from the house, add interest to the total pattern. Although color should be used daringly and with spirit, it is well to remember that too many colors may spoil the house.

Problems and activities. (1) Explore your neighborhood to find houses that seem to be imitations of architectural styles of other countries and times, and decide what period or country each represents. Which ones are good? Why? (2) Observe the types of building materials (wood, stone, brick, stucco, or others) used in your community, and decide which ones are most appropriate and which are inappropriate to the historical styles of architecture chosen. (3) Visit a new real-estate subdivision, or get pictures of houses offered for sale. Pick out what seem to be violations of principles which you have read in this section. (4) Select examples of houses that have been well planned in relation to these principles. (5) Examine houses or pictures of houses which purport to be extremely "modern," and indicate what they have lost or gained by departing from historical traditions in architecture. (6) Go on a house-hunting trip, looking for a place to rent, and select the few most likely ones for your home, as best you can from the outside, just as if your next step were to be a request for inspection inside.

VII. Areas of Action

Planning the different rooms in your home

Each scene in the drama of family living requires its own appropriate area of action. Each room in the house must be designed according to the uses to which it is to be put. Each part of the home must be planned for the comfort, convenience, and happiness of its occupants. Any design which conflicts with this normal use, or function, will lack real beauty, for beauty is largely appropriateness. For example, any bedroom which is unsuited for sleeping purposes lacks beauty, regardless of how well it may meet some other set of standards.

Not every home will contain all of the types of rooms that are analyzed in this chapter. However, a study of all the possible kinds of rooms is desirable as a basis for selection among the needs and special interests of individual students and families. Perhaps your budget does not permit you to have a rumpus room, but you may manage to have a small sun room. Someone else cannot afford a sun room but can make a dingy basement into a perfectly delightful rumpus room. Take your choice; study the problems of design for such parts of the house as your needs and interests may suggest. At least you should make a careful study of two or three of the essential and most commonly used rooms. This study may have immediate value to you and will also help you to make good choices and plans in the future as your expanding budget may permit.

You do not have to wait until you are ready to build your own home to begin using what you learn in this chapter. Every member of the family, including you, should be concerned with the use and beauty of the family residence, whether you are moving to a new one or remaining exactly where you are.

HOME

1. SANCTUARY

Designing Your Bedroom

Your own room is a kind of sanctuary—a place where you may go to be alone with yourself. There you may sleep, relax, dream, study, plan, or create. If you could build, buy, or rent exactly the type of room you want in which to express your taste and learn to know yourself, how should you design it? If you already have a room and an opportunity for choosing and arranging furniture to please yourself, perhaps you would like to analyze your handiwork and see how well you have done the job.

Air, light, and sound. Your ideal sleeping room should be so located that it can be thoroughly aired and sunned each day, and so that you can have fresh cool air at night. Two or more average-sized windows are desirable. The room should be so planned that there is no artificial light in your eyes at night. It should be as sound proof as it is possible to make it, for the sake of both rest and privacy; and, of course, it should be accessible to a bathroom.

Furniture. In every room there is one unit of furniture that expresses the purpose of the room. In your bedroom it may be either your bed, your study chair and table, or your dressing table. Pretend that you are standing in the door of your room, and in imagination place these three largest furniture units. The most dramatic and interesting unit should usually be placed clearly in your line of vision so that it dominates the room as you stand on the threshold. This most important group may be further emphasized by a wall panel, picture, mirror, lamp, or some colorful object of art that draws the eye. Your bed should be so placed that you get light and air as you wish them, and your study chair so that you have both day and night light over your left shoulder. Your dressing table or mirror should be so placed that when you use it, you have direct light on your face. A convenient and attractive place for the dressing table is in the middle of a large window. If so arranged, it should be fairly low, with an easel-top mirror that will not obstruct the light. Other pieces of furniture in the room, such as a small bookcase, an extra table or chair, should be grouped for greatest convenience.

PLANNING THE DIFFERENT ROOMS IN YOUR HOME

There should be no object in your bedroom that gets in your way, or causes extra trouble in cleaning, or whose purpose does not warrant the space it occupies. All such pieces of furniture should be eliminated regardless of their sentimental value. Life is too short to waste time in dusting a collection of objects merely because you happen to own them. Streamline your habits, eliminate clutter, and save your energies for making the most of yourself and getting the most out of life.

Which does your room resemble?

Shape and color harmony. The pieces of furniture in your room, when placed together, are a complex design. A feeling of unrest, inexcusable in a sanctuary, results when the shapes are over elaborate in outline or over decorated on the surfaces. Too much decoration, as well as too many unrelated objects, may prevent a feeling of relaxation. Simplicity is the best note for a bedroom. Do not have too many shapes in your room. Choose good basic forms which are not too ornate and which belong together. If you have a curved mirror, the curve should be repeated in the rug or some other piece of furniture. In other words, any conspicuous curve should be repeated and built into your room. Rectangular forms may be harmonized in the same way. A rectangular rug, a chest of drawers, a box and mirror, and a rectangular picture all fit well in one group because they provide a variety of sizes of the same basic form. Your bedroom furniture may thus create a pleasing rhythm through repetitions of form.

Your dressing table should never be a hodge-podge of objects whose main value is that they remind you of something else. Sentimental value is not a reason for putting any object on display. Any object on your dressing table should either be useful or good looking or both. Not only should it be good looking in itself, but it must have a relationship in shape, color, or texture to the entire arrangement. For instance, several cylindrical bottles are more rhythmic than a combination of assorted shapes.

Personality. Your room should, of course, reflect your own personality. The scale as well as the style of the furniture should be suited to the user. Bed, chairs, and table should be of a size that is comfortable for you. The shapes and colors should also be satisfying. A girl's room can show feminine charm without being full of furbelows, and a boy's room can look virile and robust without being either severe or sporty. If you choose and arrange your furniture so that it is a true expression of your personality and is also harmonious, the room is likely to be pleasing to those who visit you.

Problems and activities. (1) Inspect your own bedroom for any violations of suggestions given in this section, and decide what you can do or want to do to improve it. (2) Tell the class about bedrooms you may have seen that seemed to ignore the fact that somebody was supposed to sleep in them. What specific conditions needed correction? (3) Bring advertisements or magazine pictures of bedroom interiors to class, and pick out exceptionally good or exceptionally bad features in their designs. (4) Draw diagrams on the blackboard to show how bedroom furniture might be arranged to produce bad balance and then how it might be rearranged in the room for better balance. (5) Visit a furniture display in a big store, and compare the designs of different bedroom units.

2. ALL THINGS TO ALL MEN

Designing Your Guest Room

To be all things to all men is a difficult task. The wisest way to arrive at satisfactory furnishings for a guest room is to consider universal simple wants. In solving the problem, consider four persons of your acquaintance: a girl, a

Do you see anything in this guest room that should be changed?

boy, a man, and a woman, each one as different from the others in temperament as possible. Ask yourself how you can arrange one room so that any one of these four would feel at home in it. The following points may help you.

Furniture. Since all types of people should feel comfortable in the guest room, it should be furnished, not with heavy massive pieces nor light delicate furniture, but rather with a sturdy bed, table, and chairs, neither massive nor too dainty. Besides the usual bedroom furniture, the room should include articles which are necessary for the comfort of your guests. There should be a bedside table with a good lamp, a wastebasket, and either a small bookcase or some means of holding an assortment of books and magazines. There should also be a deep lounging or reading chair placed so that light is available both night and day, as well as a lighter comfortable lounge or rocking chair. Plan for sufficient storage space to hold your guests' belongings in chests of drawers and closets. All furniture and objects in the room should be placed so that they are accessible for use, so that there is passageway through the room, and so that one group of furniture is emphasized and subordinate groups are balanced with it.

Color. The prevailing color in a guest room should be neither too light and delicate nor too rich and heavy. Although there are exceptions, in general pinks and pale blues should be avoided, as well as too heavy browns and intense colors. Some warmth in color is desirable to create a feeling of welcome. If this warmth is toned down to warm grays, sandy beiges, rich creams, and other warm neutrals, the room will form a cheerful haven for various types of people.

Your color scheme should be arranged so that the eye is led up through a rhythm of color to interesting spots of rich color in textiles, art objects, and pictures. Spots of white must be placed carefully. Usually this color is used with no thought of its effect on the whole scheme. When you place a spot of white, be sure that the beauty of the object warrants the emphasis given by such a light value. In a guest room avoid large areas of either magenta or green-yellow, because these are pet dislikes of many people. Soft blue-greens and greens, soft yellow or yellow-orange, subdued orange, red-orange, blue, and green-blue are most popular in guest rooms. Any of these may be combined successfully with the beige and brown colors of wood.

Textiles. If the textiles used in your guest room are patterned, the units of the pattern should be of medium size so that they are neither too masculine nor too feminine in appearance. A conventionalized, simple pattern is most generally acceptable, or one-color fabric which has interesting texture is a good choice. As a rule, let window draperies be more exciting in color than the walls,

SUNROOM

Why does modern furniture offer you more simplicity, comfort, and practicality than copies of period pieces?

(Photographs by courtesy of Barker Brothers, Los Angeles)

DINING ROOM

Can you achieve convenience and roominess in your own quarters?

(Photographs by courtesy of Barker Brothers, Los Angeles)

Have you an attic which you could set up for extra living space?

but less so than the bedspread, pillows, and upholstered furniture. Unless it is exceptionally fine, the rug should be the last thing to attract notice in the room, and should be a stable support for the other objects. Textures in a room which must be adapted to many people should not be too rough and heavy, nor too slick, fine, and smooth. A well-balanced scheme which avoids extremes will be most pleasing to the largest number of people.

Pictures. Choosing at least one good picture for a guest room is a difficult problem, because you must choose something that will speak to a youth or an adult of either sex. Photographs of your own intimate friends or relatives are, of course, out of place in a guest room. Your search should be for the type of picture that will add richness of color to the ensemble and also be good company for the guest. Flowers are probably a little too feminine, but landscapes offer a vide variety of choices for this type of room.

Lighting and other comforts. You will, of course, arrange the furniture so that it provides maximum convenience and comfort. Light plugs, lamps, and furniture should be so placed that good light is available for make-up or reading both by day and night. There are other things which show thoughtfulness of your guests and send them away feeling that they were welcome and that you wished them a really good time. Such things as several sizes of pillows, different sizes of towels, and a variety of books and magazines, writing paper, pencils, pen, and ink will comfort the most weary sojourner. The small guest-room bookcase might contain books for varying tastes and moods: for instance, a book of poetry, a detective story, a book on art, and a book on world affairs. What other additions should you suggest? What additional list of comforts can you plan for your guest room?

Problems and activities. (1) Take a look at your own guest room, if you have one, and check it against the suggestions made in this section. (2) If you have no special room set aside as a guest room, check over the arrangements which you make for guests who spend the night in your home, and decide what improvements you could make. (3) Tell the class about the room and the conveniences which you enjoyed as an overnight guest somewhere, and decide how many of these happy experiences could be provided for guests in most homes. (4) Without mentioning any names, tell the class about any little oversights or unnecessary forms of discomfort or inconvenience which you have experienced in guest rooms of other families, and how these could have been corrected. (5) Make a list of the most common errors found in guest rooms as regards practical utility and another list of the errors as regards beauty of design. Which list is more important? Why?

3. HOT AND COLD

Designing Your Bathroom

Hot and cold water in quantity is the greatest household luxury of the modern age. Singing in the rain isn't half the fun of singing in the bathtub or shower, in clean, shiny, neat surroundings. Hot, warm, cool, and cold baths can do much, along with correct diet and doctor's prescriptions, for toning up the human body. Clinical cleanliness and neatness are a necessary feature of this practical room. Over elaborate decoration is out of place in a room which is essentially a place for cleansing and grooming the body. Bathrooms should combine both efficiency and beauty, and in many respects the bathrooms in typical houses (along with the kitchens) are the best-designed rooms in the house. Perhaps you have never really appreciated your bathroom. Consider the following suggestions for choosing and combining wall textures, floor coverings, fixtures, and textiles in the ideal bathroom.

Shape harmony. If our bathrooms and kitchens are the best-designed rooms in the house, it is because the fixtures for both of these rooms have been designed by experts who think of beauty and function together. Although some bathroom fixtures are certainly more beautiful than others, there are few on the market today which do not have some merit. The design of other furniture is often confused and weakened by imitation of historic styles. Not so with plumbing equipment. It is straightforward, has surfaces easy to clean, with no dirt-catching corners or ornaments, and is planned to fit well into the rooms in which it is used. Most plumbing manufacturers sell sets of fixtures harmoniously designed for use together.

Textures. You can have great fun with the textures in your bathroom. The dominant ones are likely to be smooth: fixtures of porcelain or enamel enlivened with glistening chromium or nickel; walls of tile, composition board, or plaster; floor of tile or linoleum; windows and mirrors of glass. These dominant smooth textures reflect many fascinating patterns. In choosing the textiles and other accessories for the bathroom, you have a great opportunity to emphasize this smoothness through repetition or contrast. Your window and shower curtains may both be of oiled silk—or even of cloth made of glass! For the window curtains you may prefer net or some other material that will contrast with smooth shiny surfaces. And do not for a minute forget the

Which of these bathrooms do you prefer? If the landlord asked you for suggestions for remodeling the other one, what would you tell him?

towels. Nothing adds more to the attractiveness of the bathroom than richly textured, pleasantly rough bath towels, and fine, soft hand towels.

As a rule, naturalistic decorations do not seem at home in the bathroom. It is likely to be small, and the array of textures and forms are interesting enough in themselves. Your bathroom should look as if you, rather than the plumber, had planned it.

Color. Although most good color schemes strike a balance between coldness and warmth, either one or the other usually predominates to some degree. Whether you want your bathroom to be predominantly warm or cool depends on your own tastes and preferences. Some people like to step into a bathroom which has enough yellow or red in it to remove any suggestion of chill. Others prefer cool blues and greens. Still other sturdy souls wish the bathroom in white, gray, and black. Whatever color you choose for the background, be sure that your towels, curtains, and other accessories will look well against it.

Bathroom floors, walls, and fixtures are expensive, and therefore fairly permanent possessions. Before deciding on the color they are to be, be sure that you will be able to live with them a long time without wishing to change them. Large areas of clean-looking colors, unspoiled by little decorative spots, are most apt to give you long-time satisfaction.

Distribution of color. In spotting the colors in your bathroom, think of the whole room. The floor should "stay down" as a substantial base, and the walls should not be so lively that they make you feel uncomfortable or crowded. As you step into the room, you will get a greater feeling of unity if the room gives the impression of several large areas of color—not a great many spots.

In fact, disconnected spots are a typical weakness in many bathrooms. Little, naturalistic pictures do not belong on the rugs, curtains, towels, or walls unless they are part of the whole design. The only decorative shapes used should be those which fit into the whole. For this reason, simple bands of color on the walls, curtains, or towels are generally satisfactory, and these may be repeated in the bath mat or rug.

Towels and bath mats. Bath mats and towels should be thought of as opportunities for pattern which will show off against plain-surfaced walls, or as undecorated colorful surfaces if the walls are patterned. Towels and mats may either contrast or harmonize with the general bathroom color. In either case they may add a few spots of stronger intensity to the whole color scheme.

Problems and activites. (1) Visit a plumbing shop or store that displays bathroom fixtures, and select pleasing designs, patterns, or combinations. (2) Make a similar visit to a dealer who sells tile for bathroom floors and walls, and select inexpensive designs. If possible, bring samples to class, and defend your choices. (Be sure to return the samples afterward.) (3) Make a special study of the bathroom designs in model homes that are open for public inspection, note unusual effects, how they are obtained, and how they could be adapted to your needs. (4) Compare a few old bathrooms with a few very new ones, note features that were once "the latest thing," and decide how you can best avoid building a bathroom that will be dated. (5) Bring pictures of modern bathrooms from magazines or from advertisements, rank them from the standpoint of design, and justify your ranking. (6) If possible, borrow from a department store samples of shower curtains, window curtains, towels, and bath mats, in a variety of textures and patterns, and decide which textures, patterns, and colors could be combined effectively.

4. FAMILY PERSONALITY

Designing Your Living Room

What kind of people are you and your family? The personality of the family should march right out and make itself known to any guest who enters the living room. If the living room proclaims the kind of people you are, it will attract to you persons who are at home in the same type of surroundings as you are. Your living room is the place where you and your friends should learn to know each other and where each member of your family should feel that he belongs. For these reasons the room should be planned with extreme care, and each object should be considered carefully before it is admitted into the scheme. If you hope for a chance to design or redesign your living room, consider the following points and evolve some standards for making choices.

Subordination. A room should be a background for people. Strong colors, strong contrasts in color, and bold patterns all call the background to the foreground and compete for attention. In such an environment there is nothing left for the people to do but raise their voices and demand an audience. In other words, a living room should be stimulating to your family or friends without being too exciting. You will probably not want walls of pure red, nor will you want a living room in which everything is taupe. How much color and pattern you use depends largely on the kind of family you are and the kind of friends you enjoy. Your living room, besides being what the name implies, sets the stage for much of your entertaining, and should be designed accordingly.

Furniture units. Along with the problem of selecting furniture comes that of arranging it. These are not two separate problems at all, for you will not want pieces of furniture which do not fit together, no matter how beautiful the individual pieces may be.

In placing your living-room furniture, think of two things: First, where are people going to sit? Second, how are people going to walk through and

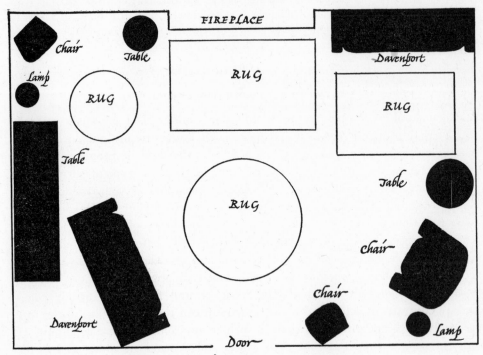

What would you change if you lived here?

around the room? In other words, you want "parking places" and "traffic ways." As far as possible, each of the "parking places" should include a comfortable place to sit, sufficient light, and a table or shelf for magazines and good books. These units should bear a definite relation to the windows and doors in the rooms.

The problem of "traffic ways" is important. Have you ever been in a room where you felt that you could not move around easily? Are there chairs or tables in your home which you and other members of the family often bump against? If so, the room has not been well laid out. Generally speaking, there should be traffic lanes between doors—for example, between the door from the hall and the door into the dining room. Also, arrange things so that you can get easily to windows, bookcases, and the fireplace, if you have one.

It is desirable to arrange the living room so that it will serve the needs of your own family when they are alone and also when they are entertaining. If you have to shift your furniture too often, you had better study the arrangement more carefully. Often, however, it is fun to try new arrangements, not only because they may work better but because changes put some variety into living. Home is one of the best places to be adventurous and try experiments, but don't go to extremes. If your experiments disrupt the family, you accomplish nothing.

Harmony plus variety. The problem of choosing things which go well together is fundamental in art, for it is this which creates harmony. Every piece of furniture in your living room should be related in some way to the others. It may be through color, size, shape, or texture. This does not mean that all the furniture has to be the same in color, size, and texture, but that each piece should have something in common with the others. There is perhaps nothing sadder than a family living room as impersonal as a picture in a furniture catalogue or the lounge of a second-rate hotel. A general feeling of harmony in the furniture is desirable, but it should be a positive and not a negative harmony. Fortunately most families cannot afford to buy complete sets of furniture all at once. The living room grows out of years of living. The important thing is to have it grow harmoniously by careful study of similarities and differences when new pieces are added.

Often a problem arises such as this: your living room furniture is of many kinds of wood which do not harmonize, and yet you cannot afford to buy new. You may bring them into harmony by upholstering the pieces in the same or related colors. They might be done in different tones of green; or green and greenish-blue might be used.

Since very heavy, solid pieces of furniture and very delicate ones are out of scale, they seldom combine harmoniously in a living room. It is far better if all the furniture can be of approximately the same weight and size, with just enough variation to give interest. However, furniture that is sturdy but of medium weight will fit well with either the heavy, large-scale pieces or grace-

Is this room properly furnished and arranged?

ful, slender ones. If you find it necessary to use heavy and light pieces in the same room, try putting each kind together. For example, if you have some light wicker furniture and some of heavy oak, keep the wicker more or less in one place, and the lack of size relation will be less noticeable.

What has been said about furniture also applies to textiles. Coarse, rough woolens are not harmonious with smooth, fine silks, for their textures have nothing in common. Textiles also must be somewhat related to the kind of wood in order to produce a satisfactory unity. Oak and knotty pine combine well with rough textures, such as heavy linen or cotton. Plate glass mirrors, shiny metals, glossy materials, and polished and lacquered woods belong together by reason of their smoothness. Between these two extremes there is a whole middle range of smooth woods and close weaves that combine with either rough or glossy materials.

Color scheme. There are no rules for the perfect color scheme in a living room! One living room may have soft gray walls and be beautifully restful; another may have walls of rich, glowing green; another walls of blue. Still another may follow a new trend and combine colors. Three walls may be yellow and the fourth brown, or three walls white and the fourth rich terra-cotta. No one of these color schemes is any better than the others except as it serves its purpose. How then do we choose colors for a living room?

First of all, decide what effect is wanted. If a quieting neutrality is the aim, then creams, warm gray-greens, or beiges will be the first thought. If cheerfulness is wanted, choose brighter yellows. If a vigorous, dramatic effect is what you want to live with, try one or all four of the walls in rich blue or green.

But before deciding, look at the room. If the room is too small, light colors will make it seem larger; if it is very large, dark colors will make it seem smaller. So think about the size. Then, there is the question of how much natural daylight there is in the room. If it is dark, light colors will brighten it. If it is light, a few darker colors may offer pleasing contrasts.

Third, consider the furniture you have or want. Against what background will it appear to advantage?

The best advice is to see many living rooms, and choose the one in which you feel at home. Then you can decide on your colors.

Value distribution. When you enter the room, you will want an immediate impression of stability and order. An easy way to achieve this is to use a dark rug, lighter walls, and a ceiling which is still lighter. The furniture can be in between the rug and walls in value. This is an easy and safe way—but it is only one way. Some ingenious decorators use light rugs and dark ceilings to give a thrilling effect. The only rule is: decide what effect you want and find out how to get it.

Contrasts of value attract attention, and should be used accordingly. A dark piece of furniture against a light wall will be very noticeable, as will a light object against a dark wall. If you have a beautiful piece of furniture, display it against a contrasting background. If you have an unattractive piece, place it against a harmonizing background. Experiment with this for yourself.

What specific changes in spacing and decoration does this room need?

If you want to avoid a confused effect, do not have many little spots of different values all over the room. White is particularly dangerous—or effective —in this respect, depending on the skill with which it is used. Study each room you see carefully. Where do you look? Why? Do you look at the most important object or at things of less importance? Think of remedies for the defects you see.

Pattern distribution. Patterns are most effectively seen against plain areas. This is an observation which you can check easily for yourself. In a living room your decorating problems will be simpler if the walls are plain or show only an indistinct pattern, because then you can use pattern in your rug, curtains, or upholstery—if you wish it. Or they may all be plain if the colors and textures are interesting.

You may, however, choose to have your walls covered with paper which has a definite pattern. If so, you will have to be careful about choosing and hanging pictures, about draperies, and about all the other patterned surfaces in your room. The contemporary trend is definitely in the direction of plain walls as opposed to patterns, but in many of the important historic periods patterns have played a great part. If your family prefers wall paper, study the whole question of patterns carefully.

Fireplace. A sparkling fire adds the final touch of cheer to any home gathering. Everyone's eyes are on the fire, and probably no one notices the fireplace very much unless it is worth noticing. The simple truth is that unless it is carefully and skillfully designed, it should be unassuming and should concede the center of interest to the fire.

An opening in a flat wall, or simple rectangular forms which are carefully related and firmly supported, will give a satisfactory fireplace design for the average living room. The materials of which the fireplace is constructed should be in harmony with the textures used in the furniture and draperies. Rough stone or brick fireplaces are not in keeping with smooth polished wood and glossy textiles, but some tile designs may be chosen that are suitable in almost any setting. Beware of the pictorial tile unless it helps your whole design. Avoid heavy overhanging mantels and any clumsy weights which are unrelated to the design. This advice does not refer, of course, to tile used in borders or bands to repeat the architectural lines of the fireplace and emphasize the opening for the fire, nor does it refer to the beautiful carved moldings of some mantels of Colonial design.

Problems and activities. (1) Check over your own living room for specific examples of good and bad design as discussed in this section. (2) Make plans for an inexpensive rearrangement or improvement of your own living room, tell the class what you propose to change, and get their criticisms of your plans. (3) Go through magazines for pictures of living-room scenes, and pick out features that illustrate or violate standards given in this section. (4) Recall living rooms which you have seen that violated one or more of the principles of good design, and tell the class what should have been changed. (Don't mention any names or speak unkindly of those who extended hospitality to you.) (5) Go through a new house or model home that is open to the public, note the permanent features of the living room, and plan the kinds of furniture and draperies that should go into it.

5. DINNER IS SERVED

Planning Your Dining Room

"Dinner is served!" or "Come and get it!" Each means food, although in one instance the food may be served on fine china and in the other on a paper plate. Good food prepared by a skillful cook deserves an attractive setting. A drab, disorderly room and a jumbled-looking table are not the appropriate background. The most creative rooms in the house can be the dining room and kitchen, where ordinary substances are mixed into delectable concoctions to tempt the eyes and appetites of the family.

Smiles and light spirits are allies of good digestion. When people are eating, their spirits need to be exhilarated rather than soothed, so the dining-room atmosphere has little in common with that of the quiet study. But neither should the atmosphere be that of the crowded lunch counter at a railway station. It should be an expression of family life at its best.

Walls. The walls in the dining room may be treated in any number of ways, depending on what effect you want to produce. Since eating should be an enjoyable activity, the decoration of the dining room is generally on the lively, cheerful side. Your decorating problems will be somewhat simplified if you paint the walls a plain color, and your furniture problems are simplified by the use of built-in cabinets. Patterned wallpaper, however, may be used to introduce color and variety. As with the living room, no special colors are suited to all dining rooms, but it will generally be found that warm colors are preferable to cool ones.

Furniture. Essential dining-room furniture consists of the dining table and chairs, and a buffet or chest of drawers. To these may be added a cupboard of some sort and one or more small serving tables. It is desirable, of course, to have the chairs of matching or similar design, but it is not necessary that all the furniture should form a suite. It should, however, have a common feeling. A Welsh dresser of pine, suggesting a cottage kitchen-dining-room, does not combine well with the delicacy and elegance of a Hepplewhite mahogany table.

Dining-room table. It is logical that the center of interest in the dining

Can you tell which differences noted in these dining rooms are due to the construction and which to the furnishings?

room is the dining table, for this is what the room is planned around. Therefore, the table and its setting become items of major importance.

A bowl of flowers or fruit on the table will always provide appetizing decorative notes provided they are well related to the color scheme of the room. The choice of table covering depends in part on how the room is furnished. If the dining room is formal in tone with polished mahogany furniture, the table-cloths should be formal in design, smooth in weave, and restrained in color. In contrast, the cloths for an informal dining room are frequently gay in pattern, rich in color, and may be rougher in texture.

With the new interest in colorful chinaware the possibilities for setting attractive tables are enormously increased. Dishes are now available not only in white and cream, but in soft grays, rich browns, warm tans, brilliant oranges, clear yellows, and varying tones of blue. When these are combined with either clear or colored glassware, any person setting a table can use color almost as richly as a painter. In addition, the colors in flowers, fruits, and the food itself can be used decoratively.

A few examples of color schemes may be helpful in suggesting what can be done. For a formal meal a white or pale damask tablecloth is generally used with dishes which have a conventionalized, refined pattern. The glassware is frequently clear, either plain or decorated, and the centerpiece may be a low bowl of the more delicately tinted flowers. An informal table might have a rough linen cloth of deep blue, dishes of soft gray, and clear glassware. Red or yellow flowers would add brightness to the scheme. Or the tablecloth might be yellow with soft green dishes and yellow and orange flowers. Because table settings are changed so frequently, they offer a wonderful opportunity for experimentation. Try different colors together and see what effects you get. Look at the pictures in magazines, or if there are large stores in your vicinity, see the tables which they set as models. You will be surprised at the great variety, and delighted to see the many ways in which you can lift your table out of the ordinary class so that your family and guests will be pleasantly surprised. Experiment with the dishes and cloths and glassware which you have at home.

Buffet. Second in importance to the dining-room table is the buffet or chest of drawers as a point of interest in your dining-room. Here is an opportunity to plan an interesting group. You may wish to hang a picture or mirror above the buffet, and arrange a few decorative objects on it. Some years ago it was fashionable to display one's cut glass on the buffet. At other periods pieces of silver were considered about the only "correct" thing. Today we are far more liberal and experimental, and display many things of low cost provided the design is good.

The design of your buffet will naturally determine what you display on it. If it is an early American pine chest, it calls for pewter plates and candlesticks. If it is modern and of bleached wood, you may use a gay pottery bowl filled with fruit, vegetables, or gourds. This can be enlivened with some small Mexican pottery figures, or smaller dishes. On a more formal, dark sideboard, glass or porcelain bowls or vases filled with flowers would be appropriate. Whatever objects you display, make certain that they are in harmony with the spirit of your whole room. The selection of suitable objects is your first step.

Suppose, for example, that you have a simple maple sideboard in natural finish, and wish to arrange something on it. You might begin with two tall plants, such as *sansevierias*, or snakeplants, as they are often called, placed in copper or brass bowls. The warm tones of the metal would reflect and repeat the color of the maple while the leaves would be a striking contrast. Between these vertical elements you could arrange rich red apples in a low wooden bowl, on a piece of blue-green textile. Or you might have a totally different scheme with colorful leaves in the autumn, or gay flowers in the spring and summer.

You can have much fun trying different objects together. A coffee service on a tray may be the center of interest, with other smaller objects arranged on each side. It is interesting to practice arranging shapes on a buffet so that you can build up to a centralized climax, balancing on either side by candles or other accessories. Beware of one thing: do not copy what every one else is doing. Experiment. Use the colors you like, and see if your friends like them too. Be yourself.

When the table is set, the buffet plays second fiddle, but between meals the carefully chosen and arranged group of objects on the buffet may be the center of interest, particularly if flowers, candles, and dishes produce a dramatic and interesting color combination. Remember that the largest masses of bright color should be centralized in the most important objects, and that strong contrasts of dark-and-light should be used to form definitely planned patterns and to attract the eye to areas of interest.

The use of white. Many people believe that white is harmless and goes unnoticed; consequently they use it carelessly in rooms where the background is medium or dark in value. White, however, attracts attention almost immediately; it is not a self-effacing color. Therefore, use white only where you want to attract attention.

Lighting. Sufficient wall light to facilitate handling of food is necessary in the dining room, but the illumination should be centered on the table. Indirect lighting is not reflected in glass and silver, and should not be used where this sparkle is desired. Direct clear light is the preference of most men. A majority of women prefer the beautiful glimmer of candle light. Whichever type of light you use, be sure that it is adequate for the purpose of seeing food and that it does not hurt your guests' eyes by glaring directly into them. Table light should be above or below eye level and should not come from too high above the table. Candles may be either considerably taller or shorter than their holders, but should never be the same length as the holders.

Problems and activities. (1) Arrange a visit to the school practice cottage, and observe how the dining room is arranged and designed. Decide what changes you would make if you were responsible for improving it. (2) Plan to use the school lunch room when it is closed, and have committees set up two or more tables or buffets for the rest of the class to judge and criticize from the standpoint of design. (3) Bring to class pictures of dining rooms and dining-room furniture, make your selections of the best designs, and justify your selections. (4) Invite an expert from one of the larger stores to explain to your class the problems of selecting and combining dining-room furniture and table service. (5) Check your own dining room for ways in which you can improve it since reading this section.

6. Bright and Early

Designing Your Breakfast Room

Bright and early is the way the day is begun if you anticipate breakfast in a colorful, cheerful breakfast room, whether it is a special room or a corner of the kitchen. Striking color contrasts and arresting patterns are good as stimulants in the early hours of the day, and a taste for gay combinations may prove satisfactory here as in no other room in the house. In order to keep from running completely wild, however, consider the following points and make a check list of do's and don'ts.

Color. Have plenty of color, but do not use every color in the rainbow; leave out one good-sized segment of the color wheel. Achieve the effect of strong color by rich small spots against white, cream, or fairly light neutralized areas, rather than by using too much heavy color. Have hue and value contrasts, but place them carefully at the spots of greatest interest.

Can you find any room for improvement here? What would you suggest?

Furniture. A table, chairs, and a corner cupboard or chest of drawers usually comprise breakfast-room furnishings. These may be of natural-colored wood or colored enamels. The lining of the corner cupboard may be painted a color that repeats the color of the draperies, and the color may be again picked up by some decoration on the table. The dishes displayed in the corner cupboard should be carefully chosen to create pattern against the background color. The

127

table and chairs should not ordinarily be extremely rich in color, else it will be impossible to achieve a center of interest in the table decorations.

Table arrangement. Colorful dishes and tablecloths are the joy of modern mornings. The fact is, we like them so well that in many homes we use them for every meal. To use these bright table accessories successfully you must learn how to combine modern tablecloths with modern dishes and you must resist buying every beautiful color you see. A good suggestion is: if your dishes are patterned your tablecloth must be plain, but if your dishes are plain, your tablecloth may be patterned. You can easily see why this is necessary, because patterns show off to best advantage against plain surfaces. Brown pottery dishes on a green-and-white patterned tablecloth create a satisfying effect, and for such a combination white and yellow flowers would form a successful center-piece. Your dishes should be of closely related colors, of the same degree of warmth, or of the same value. That is, they should have either likeness of hue, intensity, or value to tie them into the same family.

Equipment. Engineering designers have been at work evolving both practical and beautiful designs in all of the machines used in the home. Strange to say, much very bad design still persists in waffle irons, toasters, percolators, and clocks. A good criterion to help you to judge cooking-utensil design is this: "Has it any dirt-catching devices which could be eliminated?" A second criterion is: "Is its contour as simple as possible?" Each of these criteria is important in modern breakfast-room design. Well-designed equipment goes a long way toward creating a smart, smooth-going breakfast environment.

Problems and activities. (1) Consider the room or nook in which you eat breakfast, decide what you think might improve it, and see whether your classmates approve your plans. This may be the place where your family would welcome a change. (2) Try out different combinations of tablecloths and dishes on a table which you set up in your own classroom, and decide which combinations produce the best effects. (3) Go shopping for breakfast dishes, pottery, and table linens, and get all the ideas you can from the salespeople as to breakfast-room design. Report your discoveries to the class. (4) Bring several waffle irons, toasters, or other breakfast-table articles to class, judge their design, and decide what other articles of breakfast-room equipment would combine well with them. (5) Collect a number of large pictures of breakfast-room articles and accessories, and let the class judge their individual designs and the problem of combining different articles in pairs or groups.

7. Neat and Clean

Designing Your Kitchen

Neat and clean the modern kitchen certainly is, but it can be more; it can be vibrant, sparkling, brilliant, a delightful place in which to work. Some of the best minds of today have worked on the problem of designing kitchens and kitchen equipment that will answer weary housewives' prayers. Let's con-

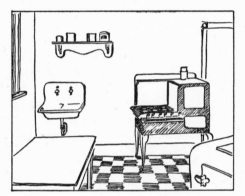 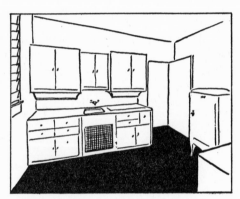

When is a kitchen well-designed?

sider a basis for choosing kitchen equipment and designing or rearranging kitchens so that they give the maximum pleasure and efficiency. If your family budget does not allow for the latest model of stove or icebox, still you can do much to make the kitchen pleasant without a great deal of expense.

Arrangement. Place yourself before your sink, and imagine that you are preparing and serving the evening meal, then washing the dishes and putting them away. The icebox and stove should be easily accessible. The doors of the stove, icebox, and cupboards should open away from you so that they do not form barriers. Salt, pepper, and other spices and flavorings should be within easy reach. A tiny spice cupboard between the windows over the sink is often a time and labor saver. The shelves for the most frequently used dishes should be most easily reached. Your job is to reduce to a minimum the amount of footwork to be done and to maintain a cool, well-lighted pleasant atmosphere for work. Cross ventilation should be planned so that odors may be carried off. This can be managed with a ventilating fan if there are windows on only one side of the kitchen.

Lighting. Illumination should be concentrated on the sink, stove, and work tables. The neatest and easiest-to-clean lighting fixtures will give the greatest and most lasting satisfaction.

Color. White and the shiny, silvery color of metal are the two basic colors in the modern kitchen, since they are the two colors in which the majority of the heavier equipment is produced. Beginning your kitchen design with those rectangles of white or white-and-black, you have the problem of holding them in the scheme as a whole, which would seem to call for a considerable use of white in the walls and cupboards of the kitchen. All-white kitchens with small touches of strong color are popular. Rich or intense areas will have a tendency to "jump" unless they are carefully designed so that they form a unified pattern. There should usually be some larger area of the strong color for emphasis, and for giving the feeling of a center of interest to which the smaller spots may be tied.

Since the food laboratory is a place for action, rich, full intensities of blue, turquoise blue, green, yellow, orange, vermilion, or red may be used in various combinations with black, white, cream, pale gray, or grayed intensities of the main color. Violet, violet-blue, and red-violet seem to be out of mood with the kitchen, since they introduce an element of mystery rather than of direct action. Medium intensities have gained popularity, and many kitchen articles (including pots, pans, and dishes) may now be bought in a wide range of hues in full and medium intensities and tints.

Even in the kitchen we find it hard to endure large areas of intense, saturated color, and we therefore often use white, pale gray, or pale grayed intensities for the large background spaces. Red, even in weak intensities, is far too stimulating for all the walls, but may be used in carefully planned spots, usually in contrast to white. Pale, slightly grayed yellow or green create satisfying kitchen backgrounds, with small contrasting areas of richer yellow, orange, vermilion, green, or black. Black is good only in shiny surfaces which relieve it of the feeling of gloom, and should be used only in contrast with light values which add sparkle. A kitchen should be gleaming, clinically clean, and light.

Linoleum. The variety of linoleum patterns on the market today is bewildering to many people who go to select a floor covering for the kitchen. A floor covering should be durable and easy to keep clean, but it should generally be the last thing you notice in the room—certainly not the first. This means two things: first, that it should not have too strong a dark-and-light pattern, and second that it should not be too strong in color. Plain linoleums are deservedly popular because they give a solid, rich base to the room, but some persons prefer patterns. Patterns composed of squares and rectangles are widely used. Any floor covering should be more grayed or darker than the other large areas of color in a room. Have you seen linoleum floors that seemed to come up and hit you in the eye? This is usually because the pattern is too startling in intensity or in dark and light contrast.

Cupboards. Kitchen cupboards may be things of joy with their bright-colored linings and interesting contents. A variation in the heights of the shelves allows for the storing of articles of different sizes, and creates a more interesting design. Shelf paper adds color, and gives variety to the line of each shelf. The background color of a cupboard should never be more important than the objects placed against it. It is easy to plan and carry out an arrangement of your cupboard shelves that will make them more serviceable. This rearrangement should improve the appearance of the cupboards and make the utensils stored in them easier to reach.

Utensils. Modern utensils save the housewife hours of work because they are rust-proof and easy to clean. Pre-measuring of liquid is eliminated if pans have the level of various cup measures indicated on the sides. The greatest energy saving is achieved by the elimination of dirt-catching crevices and unnecessary bumps and hollows. Compare old-style and new-style utensils, and consider them from the standpoint of efficiency and beauty. Note how often the highest rating for efficiency coincides with a high rating for beauty. "Form follows function."

Problems and activities. (1) Visit the kitchens in the home economics department, judge the designs of stoves, refrigerators, and cabinets, and decide which features would be best suited to homes. (2) While you are in the home economics kitchens, judge the combinations which you find there in order to decide which pieces of equipment or apparatus harmonize or fail to harmonize with other pieces. (3) From pictures found in magazines or advertisements select particularly good designs or combinations of kitchen articles and furniture. (4) Take a careful and critical look at your own kitchen to check how well it conforms to standards presented in this section, and decide what you would like to change. (5) Go through a few model houses or new houses offered for sale, compare kitchens, and decide what kinds of movable equipment you would need if you were to move into one of these houses. (6) Tell the class what kind of movable kitchen equipment should be chosen by a family which has to move often and therefore has to use many different kitchens during a period of years.

8. ROYAL ROAD TO LEARNING

Designing Your Study

The royal road to learning is a high-toll road, because it requires privacy and quiet which are difficult to get in these days of noise and bustle. The whole mood of a study or library must be quiet, and working tools must be arranged so that the study pattern is easier to follow than to side-step. If you are interested in gaining the most possible value from your work time, check the following points, and redesign your study room or corner if it can be improved upon.

Atmosphere. Experiments have shown that some persons work better when music is being played softly, but that they are disturbed by interrupting announcements such as usually come in on radio programs. Other persons prefer absolute quiet. Still others seem able to work in the midst of some noise and confusion. You are the best judge of what conditions make you want to work, and you ought to plan for these carefully. When you go to work, concentrate on the job in hand. Do not allow yourself to be distracted by noise or by a too lively wall pattern. Design the whole atmosphere so that it helps you to study, but also develop your powers of concentration.

Anyone who pretends to be a student in the true sense of the word should have a definite place for study. While you may be of the type who can concentrate in the midst of some noise and activity, it is absurd to think that you can achieve maximum results when you spend a quarter of your time listening to the radio, another quarter joining in the family conversation, and still another quarter going in search of pencils or eraser. Although few homes possess a real study or library, you can doubtless find a corner in your own bedroom,

Which room would contribute most to real mental work?

or in the living room, attic, or upstairs hall which you can claim for your own and make into a study nook.

Equipment. A library, a study, or a work corner in your room is a laboratory for reading and writing. Every study should have adequate desk or table space with good light, also drawers or racks for the materials in immediate use, and, if possible, bookcases. The table or desk should have enough surface for the orderly arrangement of materials being used. The chair should be comfortable and of the correct height, so that you will not develop a tendency to slump over the table. All the tools that you need for working should be within easy reach, with drawers or cubby holes at hand for reserve supplies. A pencil sharpener is a great convenience; it may be clamped to the table, desk, or wall in an inconspicuous place. The kind of pen and ink that you like ought to be convenient, as should the paper, paper clips, and erasers. Convenience plus beauty is a good motto for the study.

Make certain that everything which you need to work with is at hand and that eye and ear are led astray as little as possible. Your study space may be only the size of a large cupboard, but it should be a place where distractions are reduced to a minimum, and where everything is arranged so that you may stop work and begin again with no inconvenience. As far as possible, create for yourself a royal road to learning.

Lighting. Good lighting is essential in a study. The work table and a comfortable chair should be adequately illuminated for either day or night work. But there should be no glare or light shining directly into the eyes. Night light should be sufficiently bright to relieve eyestrain, and should come from more than one source. It seems good practice to have the whole room softly lighted, and brighter lights on one or two important places.

Bookcases as design. The bookcases may very well be the chief decorations in a study. Books with their rich colors, interesting titles, and varied textures make attractive patterns. The cases, whether built in or not, should fit in with the design of the whole room, and seem to belong just as the doors and windows do. They may be varnished or stained to preserve the grain of the wood, or they may be painted a color which harmonizes with the walls. It is good to remember that books are of many colors; therefore the cases themselves are more effective when neutral.

Glass doors on the cases, while they keep out dust, do not add to the beauty of the design. Very simple bookshelves can be contrived by using large bricks or tiles for the ends and laying boards across them much as a child builds things out of blocks. If the tiles and shelves harmonize with the walls or the dominant color in the room, such a bookcase is suitable for almost any type of study nook.

Color. What colors are suitable for a study nook or room? Forgetting for a moment the matter of individual tastes, it is safe to say that the study should have restful, quieting colors. Grayed hues and closely related middle values are always suitable, since they do not distract your attention. Strong, bright colors and vigorous contrasts of light and dark are definitely out of place. The colors used may be either predominantly cool or warm, depending on which makes you feel better, and also on the amount of sunlight entering the room. Blues and gray-greens are popular colors, and are good if they suit your personality. The most important thing to remember in planning a place to study—as in planning any other room—is that it should be thoroughly functional. It should also seem to be all of one piece so that the eyes will not be suddenly attracted and the mind jolted by pattern or shape contrasts. If your study corner is in your own bedroom, it should not be difficult to plan a color scheme suitable to the double use of the room.

Problems and activities. (1) Get permission to examine and criticize the study room or office of one of the officials in your school, and decide what features of its design could be copied or borrowed for use in home study rooms. (2) Tell the class about the problems which you face in your own study room or corner, and get suggested solutions from your classmates. (3) Visit the study rooms of two or more of your classmates, note good and bad features, and report to the class your most helpful suggestions for study rooms in general. (4) Make a list of the ways in which beauty and utility in study rooms seem to be opposed to each other, and tell the class how these conflicts can be overcome. (5) Bring to class pictures of the private studies of famous people, note how they follow or depart from the standards suggested here, and decide which features you would like to adopt for your own study room. (6) Have two or more committees each set up an ideal student's work corner in your classroom, just as if it were in a home; then let the rest of the class judge the merits of the different corners.

9. LET JOY BE UNCONFINED

Designing Your Recreation Room

Not many houses today have special places for recreation and games, but there is an increasing tendency to transform waste space in basements, attics, or porches for such use. If you are fortunate enough to have some such space which is not being well used, it might be worth your while to consider how it could be made attractive enough so that your friends would enjoy coming to it.

The first step in thinking about a recreation room is to decide what effect you want to produce. How do you want people to feel when they come into it? Naturally, the answer to this question is that you want them to feel gay and

Does fun in the basement depend upon wealth or upon ideas?

happy. The recreation room, more than the living room, should suggest lively activities. You will need space to move around in, substantial furniture which may be used flexibly and will not be easily marred or damaged, a floor covering that can be danced on, and walls suitable for wall games. Assuming that you have a solidly-built attic, basement, extra room, or porch that you can use for play, let's see what can be done to create a place where people like to get together and have a good time.

Ventilation. No guests have a good time in a stuffy room. How much breathable air is available for a crowd? More air is needed for ten than for two. Nothing will so dampen the spirits of a party group as being in an overcrowded, poorly ventilated room. Be sure that there are windows or other ventilating devices for your friends' comfort.

Background. If your room is in the basement, you possibly have heaters and furnaces to contend with. If these are the new beautifully designed models, which are worth looking at as decorative objects, you will not need to conceal them. If they are not good-looking, however, you may want to hide them behind screens or light partitions.

If your room is an attic, the ceiling is probably irregular, but this is a definite advantage. If properly covered with one of the new wallboards, an irregularly shaped ceiling will contribute much to a feeling of informality and friendliness. Many historic houses owe some of their charm to such ceilings.

The variety of wall treatments for a recreation room is probably greater than for almost any other room. Here you can experiment with colors and textures and materials to your heart's content. Since you can do much of the work yourself, it can be changed from time to time. What colors should you like to use? Consider the following suggestions: knotty pine walls and draperies of rough weave, burnt orange in color; rich, soft blue walls and draperies of grayed pink; clear green walls and curtains of white trimmed with green. These are only a few combinations. Think of as many others as you can.

Murals. Mural paintings on plaster or some other wall covering can create a real atmosphere of fun. They may be done either as a more or less permanent decoration, in which case you will want to consider them carefully and paint them well. Or they may be done as temporary features on large sheets of paper fastened to the walls.

The murals in your play room should have some of the characteristics which make good wall paintings anywhere. You will want to consider the size and shape of your room, the windows and doors, and the fireplace, if there is one. Built-in bookcases, seats, or cupboards need to play their part in the total design.

Keep in mind that the room will be a far pleasanter one if the paintings seem to fit into their place naturally, easily, and decoratively.

You have already observed that patterns are most effective when seen against plain areas, and this is true of mural paintings. Plan the murals so that they will be seen in relation to areas of plain color for contrast. In general, you will want spirited, somewhat playful subjects, and gay, stimulating colors. In order to get ideas, visit some buildings with mural paintings in your town or look at pictures of those in other towns.

Atmosphere. A play room should be stimulating. It should make you feel happy and carefree. To get this effect, you can have a lively play of forms and colors. The recreation room is an ideal place to express a sense of humor if you wish to, and the murals may be of humorous subjects. Humor, though, should not obscure the interest in design, for when that happens, the paintings soon lose their appeal.

Equipment. Game equipment for your play room may be bought or made and placed ready for use at any time. If you study game catalogues and books on recreation, you may plan for games that will not require more room than you have at your disposal. Games such as "Dart the dart" and Ping-pong" are universal favorites, and they are not too strenuous. Wall games are satisfactory if you also wish to use the floor for dancing. Modern department stores offer many suggestions for improving play rooms, and it would be advisable for you to look through their game departments before perfecting your rumpus-room plans.

Problems and activities. (1) Describe to the class some unusually attractive play room which you have seen, and indicate which features or elements could be introduced into the average home at small expense. (2) Draw an outline of a play room on the blackboard, indicating the locations of the main features, and get class criticisms of your plan. (3) Measure any possible play space in your own home, garage, or barn, bring the specifications to class, and get class help in making plans to convert that space to real play purposes. (4) Describe murals or other decorations which you have seen in play rooms of homes or clubs, and decide which of these could be used in homes like your own. (5) Note the arrangements and decorations in some large dance pavilion, analyze the effects produced, and decide which would be appropriate or inappropriate for a club room or party room in your own home.

10. SUN TAN

Designing Your Sun Room

Sun tan is evidence that you have been out of doors benefiting from health-giving light rays. Sickly pale plants and people are often weak merely from lack of adequate air and sunshine. Every room in which the family lives should allow for a maximum of light and air. Any room which is planned definitely as a sun room should include comfortable furniture and decorative materials which can stand the sun's rays. A real sun room is serviceable only if it is so designed that the sun can really be invited in and enjoyed. If perishable woods and fabrics are used in the room decoration, the whole purpose of the room is defeated.

Textures. Metal and fabrikoid furniture is durable and comfortable. Rattan is serviceable and long wearing. Wicker and reed furniture is not so durable, but it is cool and pleasant looking. Since bright reflecting surfaces cause eye-strain if used where there is full sunlight, mirrors and polished metals should be employed with caution in the sun room.

The matter of floor covering also raises certain problems, for sun and damp air are hard on many carpets. Painted floors, linoleum, cement, or tile surfaces resist the sun well. Navajo rugs and fiber or reed rugs are also good.

Color scheme. Since the out-of-doors is the most important part of a sun room, the rest of the room should be subordinated to the view from the windows. The whole effect should be light and airy, but there should be no glare. You have probably seen sun rooms that seemed to be a real part of the garden or the great out-of-doors, and this type creates a feeling of restful outdoor living.

For the sun room we naturally think of cool colors, such as those found in nature, as being best suited to the desired effects. Blue, however, fades easily, which is a decided drawback to its use. Greens are cool and fresh-looking, but should be chosen in relation to the greens seen in the foliage outside. White walls are likely to be too glaring because they reflect all of the sun's rays. If you wish to emphasize the warmth and cheer of the sun, yellow is the color to use—but remember that your room will be very bright! Wood, finished with wax or shellac, forms a background which has much to recommend it.

Does it cost much to let the sunshine in?

Problems and activities. (1) Collect and bring to class several pictures of sun rooms, and judge them as to suitability for their purpose. (2) Get from the stores a number of samples of materials for sun-room draperies, and rank them as to their suitability for the purpose, taking account of both colors and textures. (3) Make a similar comparison of linoleums or floor coverings, based on the sample books which you can arrange to borrow from floor covering dealers. (4) Consult the furniture departments of several stores, see what pieces and styles they recommend for sun rooms, make your best selections, and present descriptions of them to the class for criticism. (5) Check your own sun room, or the room that best serves that purpose, against the suggestions given in this chapter, and tell the class what you think you should change. See if they agree.

11. CONNECTING RODS

Planning Your Halls

Making connections between the various rooms in the house is a costly procedure. Halls cost per square foot as much as the average room, and their usefulness should justify their expense. Halls serve as reception rooms, passageways, and sound absorbers, and may be considered in each of these capacities.

Reception halls. The reception hall opens into surrounding rooms and should be definitely related to them in style and color scheme. In the smaller home, particularly, a close relationship in color scheme and value between hall and adjoining rooms gives a feeling of size to each room as well as to the hall.

The most successful reception hall is planned so that it is interesting in itself and is not merely a passageway. Perhaps there is a stairway in the hall. The stair rails and posts should be well-proportioned and simple in contour, not bulgy and ornate. Perhaps the hall contains a chest of drawers or a table and some chairs. They may add an interesting note to the ensemble, but they are too often used merely to pile things on. A wall hanging, mirror, or picture behind the table or chest of drawers may add to the beauty and interest of the hall.

Halls as passageways. Poorly designed halls are a wasteful use of house space. You may have seen houses that seemed to have almost as much hall space as room space. Smaller, better planned halls cost less and accomplish the same purpose. Many architects of today have perfected home designs that allow easy access between rooms with a minimum of waste space in halls.

Halls as sound absorbers. When you are in your own room, can you hear too much of what is going on in the rest of the house? The floor space of your home should be so designed that halls and clothes closets act as sound absorbers and give added privacy to each bedroom. When you do any redecorating, it is wise to inquire about sound-proofing materials for walls and floors. Even when one is asleep, noise has a harmful effect on the nerves. It is well to eliminate as much of it as possible if you intend to use your energies to accomplish things in this world.

Problems and activities. (1) Examine critically the halls of your own school building, decide whether they are well proportioned in relation to their purposes, and indicate anything which they suggest concerning halls for ordinary homes. (2) Judge the halls of your own home with respect to their size, shape, economy, and attractiveness. Decide what you can do to overcome any of their limitations. (3) Describe to the class any outstanding examples you have observed in which halls and stairs were poorly designed or arranged, and tell what should have been different. (4) Visit a few model homes or houses for sale, note hall and stair arrangements, and decide which ones you would like best if you were buying one of the houses. (5) While on such a tour of

Which entrance hall and room combination gives the greater feeling that the home belongs together as a unit? Why?

new houses, plan what you would put into the halls if you were to move into one of these homes.

12. THE WORKS

Designing Storage and Workrooms

The workroom and laundry may be the back porch, a section of the kitchen, the basement, or a small room by itself. Wherever it is, it is the culminating argument that "the home is a machine." Since the tools or machines compose the nucleus of the workroom, let's discuss them.

Household machines. The laboratories of the house, including the bathrooms, kitchen, laundry, and workrooms, have, in the majority of cases, stepped far ahead of the rest of the house in beauty of design. In this newer realm of machines there are no traditions from the past to blind the eyes of the customer to the beauty of simplicity and smooth-flowing contour. Washing machines, irons, vacuum cleaners, carpet sweepers, furnaces, and water heaters have achieved compact forms and shining enameled jackets which are completely functional.

Your laundry room or corner will look its best if the wash tubs are fitted into neat, rectangular cupboards that improve their appearance and make a handy storage space for laundry, soap, and cleaning materials. If your home is small, it may be possible to build all of your washing equipment into the kitchen and save space. Irons and vacuum cleaners of very light weight, with easy-to-clean surfaces, and with great efficiency of performance add to the beauty of the workroom. A good, well-designed carpet sweeper is beautiful because useful. The best-looking, most compact water heater and furnace on the market will contribute to household good looks as well as comfort. The placing of these household machines in your kitchen, back porch, or basement is as truly a problem in orderly arrangement of forms as is the placing of your furniture in your living room.

Problems and activities. (1) Tell the class about unusually neat, orderly, and attractive service porches or workrooms which you have seen, indicating how the average family might adopt some of these features without too much cost. (2) Out of your memory of several unsightly work places which you may have seen in homes, recall the specific features which made them unsightly, and tell how these features could be corrected without hampering the work of the household. (3) Get as many folders or advertisements as you can, showing washers, ironers, refrigerators, water heaters, laundry tubs, and similar household apparatus, judge these as to design, and indicate which ones would combine well in a workroom. (4) Tell the class about good arrangements you have seen for hiding unsightly materials by means of cupboards, closets, shelves, or drawers.

VIII. Comfort and Beauty

Furnishing the home

Do you take part in the selection and arrangement of the furnishings and decorations of your home, or do you "just live there"? Perhaps you feel that you are given far too small a place in the family council. When you do speak up and express a preference for a certain type of furniture, rug, drapery, or picture, are you sure that you are giving voice to more than a mere whim or prejudice? Maybe you could win the family to your point of view and do them a real service if you knew more about the art principles involved in interior decoration.

Furnishing a home in good taste calls for more than good bargaining or shopping for individual pieces. It calls for a knowledge of fundamental principles to help you achieve those groupings and combinations which look like "symphonies in form and color." This does not mean that you must buy everything new and start "from the ground up." It means that you can learn to use what you have to the best advantage. When you have achieved some real beauty with those pieces, you will be much better prepared to choose something new to add to a room or to plan an entirely new scheme of interior decoration.

1. Sold on the Old

Choosing Good Lines in Period Pieces

Do you think of period furniture as being something extremely expensive and very difficult to afford? You will be surprised, then, to learn that most of the furniture in most homes is modified period furniture. But the mere fact that it belongs to a period doesn't mean that it is good. There are poor as well as good reproductions on the market in almost every period design imaginable. You can't prove your good taste in furniture simply by getting a piece that belongs to some period. You can do so only by getting a piece that is of good construction and good design in that period.

Your choice must therefore be made between period furniture and modern furniture, or, to be exact, between the furniture of earlier times and the furni-

Italian Chest

French Table

Dante Chair

Does your personality fit the rich formality of the early Mediterranean furniture?

ture of our own age. Since the next section of the chapter will deal with the problems of modern furniture design, this one will concentrate on helping you to get good home furnishings from the more commonly available period pieces.

In order to distinguish between good and bad reproductions, you should, if possible, see some originals of the period which interests you. This is not difficult to do if you live in or near a city where there are historical or art museums. All over our country small historical museums are being established in old houses or other buildings preserved as landmarks. Some of these are furnished with original pieces of the period, others with good reproductions. Many of the larger art museums now show rooms representing typical periods of decoration in European as well as in American history. In your own home you may have a maple table, mahogany chair, or bride's chest handed down from mother to daughter through several generations. In homes on the Atlantic seaboard there are many fine pieces created by Chippendale, Sheraton, or Duncan Phyfe. Also numerous good pieces made by our early American cabinet makers traveled across the country in covered wagons and are cherished in Iowa, Kansas, Oregon, or California. In the Southwest, antiques of the Spanish period are treasured.

Armchair   *Demi-lune Comode*

Canapé

Do you possess the elegance, refinement, and restrained formality necessary to make you feel at home in a Louis XVI setting?

The word *antique* covers a multitude of sins but also of virtues. You can be either intelligent or silly about antiques. Not everything preserved from the past is good, but most of the workmanship of the old artisans and some of the design has lessons for us of the present. Genuine antiques are genuine all the way through, and they make some of our modern furniture look flimsy and false. Handmade furniture has something of the worker's own qualities in it which cannot be reproduced by machinery. Veneer was seldom used in the days of handmade furniture. Moreover, most woods acquire a color and gloss from long use which new woods do not have. So a simple maple table or cupboard made by an artisan in 1750, with its wood mellowed through the years, has more genuine beauty than can be achieved by the most expensive reproduction.

It is these qualities of genuine antiques which appeal to those people who have a sincere love for period furniture.

Periods as attitudes toward life. Are you one of those who are "sold on the old" because you admire the kind of life that was lived in some earlier period? Do you want to get away from the world as it is now and imagine yourself in harmony with the life of some earlier time?

Most of us, before we are old enough to reason about the matter, develop an unconscious attachment to certain ways of life. This is due partly to early home environment, partly to ancestry. Thus, many homes in the United States preserve an instinctive feeling for the English, Dutch, Scandinavian, French, German, Russian, Hungarian, Greek, Italian, or some other European way of living. This hereditary background probably has much to do with our individual preferences for certain periods in art and our dislike for others. But our instinctive likes and dislikes should be backed up by knowledge and conscious choice.

If you want to choose your furniture wisely, you should really know the background of history which it represents. Do you imagine you would like a living room in the general style of the Louis XVI period merely because you have a romantic feeling about Marie Antoinette? Or do you know the art, music, and literature of France in that day and the personalities and events which created them?

Some periods stress power and strength; others give a feeling of grace, gaiety, and vivacity; still others remind us of the luxury of a leisure class which once ruled a certain part of the world. But we cannot sense these distinctions and choose wisely among them without knowing something of what caused them.

Many people choose furniture the way they choose hats—merely whatever is in vogue at the moment. This is a more serious mistake in buying furniture than in buying a hat because furniture at its worst is expensive and must be used longer than a hat. Moreover, a tendency to follow fads blindly may lead to totalitarianism in taste just as it does in government.

Perhaps you have no interest at all in the past, but feel completely at home in the present. Then probably you should choose modern furniture, which expresses desire for comfort, repose, and efficient living, plus a tendency toward standardization because things are machine made. But do not make the mistake of scorning all those who have a genuine love for antiques and period decoration. Each person has a right to his own taste provided it is sincere.

Dressing Table

Side & Arm Chairs

Do you prefer the beauty of detail, the perfection of proportions, the lightness and grace of the Hepplewhite period?

Originals or reproductions. If you choose a period design for your furniture, try to secure an original or an authentic reproduction. Not all originals are expensive. You want to achieve in your room the effect which that historical style was designed to give. You cannot achieve, for example, the sturdy simplicity of a Dutch colonial dining room with flimsy imitations. It is better to search for a table, buffet, and chairs which all have the feeling of the period but which may not match exactly than to use a flimsy set of cheap reproductions exactly matched in design.

Mixing periods. Of course, an indiscriminate mixture of several different periods is bad, but some combinations are very good indeed, provided they have a common feeling. The rule among decorators that rooms must be exactly true to certain periods has given way to a freer trend. For example, you will now find modern rooms in which Chinese Chippendale or other eighteenth century

Bookcase

Side Chair

Do you entertain correctly, hospitably, and in a slightly formal atmosphere, such as Chippendale furniture provides?

furniture of classic style is used effectively. Jacobean gate-leg tables, Queen Anne chairs, and a William and Mary highboy fit just as well in a house of general southern colonial design as in a strictly English setting. Simple furniture of the Normandy cottage type may fit into a small house of no definable period. It is more of an achievement to create a room of real charm than one which is true in every detail to a certain period, whether it be past or present.

Some periods and their effect. The early Italian or Mediterranean furniture is formal and rich in decoration and is suitable for a room that seeks to express power and magnificence. Its heavy and elaborately designed forms create a magnificence which is very appropriate for some personalities, but they may utterly dwarf others and make them seem insignificant against the overpowering background.

Queen Anne furniture expresses the kind of personality that characterized that amiable, domestic queen who shied away from what was severe and

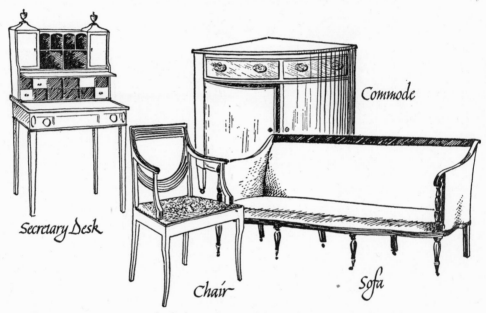

Secretary Desk

Commode

Chair

Sofa

Do your tastes run to the light and graceful simplicity of the Sheraton designs?

powerful and hid herself in brocades and embroidery which expressed her more home-like style. Do you think you are a Queen Anne type of person?

The furniture designs of Louis XIV, XV, and XVI differed from each other as did these three French kings. Louis XIV wanted very expensive and superb furniture suitable for the vast architectural setting of a very elaborate court social life. Only a socially powerful type of person can retain his effectiveness against the background of such ornate luxury.

On the other hand, Louis XV liked his furniture light and graceful with the colors in high key, with touches of gold, glints of porcelain, or even the reflecting qualities of mirrors added to dancing rhythms of line and color. This style was graceful and small in scale and is suited to rooms that are delightfully social and charmingly intimate. Would this suit your kind of family?

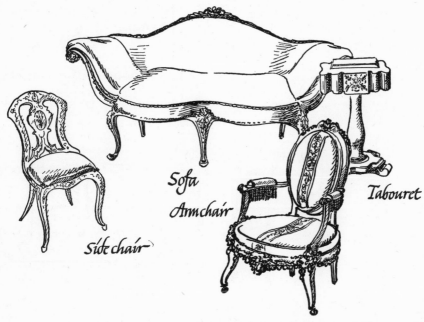

Are you emotionally in tune with the era of the horseless carriage? If so, would you be happy in Victorian surroundings?

Louis XVI and his Queen, Marie Antoinette, preferred rectangular proportions with straight, tapered legs and with curves used sparingly to offset the severity of right angle forms. The style is extremely elegant and refined and is suited to a person of exquisite taste and restrained formality.

The informality of much of our modern living is not well suited to courtly formal backgrounds. Many people feel more at home in the simple setting of the Cape Cod, English, or Normandy cottage, or with colorful furnishings such as originate in the peasant homes of Rumania or Serbia or in the villages of Mexico.

If you have a natural inclination for the Anglo-Saxon influence, you may choose the comfortable formality of Chippendale furniture, the unsophisticated

Do you like a slight echo of Greece or Rome, such as the Adam Brothers conveyed in their furniture designs?

elegance of Hepplewhite, the delicate restraint of the Adams brothers, the simplicity of Sheraton, and the Americanized modifications of the Sheraton and Hepplewhite styles done by Duncan Phyfe. Also, there is the heavy, elaborately carved Victorian furniture which utilized the forms of birds, flowers, and foliage in its design. Many pieces of this period are still stored in American attics and some have found their way into antique shops. Golden oak sideboards and severe Mission style tables and chairs of the next succeeding generation are still doing duty in many homes.

Problems and activities. (1) Make a trip to a furniture store, and ask to be shown furniture of several different periods so that you can identify them and see how each one expresses a way of living for a particular historical era. (2) While you are in the furniture store, try to select the periods that would be most appropriate for your own family. (3) With the aid of the illustrations on pages 145-52, showing the different periods, check the furniture in your own home to see how many periods are represented in it. (4) Using the furniture you have, try to distribute and group it in such a way as to give a period effect to several rooms. For example, build the living room around that good Chippendale table with modern notes in the chairs and bookcase. Or rescue from the laundry that pine chest handed down in your family and with its frank simplicity as a keynote, create an early American dining room. (5) Experiment by mixing periods, using either actual pieces or pictures which you can get from magazines or furniture catalogues, and see which periods are most compatible with each other and which are least compatible. (6) Try identifying the furniture in your classroom to see whether it conforms to any period or whether it is strictly modern in its design. (7) Visit the home economics practice cottage to observe and evaluate the combinations of furniture there.

2. The Spirit of Today

Choosing Good Modern Furniture

The adventurous young modern wants his furniture as up-to-date as his automobile or refrigerator. He wants simple designs and beautiful colors, rich textures and plain surfaces. Restfulness, comfort, and efficiency are the aims of modern interior design.

Each great period in history has had its own style of furniture which expressed the way the people lived. Modern furniture has grown out of today's needs just as the furniture of Louis XIV grew out of the needs of his period. It belongs to us just as our automobiles and airplanes, our plumbing and heating fixtures, our motion pictures and music belong to us.

Modern furniture for comfortable living. To make the home comfortable as well as more attractive is the aim of present-day home makers. Each piece of furniture must answer the test of performance with the least strain on the human beings who are to use it. Chairs must support the body without muscular strain. Tables, desks, and other equipment must hold the material being used so that it is easily accessible without forcing one to stretch or twist into awkward positions. Stretchers, dirt catchers, and other impediments to speedy housecleaning must be eliminated. Furniture is often designed in units so that several pieces of furniture may be used separately or joined together, permitting a good deal of flexibility.

Form follows function. Modern furniture is designed to be functional. Use comes before appearance in determining what shape chairs and tables are to be.

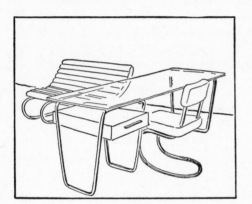 

Which do you call a *good* modern office group?

For some of the most recent chairs, countless experiments were tried to discover just which forms are most comfortable for the human body. Then these forms were refined and molded out of plastic materials so that a form-fitting chair resulted. In a similar way, tables and chests of drawers have been studied so that they will function easily and smoothly. Thus, the form of modern furniture grows directly out of the use to which it is to be put.

To be sure, not everything which is simple is good design in the modern sense. Some furniture which masquerades as "modern" is uncomfortable and inconvenient. This, of course, is not good modern.

Elimination of unnecessary details. The most obvious difference between

154

modern furniture forms and older styles is the elimination of detail. Moldings, carvings, and other ornamentation which do not serve a use are seldom found in modern design. Carvings are expensive, catch dust, and may make furniture uncomfortable. Moldings are also hard to clean and may give a restless or confused effect. Modern design gains its effect from beautiful proportions and simplicity. Simplified decoration is used when a line or form should be emphasized or repeated.

Lines in modern furniture. The lines in modern furniture show two striking characteristics: they are, for the most part, continuous and horizontal. If you study modern designs for chests, tables, and bookcases, you will notice that the lines are not interrupted either by ornament or change of direction. If you study modern chairs, you will notice that in many cases the lines of the legs or supports seem to be continuous with those of the seats, backs, or arms.

The horizontal lines found in modern furniture express stability and repose. These are welcome notes in a restless period and do much to make modern rooms seem peaceful. The horizontal, continuous lines also aid in making rooms seem larger than they really are.

Color in modern furniture. The person who goes to buy modern furniture has a real treat in store for him because of the beautiful and varied colors which he will find used. Wood is seldom painted, or even stained, but is left as nearly natural as possible to show its beautiful color and grain. In general, the lighter woods are preferred because of their more cheerful effect, but the darker woods are also used.

Upholstery materials range from black to white and from pale yellow to deep blue. The majority are grayed in intensity, with small variations in hue or value emphasized by the weave. They are more likely to be plain than patterned, although, of course, both kinds are used.

Textures in modern interiors. Today the surface beauty of material is greatly appreciated, and combinations of them are studied. Each material is frankly itself. Metal is used in the design for its metallic quality. It is not painted to represent wood. Wood is enjoyed for the beauty of its finish. Various types of paint are appreciated for their own textural quality, and paint is not used to imitate other materials.

Textures now do what was formerly done by applied pattern. Contrasts from rough to smooth, hard to soft, cold to warm, and glossy to dull add a live quality to modern interiors. Decoration is not applied, but is achieved by means of form and the use of texture and color. Brilliant highlights and deep shadows create the dark and light pattern which was formerly attempted by dark and light patterns in surface coverings.

Problems and activities. (1) Check the furniture in your classrooms, school offices, and library to see how much is of modern instead of period design. (2) Criticize the design of the modern chairs, desks, tables, and files which you find in your school. (3) Bring pictures of modern furniture to class, and choose the pieces which you think are well done and the ones which are of poor design. (4) Visit the furniture stores to observe and compare different designs of modern furniture and to decide which ones you think are really best. (5) Report to the class your family's experience with period and with modern pieces and your own reactions after experience with both. (6) Tell the class about any of your experiences with furniture which attempted to be modern but failed to be usable or practical. Explain what was wrong in its design.

3. STAYING PUT

Choosing and Placing Rugs

It is important that rugs, when chosen and placed, stay put. This means not only that non-skid suction pads should hold them to the floor, but also that they should stay put visually. Many a rare Persian or Chinese rug which would make an interesting wall hanging is entirely out of place as a base for furniture. Striking contrasts in hue, value, and intensity create compelling centers of interest and destroy the value of the rug as a background for furnishings and people. Linoleum, tile, or any floor covering creates much the same problem in dark and light, hue, and intensity as do rugs. Any floor covering in a home should hold a subordinate place in a unified room scheme.

Patterned and unpatterned floor coverings. The advantage of a patterned rug is that it does not show soil or footmarks as readily as a plain surface. Its disadvantage is that it is likely to attract too much attention. If you prefer a patterned rug, choose one that is closely related to the rest of the room in values and intensities. Large medallions create centers of interest on the floor, and are seldom desirable. All-over patterns are better choices for floor coverings. Even in this type of pattern, choose one without strong rhythmic movement, since it creates restlessness in a background which should remain unemphasized. If patterned floor covering is used, the walls should be unpatterned or be done in a pattern very closely related in hue, value, and intensity to that of the floor covering.

Paintings, flowers, and art objects are usually the most important decorative features in any room. An unpatterned background displays them to the best advantage because it does not attract attention to itself. A plain carpet allows for pattern in the draperies, walls, or other furnishings. It is desirable that there be some plain area in any good room scheme; and the carpet seems the most logical place for plainness, since it is always background. Besides, plain carpets create the maximum impression of size. A border cuts down the apparent size of the room, since the eye is stopped on the joining line. Plain carpets, walls, and draperies are good modern design. The interest that was formerly gained by means of applied pattern is now arrived at by texture combinations. This type of background is most suitable for the display of fine pictures and objects of art.

Value, hue, and intensity. A carpet, rug, or floor covering establishes the foundation on which the walls, ceiling, and furnishings rest. Darkness appears to have weight. Therefore, a dark or medium dark base gives stability to a room. A carpet of medium or medium light value is acceptable if the furnishings are light. In patterned rugs close values are best, since strong contrasts in dark and light draw an excessive amount of attention to the floor.

A carpet or other floor covering should form a neutral background. It may be either warm or cool in hue, dependent upon the mood desired for the room. Any color may be used provided the impression of a single hue dominates. Patterned rugs often present scrambled color effects of cool blues and greens with warm orange and red. When the usual value contrast is added to this, the result is a jumpy floor pattern. The all-over impression of any rug or linoleum should be either dominantly warm or dominantly cool. In this way the jumpy effect caused by a mixture of receding and advancing colors will be avoided.

157

Since the floor is background, the hue should be neutralized. Colors which are grayed in intensity as well as medium or dark in value are most easily combined in a satisfying floor color scheme. If rich colors are used, they should be related carefully to the other furnishings in the room.

Textures. Rough textures, by means of small all-over shadows, neutralize rich colors. They also tend to darken light values, and thus pull dark-and-light contrasts closer together. For this reason hue, value, and intensity contrasts are

Do you see anything wrong with the rugs in any of these rooms?

less objectionable in a rough-textured rug than in a linoleum or other smooth floor covering. Although all of the considerations mentioned above regarding hue, value, and intensity govern the choosing of a rough-textured rug, they are even more important in the choosing of smooth surfaces where the graying effect of shadows is not present.

The placing of rugs. The shape of a rug or carpet and its placing in a room are matters of shape harmony. The walls of the room create the frame for the room design. Diagonals produce dynamic, eye-arresting movement which is out of place on the floor. Therefore, rugs placed at angles to the walls are invariably unattractive. The lines of the rugs on the floor should repeat and strengthen the wall lines which form the frame for the room.

One large rug which completely covers the floor gives the appearance of maximum size and creates no additional lines to be reckoned with in the room design. Small rugs break up the floor space into small rectangles or ovals and make the room appear smaller. They also have a tendency to make the floors appear spotty. The contour line of each rug must be considered as part of the line scheme of the room as a whole. If small rugs are used, they should be arranged in an organized pattern with all edges parallel with the wall. Circular or oval rugs add curved lines to the room design. These curved lines, if used, should lead the eye to an important group of furniture, and rhythm and unity in the line scheme should be attained by repeating the curves in the furniture or important art objects.

Problems and activities. (1) Visit any of the school offices in which there are rugs or linoleum, and judge them according to standards presented in this section. (2) Borrow a sample book from a dealer in rugs and linoleums, and pick out samples which you think would be appropriate floor coverings for homes, and others which you think would be inappropriate. (3) Describe to the class rug patterns you have seen that seem to you of poor design. (4) Assume for the moment that a rug is to be installed in your classroom; select the color and style which you think will be most appropriate for it. (5) Make a similar selection on the assumption that linoleum is to be laid. (6) Note the floor coverings at hotels, motion-picture theatres, or other public buildings, and criticize their designs. (7) Check over the floor coverings in your own home, and decide which are appropriate and why. Might some of your rooms be improved by exchanging the rugs with those in other rooms?

4. Setting the Stage

Choosing and Placing Furniture

When the curtain goes up at the theatre and you see a room on the stage, you know at once what kind of people are likely to appear. If the effect is a pleasing one, you feel a sense of proportion, balance, and rhythm, all of which contribute to the total impression of the play. In somewhat the same way the rooms of a house should contribute to the drama of daily life. Can you choose the kind of furniture and arrange the pieces in such a way that they promote harmony and balance and contribute to comfortable and efficient living? In choosing and arranging furniture, consider the scale in relation to the size of the room, the design of each individual piece, its line scheme and proportion, its texture, its color, and its applied decoration in relation to the total room scheme. Setting the stage for the home drama is a matter of choosing essentials, eliminating non-essentials, emphasizing centers of interest, and creating a balanced, comfortable, and sociable atmosphere.

You are probably thinking that all this might be easy to accomplish on a stage or in a brand-new house, but how can it be done in your home with old furniture, especially if most of the family like the house and furnishings exactly as they are? This is a real problem, for a home is a co-operative enterprise and usually the tastes of several persons must be considered. Moreover, most family budgets do not allow for very much new furniture at a time, to say nothing of complete redecorating.

Remember that the principles presented in this section, as in the other sections of the book, are fundamental ones. They are intended to guide you, but they must be applied with common sense, subject to the limitations which each person faces. Even professional decorators are always faced with limitations of one kind or another. The greater the limitations, the greater is the challenge to your ingenuity.

You might begin by applying the suggestions about furniture as well as you can to your own room. If you bring about some improvements there, your family may encourage you to experiment in the living room or some other part of the house.

Removing eye-sores and obstructions. "Any place in your picture that does not speak for you speaks against you." This rule is as consistently correct in a room design as in a painting or any other work of art. For sentimental reasons or through indifference most of us allow numerous objects to clutter each room in our homes. Pieces of furniture which we do not use, ornaments which are not related to the room scheme, souvenirs from our travels and other good times, moldings and wall decorations which have no purpose, and many other odds and ends tend to accumulate in any home. Too much decoration in a room is like too much jewelry on a person. The first job of the decorator is to eliminate all objects which are not definitely useful or decorative. Only those pieces of furniture which are necessary to comfortable living should be included in the room scheme; only those objects of art which are related to the design of the whole should be allowed to remain.

However, do not begin by hiding your small brother's collection of shells or by throwing away the souvenir basket which your sister brought from Mexico. Begin in your own domain, wherever that is. Throw away those souvenirs in your own room which are dust collectors and have ceased to have value even as reminders of good times. If you like to keep old banners, badges, and programs, put them into portfolios or scrapbooks. If your mementos have real value or are part of a hobby collection of some kind, arrange them in a cabinet for display.

One way to solve the problem of too many decorative objects is to use them in rotation. Choose from among them the three or four which best suit the room scheme, the season, or your mood of the moment. Put all the others carefully away in some storage space for use at another time, when you may be wanting and needing a change. This would be a good rule for the whole household, if you could persuade your family to follow it.

Scale of furniture in relation to the room. The size of individual pieces of furniture should be in proportion to the size of the room. If large pieces are necessary in a small room, as few pieces as possible should be used. If small pieces of furniture are necessary in a large room, they should be grouped to form large masses. Large pieces in a small room should be inconspicuously upholstered. Small pieces in a large room may be gaily covered to increase their apparent size.

Design of individual pieces of furniture. Our markets today offer a greater variety of furniture designs than ever before in history. If you are buying only one new piece, choosing it can be a real adventure. Even with a small purse you can get furniture to harmonize with almost any scheme you have in mind. But remember that since most of us do not choose furniture every year, it is important to get something that you will enjoy over a period of time. Look first for good construction. Shoddy material badly put together is costly in the long run. Do not forget that furniture must stand use. A simple piece, well-built and well-designed, is worth two of the cheaply veneered, over-decorated kind.

In studying the design, look first at the proportions. Furniture which is well-proportioned leads to lasting satisfaction. If it is too tall and narrow, it looks unstable. If it is too low and squatty, it looks heavy and cumbersome. Good furniture looks comfortable and stable, but is not oppressively heavy. The outline of furniture is worth your study, for the general shape or contour is the basic element in the design. The space divisions should also be noticed, and lastly such details as drawer handles, chair legs, and the like. No hard and fast rules can be given, but careful study will help you in selecting furniture sensibly.

Texture combinations in a room. Texture combinations offer great possibilities in design today. Textured surfaces have, to a great extent, taken the place of all-over patterns or applied design. Sensitivity to textures is necessary for the home decorator of today, whether he is a professional or an amateur. For example, he will realize that smooth-textured woods, such as mahogany, satinwood, and walnut, harmonize with silks, porcelains, enamels, and smooth-textured walls. Rough-textured woods, such as oak and pine, combine with linen, semi-porcelain, pottery, copper, and rough-textured walls. Other wood textures which lie between the two extremes may be combined with textures at either end of the scale. In any event, there should be a harmony of textures among the furnishings, the room, and the decorative objects. Combinations of extremes should be used with care, but there should be enough variation in textures in wall surfaces, draperies, rugs, furniture, and art objects to give a pleasant variety.

Color in room furnishings. In any room, one color feeling should dominate, and should be offset by smaller areas of contrasting hue. If the color is mainly warm, cold contrasts enliven the design. If the effect is cool, warm hues build up the centers of interest. In light rooms dark accents are valuable. In dark rooms light values may emphasize important art objects. Strong color is often effective in small areas in a room which is otherwise neutral. If many colors are used, they should be neutralized in intensity and held closely together in value. If it is necessary to use furniture of very different woods, they may be stained one color to achieve color harmony. However, some differing woods combine very well or offer needed contrast. Harmony of color is insured if one hue is present in all except the contrasting centers of interest.

Applied design on furniture. Undecorated surfaces which rely upon carefully designed contours and satisfying textural feeling rather than applied surface pattern are becoming increasingly popular. Material for upholstery and window drapery is being created in a single color in beautiful textural weaves or with simplified geometric and abstract patterns which are related to the space in which they will be used. Screens and other decorative objects are being designed with abstract patterns that emphasize the dominant line scheme of a room.

Over dramatic designs and naturalistic panels are becoming less popular. Outdoor scenes, bouquets of flowers, and other naturalistic pictures used in decoration during a recent period of furniture design are less popular today. Too often such applied pictures were not related in form, color, or spirit to the shape or use of the object they decorated. Happily, their vogue is waning. More people are beginning to judge furniture by its proportions and shape in relation to its use and the place in which it is to be used.

Arranging the dominant furniture group. As we have observed before, the size and shape of the room determine the main structural design. In each room there is some essential piece of furniture, such as a dining-room table, a bed, a dressing table, or a library desk. This piece should be placed first, and all subordinate pieces should be grouped in relation to it in such a way as to insure most comfortable and efficient use. Large, unbroken wall areas should be considered as frames in which furniture pictures may be created. The furniture groups as they are silhouetted against the wall produce dark-and-light patterns. Emphasis, subordination, and fine proportion are as important in this type of design as in any other. Diagonal arrangements oppose the original structural lines within which the furniture picture is being created. Criss-cross arrangements are likely to give an impression of disorderliness. For this reason it is desirable to have all large rectangular pieces parallel the wall lines and thus strengthen the main structural lines of the room by repetition.

Obtaining balance in furniture placement. All four sides of the room should present a feeling of balance or equilibrium. The largest, most important group of furniture, if unsupported by secondary groups, gives a lopsided feeling in the room. In the dining room the side table and the cabinets are balanced in relation to the table. In bedrooms the dressing table and study space may balance the bed. In the living room the fireplace and easy chairs may be balanced by a group of chairs or a table. This balance in a room is not always easy to attain because doors and windows must be considered. Colors in varying values and intensities may be used to add emphasis to the weaker side.

The purpose of unfurnished areas. Undecorated wall areas and uncluttered floor spaces are resting places for the eye. They are necessary to give the furniture groups a chance to show up well. Textiles, furniture, and art objects should be thought of as dark-and-light colored pattern framed in the neutral areas of the floor and wall. In this way the furniture groups may be more clearly felt as design elements in the room picture. Do not be afraid of some empty spaces.

Problems and activities. (1) Try your talents at room arrangement by moving the pieces around in your own room until you get the best possible effect. If it is not ideal, plan the changes you will make if and when you can. (2) Using easily movable pieces of furniture from other rooms in your home, experiment with new combinations and additions, and report to the class what effects you are able to produce. (3) Study suites of furniture as arranged in stores, and pick out combinations or arrangements which you think are especially effective. (4) Tell the class about unfortunate or unhappy combinations of furniture you have observed in homes you have visited. (Do not mention any names.) (5) In the home economics practice cottage, experiment with arranging and rearranging the furniture until you know what makes the room unbalanced and how to correct it.

5. Walls and Windows

Choosing and Arranging Draperies, Textiles, and Mirrors

The walls of any room are broken into spaces by the doors and windows. Therefore, the design of the room is definitely affected by the kind of curtains and draperies you use. In fact, many amateurs in home decoration think of the window draperies as the most important part of the whole scheme. "Some gay curtains would do wonders for this room," they say, or, "If I could only afford that expensive stuff for draperies, I could make something of this place."

These are half-truths, and like all half-truths, are misleading. Draperies (a better word than "drapes") do play a large part in creating the atmosphere of a room, but gay or rich, heavy materials may not be the sort which the room needs.

The important thing to remember is that the doors and windows are a part of the architectural plan. Their rectangular shapes and the shapes of the wall spaces between them form part of a design. Textile panels, mirrors, and other wall decorations, as well as window draperies, may be used to create dominant and subordinate areas of interest within the rectangular spaces of the wall. The first step is to decide the treatment to be used on the openings, the doors and windows. Then the spaces between these openings may be used for decorative panels or textiles, pictures, or mirrors. Various ideas which should be considered in the choice and placing of these objects will be discussed in the following paragraphs.

The line scheme. Horizontal and vertical lines in draperies and wall decoration support and strengthen the structural lines of the wall. Verticals should be stressed if height and the feeling of dignity are desired. Horizontals may be emphasized around the entire wall area to stress apparent widths, to lower the apparent height of the room, and to create a mood of restfulness. Transitions at angles, or the use of circular or oval forms, add a feeling of smoothness to the line scheme. Obliques or diagonals are generally dynamic and restless. They should be used chiefly in definite centers of interest, as in a textile behind an important group of furniture.

Window and door draperies. The draperies used at windows and doors should be closely related to the architectural background, that is, to the shapes of the doors and windows themselves. Because almost all doors and windows are rectangular, draperies which fall into vertical or horizontal patterns are best for most rooms. At times, however, there may be a good reason for some deviation. For example, if a room is definitely feminine in spirit, ruffled curtains tied back in soft folds may be perfectly in harmony with the scheme. There should be some good reason, however, for departing from the rectangular shape of the doors or windows on which draperies are hung.

Draperies can be used to make openings seem either wider or narrower. The material may be hung so that it covers some of the window or door frame and some of the wall, or it may cover the opening itself. It may reach to the floor or only to the window sill. Horizontal stripes will make the opening seem wider. Vertical stripes will make it seem higher. Choose the one which will give the effect you want to secure.

In selecting colors and patterns you will want to find something to make your room more attractive. If your walls are covered with a vigorously patterned paper, plain draperies will probably be more effective. If you have plain walls, you may choose either plain or patterned materials. The modern trend is to use plain textiles, interesting in texture and color; but some rooms can be livened by using richly patterned draperies. Study photographs in current magazines to see the many effects that are possible.

If you are planning a period room, the draperies should carry out the spirit of the period. Silk, damask, or other rich textures are, of course, out of place in a Cape Cod cottage just as gingham or printed calico is inadequate for a Louis XIV room. These are extreme examples. In most cases you must really understand the period and have a genuine feeling for it, in order to choose appropriate textiles.

Another problem in handling window draperies is that of the curtain or shade to be drawn when privacy is desired. Venetian blinds are now in vogue in place of ordinary shades, but your choice should depend upon the scheme of the room, the amount of light desired, and the need for privacy. For some windows Venetian blinds or glass curtains may be desirable to soften the light or to shut out an undesirable view. At other windows the view should be framed and emphasized. Many persons now prefer the kind of draperies which can be drawn at will and thus serve the purpose of both curtain and decoration.

Textile panels. Textiles may be used on wall spaces as well as at windows. A satisfying center of interest may be created by using a textile panel which stretches from the floor to the ceiling behind an interesting group of furniture. It may be in one unbroken color, or may have an all-over pattern, or may be composed of a single abstract design. Interesting textures in one color make excellent backgrounds for a mirror or picture. All-over patterns should usually have colors closely related in value and intensity unless the panel is intended

166

as an emphasized decorative feature. In case it is to be a dominant interest, the dark and light and intensity contrasts may be sparkling. A single abstract design takes the place of a picture and should be part of the design of the room in order to insure unity.

Mirrors. Enlarging and lightening a room is often successfully done by the use of mirrors. They have the additional advantage of making further interesting wall breaks without adding color notes. Since the color of a mirror is silverish, a repetition of the silver quality in the frame is more harmonious than gold or any other color. However, much depends on the effect you desire. Unframed mirrors or metal frames of a silver tone suit modern furnishings. An antique gold, mahogany, cherry, or rosewood frame of Chippendale design may suit the period of the room you are creating. Mirrors are pleasant on an unpatterned wall or against an unpatterned or all-over-patterned textile. Their glossy texture reflects the furnishings of the room, helping to give a unity of feeling throughout.

Problems and activities. (1) Study your own classroom and decide what are its needs for draperies, textiles, or wall decorations to break the plain surfaces and to create better design; or evaluate those already in the room. (2) Observe and criticize the methods used to break the plain surfaces of walls in the office of the school principal or other officials in your own building. (3) Study the rooms of your own home to decide in what ways they do or do not conform to suggestions made in this section. Decide what draperies would be best for your own room. (4) Pay special attention to the use of draperies, textiles, mirrors, and other wall decorations in the lobbies of hotels and theatres in your town, and decide which features could be adopted for home interiors. (5) In magazine pictures of rooms point out specific illustrations of good or bad design in draperies and other wall decorations.

6. LANDSCAPE, STILL LIFE, OR PORTRAIT

Choosing and Hanging Pictures

The walls of some homes are cluttered with pictures of all sorts, from portraits of great-grandparents to water-colors by Aunt Susan and enlarged snapshots of all the places the family has visited. Other houses have a bare and empty look because the walls lack all attempt at decoration. There is, of course, a happy medium between these two extremes.

167

Pictures are a part of the decoration of any room. They should suit the purpose and mood as well as the general style of the room. They should be framed and hung in such a way as to fit into the room design.

Today there is little excuse for not owning some really excellent pictures. Good paintings by contemporary artists are not all prohibitive in price. Original

What would you like to do about the pictures in this room?

paintings by the masters are, of course, too costly for most budgets, but excellent color reproductions can be obtained. In fact, some good ones have appeared in magazines. Besides, one has the choice of etchings, lithographs, woodcuts, and other prints in both black and white and color. Camera studies also have achieved artistic excellence and offer interesting decorative effects.

Using pictures decoratively. People like pictures for various reasons. Some people find certain landscapes attractive as reminders of things they like, such as the sea or the woods. Others like pictures because of the color or the design. When you hang a picture on your walls, make certain that it really contributes in some way to the decoration of the room. Do not be satisfied if it merely reminds you of something. Select a picture that is good in color and design, and that really seems to fit into your room as though it belonged there. It may or may not be realistic, but it should never be chosen merely because it is a good imitation of nature. A picture should do more than imitate nature. It should arouse a real emotion in you.

Pictures related to purpose and mood. Because pictures do have emotional appeal they should be chosen to suit the purpose and mood of the room. Prize fights and flowers, for example, represent opposite extremes in subject matter, and should be chosen for very different types of rooms. One, being definitely masculine, is suited to a man's den or club room, while the other, being somewhat feminine, is in harmony with the social rooms in the home. A picture which arouses emotional reactions of a very personal nature is suited to one's own room but not to the family living or dining room.

In your own bedroom you may well choose to have at least one picture that is definitely expressive of your own personality. For example, in a woman's room a fifteenth-century portrait or a rich Venetian painting might be appropriate. A man, on the other hand, might be better satisfied with a portrait by Raphael or Rembrandt or by a modern artist whose work he admires.

Pictures for the rooms of young children might emphasize people and animals. Avoid pictures which merely tell stories but which have little beauty as works of art. Some of the great painters of the past have created decorative pictures which are both satisfying to children and beautiful as room decorations. For your library or study place which is a spot for serious work, you will find that pictures which stress horizontal lines, whether they be formed by big curves, large angles, or a series of small curves, create serene designs. Subdued colors with slightly grayed intensities have the same effect. On the other hand, you may want to use a picture which is definitely stimulating as a focal point in your room.

Rooms which are dedicated to social gatherings should have pictures of interest to the various people who gather there. As a rule the pictures should be rich in color, vivid, and interest provoking. Upward reaching diagonal lines create this sort of dynamic feeling, as do also vivid colors, particularly in the warm range of reds, oranges, and yellows. Of course, it should be remembered that no fine picture is restless throughout, and that vivid colors are offset by more grayed areas, warm hues are balanced by cool ones, and strong dark-and-light pattern is set off against spaces where the values are most closely related. Part of your problem is to consider the mood you wish to evoke in your guests and in those who use these various rooms, then to choose pictures which have a design scheme appropriate to that mood.

The dining room and the breakfast room call for a mood of lightness and gaiety as an aid to pleasant eating and good digestion. Small curves and angles leading upward are the types of line that provoke the mood. The colors may be pale or strong and may be stimulating or merely light and alive, depending on the other features of the room design. In choosing pictures for this type of room, you must decide how dominant you want the wall decorations to be, because powerful contrasts of dark and light may throw too much attention on the wall and away from the dining table where it rightfully belongs.

Pictures suited to the style of the room. Your pictures should be in harmony with the style of the room, but it is not necessary to have the pictures all of the same period as the furniture any more than it is necessary to have every piece of furniture of the same era. The important thing is that the feeling conveyed by pictures and furniture should be harmonious and compatible.

If you will review the discussion of period furniture, you will find that much of it applies to paintings as well. Thus, one group of artists may express a note of rather rich, heavy formality appropriate to the early Italian and the Louis XIV type of furniture, while other artists, with their domestic scenes and bright-eyed children, suggest the Queen Anne or Victorian room. Some pictures are suited to the strong simple usefulness of a cottage; others have the delicate and restrained elegance of the eighteenth century drawing room.

Spend as much time as possible studying specific artists and their work if you want to find pictures that you really enjoy and that will exactly suit a certain room. Do not neglect the work of modern artists.

Framing pictures suitably. After the picture is chosen, the problem of framing it arises.

A mat and frame create a transition area between the wall and the picture.

If the wallpaper pattern is strong, the mat on the picture should be large, to surround the picture with a plain area against which it can show. This mat should be subordinated to the tone and color of the picture and should not be more intense in color than the picture is. A pure white mat will stand out in too striking relief against most walls. For this reason cream and slightly grayed mats are preferable except in high-keyed interiors. A mat may also be used to change the proportions of the form so that the picture will create better shape harmony in relation to the wall. Small pictures may be brought more into the scale of the large room by the use of mats, whereas large pictures may have smaller frames if this will help to reduce them to the best scale for the room.

The frame should be in harmony with the style and color of the picture and in scale with its size. Gilt frames are suitable for pictures heavy and rich in color, but there is an increasing tendency to use simple wood molding, often finished with shellac and wax. Black or very dark frames usually stand out too sharply from the background, and should be used with due regard for their effect in the room.

Hanging pictures. If several small pictures are to be used, they should be hung as a group rather than as individual spots. If the wall space in which a picture hangs is definitely a horizontal area, the picture should be a horizontal rectangle to conform to it. Likewise, panels call for pictures which are vertical rectangles.

Pictures should be placed at about the level of the eye, so that they can be seen without craning the neck. Placing them above doors, or above high pieces of furniture, or anywhere higher than the eye level of the average person, will center the interest too high on the wall. Also, it will cause the picture to be lost as a unified part of the design formed by the other furnishings.

With a few exceptions, all pictures in the room should be hung on one line. This may be the line which passes through the center of each picture or which is formed by its upper or its lower edge. If there is already a definite horizontal feeling in the room, it may be further carried out by the horizontal lines of the picture frames.

Problems and activities. (1) Bring to class a number of mounted prints of famous paintings, and classify them into three or four major groups according to the style of room for which each one would be suited. (2) Make a second classification of the pictures according to their suitability to the purposes and moods of different rooms. (3) Arrange for a loan of framed pictures from an art store, and try each picture in several different places or panels on your classroom wall to see where it would fit and where it would be out of harmony with the lines of the room. (4) Try placing the same picture at different heights or distances to the right or left to see where it creates the most pleasing effect. (5) Let each student bring from home one picture which he thinks is exceptionally good, and get reactions as to the types of rooms in which it would be most appropriate. (6) Arrange for a loan from a store of some very cheap and some expensive pictures, and have the class decide which ones are really fine and which are not so good, by judging each on its own merits without knowledge of the price. (7) Experiment with the effects produced by mounting the same picture with different widths and shapes of mats, to decide which is the most effective for a particular place where the picture is to be hung.

7. EXTRAS

Choosing and Arranging Art Objects and Flowers

When you have done your best to furnish your room or your home in good taste and have arranged your furniture and pictures to the best of your ability, you have the background for living. Daily life involves the use of these things and many others, such as dishes, books, lamps, toilet articles, vases, book ends, screens, cushions, ceramics, figurines, plants, and flowers. Can you choose and arrange the forms, colors, and patterns of these smaller articles in relation to the room and avoid creating a cluttered, disturbing effect?

The design of art objects. The fact that a lamp shade, vase, or pair of book ends is smaller than a table or chair is no excuse for ignoring the basic principles of design in making your selections. There are plenty of badly designed things on the market. Excessive curves and too many or varied angles destroy the unity and rhythm of a form, as do bad proportions of height and width. A lamp shade that is out of proportion to the lamp creates a disturbed feeling. Moreover, the structural design of the article and the applied pattern upon it should hold together and create a single unified effect in harmony with the design in the room. For example, the outline of a lamp shade may be repeated in the design stenciled on the shade so that the whole is harmonious.

Art objects as part of the room design. Decorative objects should be chosen and placed so that they create areas of interest in the room. You get better design as a rule by using few objects than by using many. If you have too many, they are hidden one against another, and none of them shows up to good advantage. It is better to have a few well-chosen and well-placed objects than a great many which are carelessly scattered.

Would you choose either of these jars for a decoration in your home?
Why?

Any object which has a lively color scheme or a strong pattern of light and dark should be placed against an unpatterned area such as the undecorated wood of a table or wall surface. The colors may be vivid but should repeat colors in some dominant center of interest, such as the main painting in the room. They may contrast with the general tone of the room, thus adding sparkle and attracting attention. Crystal or colored glass which catches the sunlight and copper, brass, pewter, and silver which reflect firelight or the gleam of candles offer other opportunities for dramatizing decorative objects.

Plants and flowers in a room. Something green or growing fits into the de-

173

sign of almost every room. However, plants and flowers, like other kinds of decoration, can be poorly chosen or quite overdone in number and arrangement.

Since most plants require sunlight, they are usually placed in or near a window. A sunny window full of vigorous greenery may add interest to a

Which of these bowl and candle sets would you buy for your dining-room table?

room, but if the plants and their containers are jumbled and crowded, or if they seem to clutter and fill the room, they probably need to be sorted and reduced in number. Two or three really lovely plants are more effective than a dozen massed together so that their contours and colors are lost. And nothing is more depressing than sickly, anemic-looking plants occupying a conspicuous spot in the room.

Flowers are at their best when the bouquet shows in relief against the soft wood of a table, a table cloth, wood paneling, or an undecorated wall. They should not be placed in a jumble of ornate forms with vivid colors or strong dark-and-light pattern that will compete with them for attention. The colors of the bouquet should be carefully chosen to produce a definite effect. They show to good advantage when combined with mirrors or pictures which are less striking in color. The mirror adds a pleasing texture and repeats the lines of the flowers without competing with them. If flowers are used near a picture, both gain interest if the flowers continue the colors of the picture in

Which of these bowls is suitable for flower arrangement?

stronger intensities. Ceramics or small carved figures may be used near the bowl of flowers to repeat the colors and enlarge the design.

Are artificial flowers suitable as decoration? Nowadays they are so perfectly made that they often deceive the eyes at first and even at second glance. Some people feel that they may well be used during the months when garden flowers are not in bloom and hot-house flowers are expensive. Other people maintain that because they are a mere imitation of nature, they bring a false note into any decorative scheme. If artificial flowers were frequently changed or rearranged as real flowers are, there might be less objection to them. Too often they are perennial dust catchers in rooms already cluttered with excessive decoration.

Choices of containers for flowers. Ornate shapes, or containers with striking applied pattern, do not often show flowers off to good advantage. If such vases have beautiful form and pattern, they may be used as individual decorative pieces, but they are frequently too insistent in design to subordinate themselves to flowers. A container should generally be less dominant in line scheme,

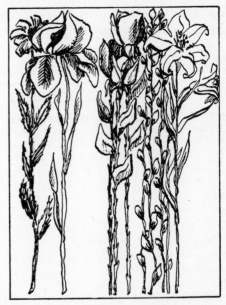

Would either of these bunches of flowers be well adapted to flower arrangement? Why?

color, and dark-and-light pattern than the flowers it contains. It should have a simple shape that allows the flowers to play a leading role. It may be related to them in color, or be directly contrasting, but it should be either more grayed or more receding and cool. The texture or material of the bowl should be harmonious with the flowers. For instance, silver and fine porcelain are suited to gardenias, roses, and orchids. Geraniums, calendulas, zinnias, and heavy-textured flowers are good in earthenware bowls. The delicacy or hardiness of the flowers and the texture of their leaves are clues to the type of container which is suitable for them.

176

Flower arrangement. A few roses in a vase by themselves or yellow daffodils in a bowl require little arrangement. One rule should be remembered. Do not crowd flowers. A few loosely arranged are always better than too many massed together. If you are interested in flower arrangement as a specialized art, consult authoritative books on the subject.

If you are combining different kinds of flowers in a bouquet, consider both the color and the shape of the blossoms. Some flowers are circular, others are cone or steeple-shaped, while some, such as the orchid or lily, have ungeometric contours. Large, middle-sized, and small circular flowers create interesting flower patterns when used together. The heavier forms and darker colors should be at the base, with a progression upward to smaller sizes and lighter flowers. Cone-shaped flowers may be arranged so that each flower is seen in silhouette. Variety is achieved by the use of tall, medium, high, and short flowers in the bouquet. Flowers of irregular form should be used sparingly so that their contours show to advantage.

Problems and activities. (1) Let each student bring from home an art object such as a vase, bowl, small lamp and shade, pair of book ends, or similar article and show it to the class for criticism and judgment of its perfection of design. (2) Experiment with combinations of such objects to see which combinations are appropriate and which are inappropriate. (3) Divide the class into four or five committees, and let each committee make a selection of articles which would be compatible with one another; then have the class as a whole judge these several exhibits. (4) Deliberately arrange such art objects in inappropriate combinations so as to draw attention to the errors which should be avoided in the use of such objects in the home. (5) Have each member of the class bring from home a few flowers which may be used by class committees in setting up flower arrangements to be judged by the rest of the class. (6) Experiment with several different flower arrangements in combination with different kinds of vases and accessory art objects to show your class members which combinations are pleasing and which ones are not.

Part III
SCHOOL

IX. Beauty and Brains

Using art in school activities

During the major part of the year you spend at least a half of your waking hours in school activities of one kind or another, either in the classroom or in school surroundings. Do you use your knowledge of the principles of art, or do you leave it behind in the art classroom? Can you prepare attractive posters to advertise school parties, club meetings, or perhaps the merits of your favorite candidates for student offices? Can you help decorate the auditorium or gymnasium for some very special occasion and make the setting really suit the occasion? Do you add your bit of constructive service in making the grounds, buildings, and classrooms attractive? When you offer written work to a teacher, is it not only correct and neat, but also so attractive that it invites reading? Perhaps you would like to learn how to make art your ally in all your school activities.

1. EVERYBODY COME

Making School Posters

When you put up a poster of your own design and execution, there is one good test of its success. Does it get attention, or do people merely pass it by?

Appeal. Your chief problem is to make a poster so striking and so beautiful that as people come into the room or pass along the hall they will want to look at it. Why should anyone vote for your candidate or come to your dramatic club play just because the name, picture, or date is posted in a public place? The poster must not only set forth the facts; it must invite and persuade people. It must get results in action. It must cause people to *do* something.

You will want to use color strikingly but harmoniously. Bright colors and simple forms are likely to attract attention. Diagonal lines arrest the eyes. Simple lettering is easy to read. All of these things are known by professional advertisers. What can you learn from billboard advertising that will help you to make your posters produce results?

What changes would you suggest for either of these posters?

Lettering. In planning a poster, you have to choose between machine printing and hand lettering. Printing on a press is usually too expensive for a small number of posters. Therefore, your message is most likely to be conveyed by means of hand lettering. In making a poster, try not to be too ambitious. Stay within the limits of what you can do well. Do not be satisfied with crude work, but do not make over-elaborate letters. Good lettering alone, combined possibly with some simple decorative lines, will make a telling poster.

Good lettering requires, first of all, uniformity of lines and spaces. If the lettering is vertical, then the letters should all be vertical, not varied from forward slant through vertical to backward slant. If you choose a forward or a backward slant for the upright lines, then be consistent and give them all the same slant.

The same is true for the horizontal lines, or crossbars, of the letters. They should all be horizontal or all slanted to the same degree. Furthermore, the crossbars should be placed at an interesting height above the base line of the letters. The effect of crossbars in the very middle is as uninteresting as that of a costume or a room divided into two equal parts. If, for example, the crossbar is placed two-fifths of the way from the top to the bottom of the letter, the ratio is more complex and the effect is more challenging. The crossbars need not all be on a line. Certain letters may be consistently printed with the crossbars above the middle and others with the bars below. But whatever is done should be done according to a plan, and not just at random.

There are many different styles for hand lettering just as there are different faces of type, ranging from the black letters of the earliest printed books through roman, old style, and modern to the sans-serif letters in ultramodern layout. Study different samples of hand lettering or different faces of type to find the kind of letters best suited to the purpose of your poster. Quaint Gothic letters, for example, might be suited to advertising the revival of an old play, but would hardly do for announcing a football game.

Page design. The layout of your poster should be carefully planned. It is generally best to make a number of small sketches showing different ways that the lettering could be placed. These need be no larger than two by three inches, and can be made very rapidly. When one of these suits you, it can be used as a guide in laying out your poster. Be sure to check your spelling. Words incorrectly spelled, divided, or abbreviated may destroy the appeal of the finest art work.

A good way to do is to sketch the whole design very lightly in pencil on the sheet. Then look at it carefully. Does it satisfy you? Is it comfortably balanced? Are the most important parts emphasized? Does it have an interesting rhythm? If it seems as good as you can make it, then sketch the letters more carefully.

Decide where the crossbars are to be. Use vertical lines to guide your sense of direction. Good lettering is something of which you can be proud, and it is worth doing well.

Spacing. The use of spaces is as important as the use of lines in lettering. Allow the width of one letter between words. Allow enough space between lines to separate them for easy reading but still keep the total area of lettering unified in block form. Too wide a space between lines makes the individual lines look lonesome and destroys the unity of the design. Marginal space is also important, just as it is in any printing layout. Allow enough blank space on your poster to set off the design but not so much that the printing looks lost and lonely.

Illustrations. The use of pictures or designs to suggest objects or ideas is a bit more challenging than straight lettering, yet not too difficult for most amateurs. A new moon and a few stars may suggest a night program. A witch and broom for Hallowe'en can be done in simple outline drawing. A large football speaks for itself. If the drawings are strong and simple, they will harmonize nicely with the lettering. It is best not to make drawings too naturalistic or too detailed. A poster is meant to attract the attenion of someone passing it.

Remember that no one ever sets out to find your poster. It must find him—and speak to him loudly and clearly. One way to attract attention and to put across your message is to use exaggerated or distorted forms. Exaggerating the most important part of an object is a favorite device with artists of all ages. The primitive men who left drawings in caves used it, and the greatest painters in the world invariably exaggerate some part of their subject. So do cartoonists and comic-strip artists. Learn from all of these men.

Problems and activities. (1) Bring several school posters to class, and try to determine whether they were or will be effective in getting the actions desired. Analyze the designs to determine what qualities helped to produce their effects. (2) Bring several samples of alphabets to class for comparison as to simplicity and effectiveness for poster work. Which letter styles should you try to imitate? (3) Have the members of the class sketch the general outlines of some posters for a school event; compare these, and select the best to be developed and used.

2. THE PLAY'S THE THING

Putting on Dramatic Entertainments

When you help with a school play or a marionette show, can you make a real contribution to the work of your group, or are you just a dead weight? Do you have ideas about stage sets, costumes, or puppets which will help your group give better performances? Whether you expect to do much work in dramatics or not, you may profit by learning a few of the elements of good design in order to increase your enjoyment at the theatre.

Puppets. From the old days of Punch and Judy, to the modern days of Charlie McCarthy, people have enjoyed puppets. If you are enough of an artist and mechanic to work with puppets, you can have a great deal of fun and provide excellent amusement for your classmates and the whole community.

Of course, you must first understand how to work puppets. There are various kinds, as you know. Some are controlled by strings; simpler ones are operated directly by the fingers.

Before making your puppets, you will probably decide on the play they are to present. While you may write a play for them yourself, it is safer for amateurs to follow the puppet fashion and use an old familiar tale to be acted. The audience usually prefers such a story because when they know what is coming next they can give all their attention to the antics of the puppets. "Little Red Riding Hood" or "Jack and the Beanstalk" from old fairy tales and "Little Black Sambo" or "Ferdinand and the Bull" from modern favorites are suitable for puppet shows. It is best to select a story with plenty of action and not too many characters.

When you have decided on the story, study the characters carefully and select the most outstanding and dramatic trait of each one. Then design your puppets to reveal these traits. Exaggerate the characteristic of each to such an extent that everyone will recognize it even though he does not see the puppet in action. For example, the nose is a particularly expressive part of the character and may be made very bulbous, or long, slender, and pointed, or tiny and tilted upward. The chin may stick out to suggest a very domineering character or recede in extreme degree to suggest weakness of will. If you are a good student of shapes and forms, you can make the ears, the eyes, the eyebrows, and other features of the puppets equally suggestive of the parts they are to play. If one of the little characters is a pessimist by nature, present him as a very extreme pessimist; then give the optimist all the optimism you can put into him. Also choose gay startling colors for the cheerful character and dull or somber ones for those who express somber moods. The main characters

Which of these puppet show stage sets would you choose for "Little Red Riding Hood"? Why?

can be made to stand out from less prominent ones by the use of more vivid coloring, and even by differences of size.

Stage sets for puppet shows. The puppet-show stage should be shallow, with all the scenery as flat as possible. The vision of the audience should be blocked off from the wings and the overhead stage area so as not to spoil the illusion of size. One single object on the scale or size found in normal life, if seen by the audience, will immediately dwarf the puppets to the tiny size they really are. For this reason even the lights should be on a small scale, consisting perhaps of Christmas tree bulbs or flashlights covered with colored gelatin or cellophane.

USING ART IN SCHOOL ACTIVITIES

You can make a puppet-show stage set very simply by arranging backdrops, windows, doors, and steps. Columns and arches may also be included. These are all basic elements that can be used in almost all scenes. The sets need not be realistic. The lines and colors, however, should suggest the moods of the play. If the dominant lines are vertical, they will help to give an impression of power, nobility, and dignity; horizontal lines may be used to suggest peace, repose, and stability. For plays which feature conflict and struggle, utilize horizontal, vertical, and diagonal lines in opposition. Comedy scenes are suggested by well-rounded robust curves in the background, as if they stood for jolly innkeepers and cheerful pranksters enjoying life in a rather overfed way. Graceful and more restrained curves may be used for lighter types of plays, and these curves should suggest, as nearly as possible, the object, thing, or situation which is most typical of the play.

The colors for the stage setting may also be chosen to match the spirit of the play, if you are good at judging what color goes with what mood. Blues and grayed cool colors convey a quiet or even a melancholy note, while grayed warm colors are good for a faster tempo of acting. Very slightly grayed pale colors may be used to create an ethereal quality. Countless other color effects are possible; there is almost no limit to what may be done when you learn how to combine colors skillfully.

Stage costumes. When your play is given by life-size actors instead of by puppet characters, the costumes involve the same principles but raise a few additional problems. For example, in a play of the thirteenth century, the costumes should really resemble or suggest the clothes worn at that time. Books and the picture file in the library will give you accurate ideas of what people wore at different times and in different countries; from these pictures you can make your play costumes even though you use inexpensive fabrics or, in some cases, crepe paper. You do not need to copy every detail, but you do need to get the general effect. Study each historical costume for that feature which is outstanding and which attracts the eye most readily. Be sure to work this feature into the costume so that it is promptly noticed, even though you have to exaggerate it.

187

All that was said about lines and colors in connection with puppet shows applies to costumes for life-size characters.

Stage sets. The sets of a play may be either realistic or symbolic. For example, if part of the action takes place in a comfortable American living room, you may reproduce such a living room with all the comfortable details, or you may suggest the comfort by one or two symbols, such as a glowing fire and an easy chair. In either case the setting should stress the central idea of the play.

If you prefer realistic settings, you may give emphasis to the main idea by color, repetitions in form, and various details selected from real life. If your setting is symbolic, you may enlarge or distort one object as a symbol of the main idea and thus emphasize it. For example, an adding machine used in a play of that name was made so large that it practically filled the room in order to stress the theme. In choosing such a symbol for a play, you must first ask yourself: What is the main force molding the hero's mind? Is it love, hate, fear, ambition, or something else? Then select a symbol to represent this power and build it with overwhelming force into the stage setting. The background thus becomes a symbol of what is happening in the hero's soul or of the forces which are working for or against him.

In Russia a type of stage set has been developed which leaves a great deal to the imagination of the audience. It is called constructivist. Such stage sets are merely skeletal frameworks with no skin drawn over them. For example, the framework of stairs, platforms, porches, automobiles, or other parts of the set may be left exposed. There is no decorative ornament whatsoever. This does not mean that the stage is necessarily ugly. The frameworks are carefully designed and well-proportioned. You might try using such a stage set for an audience which would like to do its own thinking and feeling rather than have everything completely explained.

Problems and activities. (1) Bring some puppets to class, tell what plays they were used in, and criticize their design and construction as to suitability for the parts played. (2) Sketch the facial silhouette for a puppet that would represent pride and haughtiness and another contrasting one to represent meekness and humility. (3) Choose a play or story which you believe would make a good puppet show, and discuss

School Room

(Photographs by courtesy of Visual Education Department, Los Angeles City Schools)

Exhibit of School Posters

School Banquet

Can you decorate for a school banquet or breakfast without using crepe paper?

(Photographs by courtesy of Barker Brothers, Los Angeles)

School Breakfast

the types of puppets you would construct for some of the main characters. (4) Bring to class the assembled stage settings for some puppet show that has already been put on, and decide what changes you would make in them. (5) Go to the library, and find some books with pictures of characters from other countries and periods which you think you could use for planning life-size dramatic costumes. Compare different books as sources for this kind of help. (6) Report to the class the outstanding features of the stage sets used in plays which you have recently seen, and indicate what features were particularly effective in supporting the theme of the play. (7) Invite to the class a teacher of dramatics, a stage manager, or some other expert in dramatic activities to discuss questions of stage costumes and sets. (8) Recall a few well-known plays which most of the class have seen, and discuss what kinds of line and color you would use in stage settings to support the central idea of each.

3. "Life Goes to a Party"

Decorating for School Social Events

When the school entertains its friends at a carnival, a tea, a dance, or other social affair, there is always a committee that has to be responsible for the decorations of the room in which the party is held. Too often the committee is overambitious and plans decorations which only the purse of Midas and the genius and time of an interior decorating crew could achieve. Unfortunately, humorous murals or beautiful chandeliers do not grow like mushrooms overnight. A committee of decoration must consider the cost of materials, where they may be obtained, the uses to which they can be put after the party is over, and the talents of the committee members who are to do the work. Also, there is an important item, too often forgotten—the time outside of class hours necessary to produce and install the decorations. However, in spite of these various hazards, it is possible for a committee to achieve decorations which will help give life to the party, which are effective but not too elaborate, and which suit the time, the place, and the event.

Decorating for a party is different from decorating the living room. Inexpensive material should be used, but it need not always be crepe paper. What you do will be seen for only a short time, and you can therefore be daring and experimental to a high degree, provided you do not waste money and time. Try something new. Innovations are often the life of the party.

189

The theme of the party. Why is the party being given? Is it for Hallowe'en, a football celebration, or a spring dance? The theme of the party immediately suggests what type of decorations would be appropriate, and this is the point at which to begin your plans. How can you best carry out the theme? What colors will you want to use?

For a patriotic party one school chose to emphasize Pan-American spirit. The balcony of the gymnasium suggested the idea of making the room into a Spanish patio with a gallery surrounding it. Pillars were imitated in wall board painted to look like crumbling old stucco. Plants and vines, some real, some artificial, were introduced to give an outdoor effect. Spanish and Indian rugs and serapes, thrown over the benches and gymnasium equipment, furnished warm color. At either end of the patio were hung groups of flags of the various Latin-American countries with the Stars and Stripes in the middle. The students were asked to come in costumes suggestive of those of our Latin-American neighbors.

Line and pattern. The party decorations, whatever their theme, should be orderly and should follow some definite pattern. They should relate to the size and shape of the room and to any important architectural features. If possible, these features should be utilized, as in the party just described, but at times it may be necessary to conceal or camouflage them completely.

If the room has definite architectural beauty of its own, it is often possible with the aid of plants and flowers to set it up in the spirit of your party and get a pleasing effect with very little cost of time or labor.

If the theme of the party or the room itself does not suggest a natural unity for the decorations, it is a good policy to choose some principal design feature for the center of the room or for one wall and then to repeat this motif in subordinate designs at intervals on the walls. Thus the whole decoration scheme is held together and a confusing impression is avoided. Naturally the color scheme should be chosen with this same desire for a unified impression throughout. Either warm or cool colors may dominate, while small areas of contrast may be used for sparkle, but the room should not be cluttered and confused by the use of one dominant color effect in one part of the room and another somewhere else.

USING ART IN SCHOOL ACTIVITIES

The carnival spirit. For one type of school party it is rather difficult to achieve unity in the decorations. This is the carnival, fair, or circus with its concessions, side shows, fortune-telling booths, fishing for prizes, tests of skill, puppet shows, and other attractions. This kind of social affair is actually several parties in one, and the decorations are correspondingly difficult. Whether held indoors or outdoors, it is likely to require considerable space and to consist of several parts. If there are a number of displays or exhibitions, such as pet shows, hobby shows, or booths for this and that, the booths should be arranged in some orderly form and not be allowed to create a helter-skelter effect.

Since the groups responsible for various booths will create their own decorations, there can be no perfectly uniform color scheme in a big school carnival. But the central decoration committee may at least decide on a few colors for booths and canopies so as to have one dominant color note running throughout the carnival. School colors may be featured, but if they are not chosen, a wise selection might be from the warm colors—yellow, orange, and red—with only small areas of cool colors—green, blue, and violet—as subordinate contrasts. The warm colors are most appropriate for the feeling of gaiety which the party requires. Black and white may be used throughout the carnival as neutrals and as a unifying touch.

All signs put up in or above the various booths and concessions should stress the same type of line, and each sign should be placed on a level with the others that are posted. A visitor, viewing the signs of several booths in a row, should not get the confused impression of many show cards placed at all levels and angles. Either the bottom, the top, or the center of each poster should be placed on a line continuing through all the other posters in the group.

Elaborate costumes are unnecessary for a carnival. Paper hats and paper hair ribbons or other simple articles of dress can be made by the students themselves at little or no cost in time and money. An enterprising group, such as your art class, might make hats and bonnets, carrying out the dominant color scheme, and sell them to visitors to add to the carnival fund.

Refreshments. To most people the refreshments are the peak of the party. And strange to say, the way in which they are served often makes more impression than the food itself. Refreshment and decorating committees should, of course, work together to produce the most satisfactory results.

The kind of refreshments is determined by the nature of the party, but certain things are important whether you are serving fruit punch, tea and cakes, cider and doughnuts, a buffet supper, or a formal dinner. A fresh tablecloth, carefully arranged table service, and flowers give a note of festive cheer to good food. Place cards and favors are pleasing additions for a dinner or banquet. The table service should be arranged so that major lines are parallel with the structural lines of the table. Napkins folded in squares and rectangles are more harmonious than triangles, because they conform to the design of the table. Plates, glasses, and silver should be placed so that the line forms are also parallel with the table edges. Other necessary articles on the table should be planned so that they balance. For example, at a tea or a buffet supper, the tea and coffee services are usually placed at either end of a long table with the plates and bowls of food between. All of these may be subordinated to a beautiful flower arrangement.

Flowers and favors. A bouquet is the center of interest on almost any table. Bouquets may be wide and moderately high, but should always be kept low enough to allow conversation across the table when the guests are seated. The texture of the flowers should be in harmony with the container, the linen, and the china. For example, heavy strong-fibred flowers, such as calendulas, may be used with heavy linen and pottery, while delicate flowers, such as sweet peas or roses, are suited to china and a daintier type of container. The flowers should maintain the center of interest by being either the lightest, the darkest, or the richest large area in the design. The color of the flowers may be repeated in subordinate centers of interest, such as the conserve, bowls of fruit, or favors.

Since the making of elaborate place cards is usually out of the question for a large school party, small rectangular name cards should serve the purpose. The names may be lettered in any of numerous designs and should be inscribed slightly above the center of the card. A small flower slipped through a slit in the corner of the card may repeat the center bouquet and add a sparkle of color to the white area of the table. If favors are used, they should build up the theme of the party and should usually be humorous to add to the note of gaiety. Favors should repeat the color of the flowers and be carefully considered in the color scheme.

Problems and activities. (1) Recall a school party which you attended recently, analyze the decorations used, and describe unusually successful features. (2) Without being personal, point out mistakes you have observed in designs and decorations at recent school parties. (3) Imagine your class as the decorating committee for a certain type of school party, and make plans now for the decorations you think should be used. (4) Bring several types of place cards from a stationery store, criticize their suitability to different occasions, and decide which types would be best for school parties. (5) Make class plans for a party in the carnival spirit which you might carry out in your own school. (6) Either set the table or draw on the blackboard the arrangement you would use in setting the table for a school tea. (7) Do the same for a large banquet table for your class party.

4. TEMPLE OF LEARNING

Beautifying School Buildings and Grounds

The phrase, "temple of learning" is an ironic one if you do not apply what you learn to the improvement and upkeep of your immediate surroundings. Do you do your part toward making the school buildings and grounds attractive and keeping them so? Perhaps you have assumed that these matters are the responsibility of school officials, custodians, or teachers. But the public schools of America are the property of the public, and therefore you are one of the owners. Are you a careful property owner or a careless one?

Landscaping. Any building is improved by lawn, trees, shrubs, and flowers. Does your school have as many of these as it needs? Are they arranged attractively? Can they be improved? If your class were about to buy and plant some shrubbery, should you know how to add to the attractiveness of the landscaping pattern?

Most of the general principles mentioned in connection with landscaping grounds around a house (see pages 94-99) apply to the school grounds as well. There are areas, such as the front lawn, which are primarily for beauty. They give the building a good setting. Trees and shrubs help to fit the structure into the landscape. Tall shrubs, low trees, and colorful beds of flowers may accent the entrances to buildings. If flowers are used, they are more effective against a good background of foliage or walls than in isolated spots. There are other areas of the grounds primarily for use; play fields, service entrances, and parking areas. These are often screened from view by trees and shrubbery.

Upkeep. The main thing that the student body can do toward beautiful grounds is to be careful about their upkeep. The lawns will not stand trampling by hundreds of feet. The walks should be used as passageways instead of the grass. Bare spots and paths where students cut across and wear out the grass are always ugly. Places which for any reason need to have heavy wear should be planted with tough grass, and even then they should be roped off occasionally to give a chance for regrowth. Most defacing of all are papers, lunch remains, and refuse carelessly dropped on paths and lawns. The finest landscaping in the world can be ruined by such practices. No corps of custodians can possibly clean up after a careless student body which so far outnumbers them. If you and your fellow students have to have a large extra body of paid helpers to keep your grounds presentable, you have not yet learned the ABC's either of art or of true democracy. The democratic way of life functions only if people assume responsibilities as well as demand rights.

Halls and corridors. The entrances, halls, and corridors of the school building may seem mere passageways to you, but actually they are as important as the title page and table of contents in a book. They tell the user what to expect. Is the main entrance of your school a fitting title page? Can everyone recognize it as the doorway to great opportunities? Is there something about it to suggest that education leads upward and outward? It may be a fine picture, a table holding a bowl of flowers or branches, a wall hanging, or a piece of sculpture. Farther along the hall other good pictures, well-organized display cases, and bulletin boards may reveal the varied activities of the school. Posters of coming events may add interest and remind students and visitors alike that the school is a world worth exploring.

If you use a table or bowl of flowers as the main attraction in your hall, the table should be large in size, simple in form, and of very durable material. In a passageway where there is much going back and forth, it needs to be strong rather than delicate. Oak and walnut are good table materials, and copper or heavy pottery is suitable for the bowl. The flower arrangement which it supports should be large in scale.

If wall hangings are used, they should be of such textiles as will be suitable backgrounds for the flowers, pottery, or decorative objects on the table. It is well to avoid having two different patterned materials next to each other. On the other hand, a one-color hanging may easily harmonize with a patterned design. Also, a strip of unpatterned material is good behind branches of flowers so that they may show in silhouette. The hanging should be either dominantly cool or of grayed colors with small accents of contrasting hues. Careful buying is necessary in order to acquire a hanging of this type.

Pictures for the halls. No formal hall decoration is more colorful and satisfying than good pictures. The pictures should be strong in design and cheerful in color. Large colorful prints are available at prices which any school can afford. Your art class might contribute much to school beauty and also much to your own appreciation of art by undertaking to select pictures or hall decorations.

Display cases. Are the display cases in your halls attractively arranged? What could be done to improve them? The first question to ask about any display is: Does it have unity? Does it all seem to belong to a central theme? Every display is or should be built around a main idea. It may be concerned with athletics, health, science, gardening, dramatics, books, or art. Color should be used in such a way as to make the exhibit harmonious and interesting. The separate objects should be so arranged that each shows to good advantage and makes a pleasing composition with the others. Sizes of objects may be varied to attract attention. Grouping the larger and small objects together helps the appearance of the whole exhibit. After you have arranged it, stand back and look at it critically. Will it attract attention? Does it tell its story clearly and pleasingly?

For any exhibit it is better to choose too little than to much. While it is better to stress one idea than to give a scattered effect, the exhibit will be more interesting if there are subordinate centers of interest as well as a main center. Because too much repetition and harmony are monotonous, the secondary centers should be contrasting in spirit and color. For example, in a nutrition exhibit arranged by one class, interest was centered on the part played by nutrition in maintaining health. The color scheme was built around foods. A subordinate center of interest was created by stressing health as a patriotic duty. Red, white, and blue were used in small amounts to accent this part of the exhibit.

In color you can afford to be daring. The exhibit should be changed often and you will want to let people know that a new exhibit has been arranged. In choosing your basic color scheme, consider carefully the effect you want. Do you want it to be cool, dignified, and restrained? Then use blues, greens, violets, and grays. On the other hand, if you want it to be stimulating and eye-arresting, you will find reds, oranges, yellows, black, and white just what you want. Your exhibit will probably be more unified if it is either predominantly cool or predominantly warm in hue.

It is general practice to use neutral colors in the background with strong notes of color contrast in the main center of interest. These contrasting colors may then be repeated in weaker intensities and smaller amounts in other sections of the display. A strong pattern of dark and light, as well as bright colors, will attract attention to the center, and it can be made more important by leaving plain space around it for contrast. The background, though, should not merely look empty. It should play its part in the whole design.

Bulletin boards. Some school bulletin boards look as though notices had been thrown at them and had simply stuck where they landed. This disorder makes the notices hard to read, as well as making the board unattractive. A good-looking bulletin board is not produced without time and thought on the part of someone.

The bulletin board should seem to be part of the wall against which it is fastened, and should be in harmony and alignment with any nearby doors, windows, or cases. As with the display case, there should be a definite center of interest and an orderly arrangement of sizes. Bulletin material is necessarily varied in size and kind. It is sometimes necessary to combine posters with typed material. There may be irregular forms, such as pictures of fruits and vegetables for cooking classes. Such a miscellaneous assortment of notices and pictures may create a nondescript form and color pattern. This effect can be reduced somewhat by mounting the odd-shaped and irregular cut-outs on sheets of paper or cardboard. By this means rectangular shapes are created which can be organized into uniform patterns to harmonize with the frame of the bulletin board and of the hall in which it stands. Mountings of uniform height are more easily arranged than those of varying heights and sizes. When pictures or dia-

Can you help improve your school's exhibit cases?

grams are to be mounted, they should be placed slightly above the center of the cardboard, with the side margins equal. Richly colored mounting paper is effective for vigorous designs. Neutral colors will give the material itself a better chance to speak up and deliver its message.

You can arrange your bulletin board much more easily if you will draw main axis lines to divide the total space into four large areas. The vertical axis should be through the very middle, while the horizontal one should be slightly above the middle of the bulletin board. Permanent or semipermanent material should be balanced on either side of the center of interest, which obviously is at the intersection of the two axis lines. A row of large notices may be arranged to form a center line between two rows of smaller ones. Or the notices may be arranged so that there is a transition of widths from small to large, or a transition of heights from short to tall. Should you like to try rearranging the bulletin material as a class project in order to fix these principles more clearly in your mind?

Problems and activities. (1) Decide what changes could be made to improve that portion of the school ground which you can see from your classroom windows. (2) Walk around your school grounds and study the effectiveness of the landscaping and planting from various angles in order to decide how it could be improved. Then make plans for improving those parts of the school grounds to which you think your class could make its best contribution. (3) If your school plant has more than one building, compare the entrances of the different buildings and decide which could be improved by means of students' efforts and help. (4) Decide what your class could do to give the front hall of your building a better effect for incoming guests. (5) Appoint two committees from your class. Let each committee arrange a bulletin board; then let the rest of the class decide which of the committees achieves the most pleasing design. (6) Examine the display cases or exhibition cabinets in your halls, and decide what improvements could be made in each.

5. LABORATORIES FOR LEARNING

Making Classrooms Attractive

Does the room where your art class meets show to the rest of the school and to visitors that you know how to apply the principles of art? Does the room look organized and orderly? Is there anything you and your classmates could do to improve it in this respect? Is the art equipment easy to get at and ready to use? Are there two or three beauty spots in the room in which you take an interest?

If the art room is already as attractive and convenient as you can make it, what about other classrooms? The teachers are not wholly responsible for a cheerful work atmosphere. Part of the responsibility is yours. As a student of art perhaps it is up to you to take the lead in a movement for beautifying your classrooms. The best way of starting any good movement is to demonstrate quietly that improvement is possible. Actions always speak louder than words.

In an English class in one school two students decided that a disorderly and ugly room was not an appropriate place for the reading of the world's great literature. With the co-operation of their teacher they arranged a book corner. They painted an old set of shelves a soft grayed blue-green and filled them with some interesting books borrowed from the library. Above the bookcase they hung a blue-green textile in an all-over pattern of lighter value than the shelves. Against this as a background they arranged some bronze bookends holding a few small volumes, a terra cotta bowl containing a pot of ivy, and a group of brightly colored figurines supplied by the teacher. Their class was delighted. Almost at once they saw that disorderly desks, papers on the floor, and window shades awry somehow did not suit the book corner. They began to co-operate in improving the room, and soon an enthusiasm for more attractive classrooms spread through the school.

Special problems of the art room. Colorful pictures and exhibits show to best advantage against neutral backgrounds. If the walls of the art room are too striking or vivid, they will overpower the drawings and paintings which students create or display in the room. Light gray, gray-green, and cream are good neutral colors for this background purpose. There should be no accents of bright colors on any of the permanent equipment that is continuously in sight, because you may wish to plan exhibits in color schemes which do not harmonize with them. All your permanent equipment, then, should be painted in such neutral colors as white, gray, cream, or black, or in such grayed cool colors as grayed green or grayed blue-green.

Exhibits of pictures and illustrative materials should be mounted on cardboards or paper of uniform height so that their edges will repeat the architectural lines of the room. Thus, the exhibit may form a continuous border of a uniform height, even though the pictures are of varying widths. An interesting variation of this for the art room is an upper and lower row of small pictures with a central band of larger pictures. In order to make it easy for you to change your exhibits quickly, it may be well to draw light red lines on the walls at the levels at which you wish the pictures to hang.

Paints, water pans, crayons, ink, and other art materials which you and your fellow students use continually may be combined and fastened to a single board which fits the desk. Tin cigarette boxes may be enameled in black or soft colors and used to hold crayons. A square ink bottle with a colored enamel top may be fitted into a wood cut-out designed to hold it. The water pans which will assure clean water for painting may be fitted into another cut-out block. These articles and the paint box may be nailed to a single board. Care should be taken to plan them for practical use as well as with pleasing design. A number of cans and bottles for collecting and distributing water may be organized and combined into a single wooden case cut to hold them, and the whole may all be painted in a slightly warmer color scheme than the room background, since it is movable and may be put out of sight. The regulation large blue ink bottle is an effective addition to this design, particularly if the container is placed near the windows where the light may shine through the bottle.

A great contribution which you and your classmates can make toward the beauty of your art room is the exercising of restraint in handling your materials so that you do not leave crayon marks, spots of paint, ink, scratches, or scars on the furniture. Careful use of sandpaper, varnish, and enamel will remedy ordinary wear and tear so that you and the others who use the room may have an attractive place to work.

General problems of other classrooms. Fundamentally, the beauty of any schoolroom grows out of having a place for everything and seeing that everything is in its place when not in use. Disorderly books, a confusing arrangement of furniture, paper on the floor, disorganized wall areas, window blinds at all levels, and badly mounted or badly displayed illustrative materials cause restlessness in a class. Although poor color schemes, disturbing line arrangements, and jumpy dark-and-light patterns may not be recognized as a cause of physical strain or nervousness, they do contribute to a general feeling of uneasiness. You and everyone else will be less likely to grow restless and irritable if you take the trouble to make all your classrooms orderly and attractive.

Window blinds or shades are common offenders against order. Since they form an important part of wall design, the bottom of each blind should form a continuous line with the bottoms of the others. You might begin improving your classroom by pulling all the blinds down just the right distance from the top to admit sufficient light and to create an attractive proportion.

Since orderliness is one of the major principles of classroom art, furniture and equipment should be carefully arranged. Plants, if there are any, should be pleasingly spaced. Posted material should form continuous lines parallel with the lines of the room. After some order is achieved, curtains, pottery, flowers, pictures, and interesting arrangements of books may add to the beauty of the room.

Is this schoolroom a tonic for tired nerves?

The same general principles that were mentioned in connection with a center of interest in the hall apply to a beauty spot in the classroom as well. The same problems that are involved in displaying materials in the art classroom apply in the mounting of pictures that are used in courses in science, English, or history. The general wall design should form a more or less neutral background. There will always be highly colored objects or articles for display in the modern classroom, and these should have a chance to speak without being overwhelmed by too lively a color scheme in the room itself.

Selecting pictures. Good pictures can do much to enliven the walls of your classroom. If they are to do this well, they must be thoughtfully chosen. What is a good picture? Perhaps we can best answer this by saying some things that a good picture is not. A good picture is not merely a record of facts or of objects; it is not a photographic reproduction of things seen. You have plenty of drawings and photographs in your textbooks to give you realistic images of things. A good painting shows you how the painter felt about something. Let us take as a specific example a painting of a tree. It will not be merely a copy of the appearance of the tree. It will express some feeling, some emotion, through the way in which the tree is painted. The artist may make the tree tall and broad to suggest strength and vigor, or tall and slender to give a feeling of grace, or soft and misty to produce a dreamy impression. He may make the branches more angular than they really are to give it a rugged, lively quality; or he may emphasize the roundness to make it seem rich and full.

The one thing the artist will not do is merely to copy the tree as he sees it. A good painting is a record of *how and what the artist felt about his subject.* The picture does not have to tell a story. It does not have to present many details accurately. It should, however, arouse in you an emotional response, and be a decorative spot on the walls. To be sure, a picture may tell a story or represent objects realistically, provided such representation also has beauty of design.

The subject matter of a picture may include human beings, outdoor activities, home scenes, moods of nature in the morning, at sunset, or by moonlight. Plains, mountains, and deserts, offer material to the artist, as do growing plants, trees, shrubs, flowers, and still life. Any of these subjects may be suited to the classroom.

All pictures which have a fairly general appeal may be used in classrooms regardless of the subjects that are taught there. Particular types of pictures may be more appropriate to one classroom than another; for example, geographical pictures for social-studies and portraits or landscapes for literature classrooms. No picture should be chosen, however, just because it is a good factual document and is believed to represent the costuming and setting of other times. Such works, if they are valuable in illustrating history, should be kept in a folder or file and used when necessary. A music room is not necessarily improved by a display of portraits of musicians; few of these are actually fine paintings. It would be better to replace them by lyrical pictures which stimulate moods, or by modern abstractions which have close parallels with music.

USING ART IN SCHOOL ACTIVITIES

Since the schoolroom should be a happy and stimulating place, it is natural that the majority of the pictures should be chosen with strong color and dynamic pattern. The art shops and stores will be glad to help you make choices, and you can learn much by calling upon experts for advice.

Hanging pictures. The pictures you use should be chosen and placed so that they are related to the lines, dark-and-light scheme, color, and texture of the room. They should be in scale with the size of the room and harmonious with the other pictures. For example, in a very small room an exceedingly large picture is overpowering, while in a large room a small picture is lost.

Pictures should be mounted or framed so that they show to best advantage. Very small pictures can be mounted to increase their size; or several may be grouped in one large unit to fit a space that would be too large for one alone. Mats and frames can be used to convert pictures of pleasant sizes into decorative designs which conform to the shapes and lines of the spaces in which they are to be hung. Mounting a picture on a mat helps to set the picture apart from the room and creates a neutral area against which it shows to advantage. This mounting should not be of stronger intensity than the color effect of the picture.

If possible, pictures should be placed close to the eye level so they may be studied comfortably. The most important and beautiful ones should, if possible, be seen by those who pause in the doorway, or as a first welcome to those who enter the room. Pictures should be hung so that they do not tip forward, because when they lean away from the wall they are not related to the plane of the wall. Also the edges of the frames or mountings should be parallel with the floor and with the vertical lines of the room. Pictures that are out of line create a feeling of unpleasant disorder.

Flowers and figurines. Bringing flowers to teacher has long been laughed at as a strategy for getting better marks and perhaps a little leniency when you have misbehaved. It is good strategy today for better reasons. Flowers and plants help greatly to keep your classroom bright and cheerful. And along with flowers you can use decorative objects of terra cotta, plaster, porcelain, ivory, jade, wood, glass, bronze, or other metals.

The problems of flower selection and arrangement for the classroom are essentially the same as those involved in the decoration of the home. Likewise, the little figures present problems of line, form, color, and texture, involving all the principles which you have been studying. The figurines may be varied in subject, but they should be designed with respect for the material of which they are made. Glass figures, for instance, present the beauties of glass and should not try to imitate the shaggy coat of a dog or the soft skin of a girl. Beautiful little figures from the countries about which you are reading, or expressive of the work which you are studying, will be a valuable addition to the classroom and may appropriately be used without any other excuse than that they are attractive. Changing them from time to time will create interest and give you new problems in forms, line, color, and texture.

Problems and activities. (1) Check your art room for ways in which you and your classmates could improve its appearance. (2) Do the same thing for one or more of the classrooms in which you meet for other courses. Then try to carry out the improvements tactfully. (3) Experiment by raising, lowering, or changing pictures from one position to another in your classroom to determine which arrangement produces the most pleasing effect. (4) Bring several framed pictures from home, or arrange for a loan from the stores, and make selections of the types which you think would be most suitable for classroom use. (5) Experiment with different types of plant and flower arrangements and locations for your classroom, and decide which are most effective and why. (6) Bring a number of different kinds and types of figurines to class, and experiment with different combinations of figurines and flowers in order to work out ideas for pleasing effects.

6. THE DAY'S WORK

Doing Assigned Work in Good Taste

Do you expect the teacher to judge your accomplishments by your good intentions, or by what you submit for the eye to see? Mastery of school tasks is best proved by what you can show. Your daily written work may be well thought out, but if it looks scraggly and jumbled, it starts with a handicap which may never be completely overcome. Your notebook may be a treasure house of wisdom, but the teacher cannot appreciate the treasure if the visual effect is too much like that of a junk pile. The way you plan and carry out your various projects and assignments has much to do with the impression you make upon your teacher and your classmates, but most of all upon yourself. Can you respect your own work when it does not merit or win the respect of others? When your work leaves your hands, it speaks for you. It is your agent. You never know when someone is secretly measuring and judging you for a higher station in life. If you form the habit of doing your school work not

How do the size, slant, and form of your letters affect the appearance of your writing?

only accurately and thoroughly but also with a finished look, you can qualify for the big opportunity when it arrives.

Handwriting. When you turn in a paper in longhand, is it both legible and attractive? Study your handwriting in the light of these questions: First, can you write a word on a straight line? Frequent testing with a ruler will make you conscious of this point. Second, can you keep your writing in the same scale? Large and small letters do not mix well in the same work. Someone will suspect you of lack of control. Third, can you make your letters slant in the same direction? Chaos and disorder are suggested by writing in which the letters slant in several different directions. Test this phase of your writing with a small triangle made of folded paper, and see that the letters are all parallel with each other. Fourth, are your crossbars cut through at the same height? If they are not, take a little more time to establish uniformity in this respect.

When you use lettering instead of longhand, are your letters simple instead of ornate and complicated? The old English lettering is not simple in form and is not easy to read; it should be used only when a very special style of material calls for it. Roman lettering is practical and effective, and the modern sans-serif writing is even better because it dispenses with the serifs, or little feet, on which the roman letters rest, and depends for its effect on simple circles, ovals, rectangles, triangles, and well-spaced straight diagonal lines. Whatever the design of the alphabet you use, it should be consistent throughout in both weight and style of letter.

Margins. Plain space around the rectangle of writing contributes to ease of reading and makes the dark mass of written matter more attractive to the eye. These light margins on both sides of the page help the eye to regulate its swing from one end of the line to the other, and they also shorten the line of writing so that it is easier to read. It is preferable to have the bottom margin a little wider than the top margin. If the bottom margin is smaller, the weight of the rectangle of written material seems to be slipping off the page. On loose sheets side margins may be even. In a bound book they should be smaller toward the binding side because the facing pages form a balanced design which should not be broken by too much blank space down the middle. No pictures, diagrams, or lettering should break into the margin unless they are very carefully planned as a part of the design of the whole page. Unless you are quite talented in matters of design, you had better stick to plain margins surrounding carefully balanced rectangles of the manuscript. In handwriting it is impossible to make the right-hand margins absolutely straight, as in typewriting. Merely keep them as straight and uniform as possible.

Notebooks. What has been said about written and hand-printed pages applies, of course, to all notebooks containing notes and other written material. Often, however, you are called upon to prepare a notebook as part of a project.

You may wish to give it a specially designed cover and binding and to include illustrations. Even this special kind of notebook should be simple in form. Simplicity is more effective than over-decoration.

Such a notebook may be constructed in different ways; there is the regulation sewn book, the popular loose-leaf type, the portfolio containing individual

page two

that our history started and continued to be an adjustment of immigrants and settlers to new and terrifying environments. It was the courage, faith and struggle of these people, regardless of their ancestral creed that is the nucleus of our history. In our frantic search in foreign lands for an art that in some way would substitute for our lack of cultural heritage, we have almost overlooked some of the most exciting primitives yet revealed.

This great American art still lacks a descriptive definition. It has been called "Spanish-American Folk Art", "Early American Catholic Primitives", "Early American Southwestern Art", etc. It is doubtless of little importance what it is called, and unfortunately its significance has been known only to a few artists and a still smaller number of other appreciative individuals. Among the latter are Mrs F.M. Potter, whose intelligent generosity has probably saved many of these works from oblivion. Also Mitchell Wild, curator of the Potter museum

page 2

that our history started and continued to be an adjustment of immigrants and settlers to new and terrifying environments. It was the courage, faith and struggle of these people, regardless of their ancestral creed that is the nucleus of our history. In our frantic search in foreign lands for an art that in some way would substitute for our lack of cultural heritage, we have almost overlooked some of the most exciting primitives yet revealed.

This great American art still lacks a descriptive definition. It has been called "Spanish-American Folk Art", "Early American Catholic Primitives", "Early Southwestern Art", etc. It is doubtless of little importance what it is called, and, unfortunately, its significance has been known only to a few artists and a still smaller

Which paper would you prefer if you were the teacher?

leaves, and also the continuous-fold Japanese form. The back hinge should be of cloth and tough paper that will really serve the useful purpose of a hinge. The thickness of the book will determine the width of the back hinge.

Rough paper is sometimes used in preference to smooth for the pages of such a book, especially if pictures are to be mounted. Durable material, such as heavy paper, cardboard, cotton or linen cloth, or leather, may be used to make covers that are suitable to the purpose of the book.

Silk or gold cords, ribbons, and bowknots are not suitable for lacing book covers. They suggest a daintiness or preciousness out of harmony with the utilitarian nature of most notebooks. Heavy cotton or linen cords or strips of leather are much more appropriate for book binding.

The color of your notebook should be kept neutral in intensity and harmonious throughout. A mixture of colored pages including very strong intensities of both cool and warm colors may be confusing. A reddish color, even if rather subdued, is seldom a good background, since red is an aggressive hue which may overpower the message written upon it. If you use strong colors, it is best to use them in small areas for contrast or accent.

Illustrations. Pictures are seldom good designs for notebook covers. A picture is more appropriate inside the book than on the front. Well proportioned, plain, undecorated covers, or covers with simple well-balanced lettering and all-over patterns make satisfactory cover designs.

Illustrations inside the notebook may be of various kinds: pictures cut from magazines or travel folders, your own snapshots, or your own drawings. The last are, of course, much to be preferred. Such sketches should be your own first-hand impressions of things you have seen or thought rather than designs copied from a book. Such copying is seldom art or education.

The illustrations of whatever kind should be designed in rectangles, and these rectangles should be balanced with the rectangles of writing or printing on the page and with the rectangles formed by the boundaries of the page itself. In this way unity is developed for the entire book. When large illustrations are used, they should be so planned and spaced that they are the most important thing on the page.

Captions and legends for the illustrations should be printed in such a way as to fit into the whole design.

Maps. Are you sometimes called upon to reproduce maps in simplified form, presenting various geographical, historical, industrial, or agricultural facts? If skillfully done, even such factual maps can be beautiful. Maps also make attractive illustrations for a notebook, or they may be used as decorative panels for the wall.

Merely reproducing the boundaries and main divisions of a country or geographical region is no art problem; it is a mechanical job which the printer can do more effectively than you can. Trace the outline of your map from a printed one by means of carbon paper. If you must reduce or enlarge it, do so by measuring and reproducing it according to a uniform scale. When your outline is as nearly perfect as possible, you are ready to proceed with the rest of the design.

Keep your map as simple as possible, and emphasize just those places that are essential to your purpose. Do not weaken your effect by including too many confusing minor details.

Names of oceans, countries, rivers, mountains, and cities make an intricate pattern. You had better sketch them in lightly before doing them in ink. Before starting, decide carefully on the style of lettering best suited to your purpose.

If the map is to be pictorial, you may designate important places by symbols which allow for an additional bit of color. Wave borders are effective in representing water. Conventionalized trees, buildings, products, and people may be spotted over your map in an effective though informal all-over pattern.

Color makes almost any map decorative. Cool or bluish colors naturally give the feeling of water. Use these for oceans, lakes, and rivers. The land should naturally contrast with water, and therefore should be done in the warm colors. The land itself should be less noticeable than the pictorial details of people or objects. It should, therefore, be done in subdued or grayed warm colors in order to let the more brilliant pictorial symbols stand out. If you want a few areas of contrast in a wide expanse of blue ocean, you can insert a few boats, Neptunes, or other symbols in warm colors but in small areas only, and thus tie this part of your design in with the larger areas of land. The total effect of your map should be predominantly cool or predominantly warm with a lesser amount of the contrasting color. There should not be an even amount of warm and cool colors in the design as a whole.

Relief maps may be built up by mixing salt and flour in equal proportions, with enough water to make a thick dough. This makes an excellent working material. After your map has hardened about three days, it can be painted with calcimine, water colors, tempera, or oils.

Projects. Are you being asked more and more in your school work to turn in, not something written on paper, but something made with your hands? It is now popular in education to integrate art, music, shop, science, mathematics, and other academic subjects around creative projects. In these projects you have a chance to reveal your talents in various ways and to apply the principles of art you have been learning.

Clay modeling, for example, is often used as a means of expressing ideas gained through the study of history, science, and literature. There is little point in making a clay model of something exactly as it is portrayed in a book or a museum. To be sure, making a model of a Greek temple, a saber-toothed tiger, or a frontier blockhouse may teach you to observe more accurately, but such work often becomes more a mechanical job than an art challenge. Creative modeling is an expression of your own way of feeling and never merely a task in copywork. Your problem is to discover what quality makes an object different from all others and then to accentuate or exaggerate that quality until the feeling you have about it is communicated to others. Thus, a cat whose cat qualities are accentuated so that his "catness" is evident to everyone becomes more truly a cat than one just copied in some accidental pose from real life. In drawing and painting as well as in modeling the same thing is true if your project is to be truly creative.

Again, if your project calls for a dramatization of scenes or situations from other lands or in other times, your problem is that of selecting and portraying the unique spirit and meaning of the events and characters.

If your class combines to express in pageantry the spirit or moving force of some great episode in the history of the race, you will probably want to combine your talents for drawing, color combination, and dramatics, with a good deal of music thrown in. Again you will do well to try to create a certain emotional effect or impression rather than to present something so factual and realistic that it might have been a page of statistics instead.

210

USING ART IN SCHOOL ACTIVITIES

Problems and activities. (1) Hold up samples of good manuscript, two at a time, and make judgments as to which one of each pair is better from the standpoint of design on the page. (2) Make similar comparisons, particularly with reference to the question of margins. (3) Likewise, compare and evaluate pairs of notebooks in terms of external features of binding materials and cover designs, and then from the standpoint of their page design and make-up. (4) Show to the class, one after another, maps which students have drawn, and select the outstanding good features of each. Likewise, suggest possible improvements where they are most needed. (5) Bring to class samples of your own project work, or borrow samples from other classrooms, and decide which ones have outstanding qualities of design, and why.

Part IV
WORK

X. Art on the Job

Using art principles in the workaday world

Since the first decade of the twentieth century the world has become more and more design-conscious. When your grandparents bought a table or a piece of dress goods, their first question usually was: Will it stand up under use? Will it wear well? Today your first question is likely to be: Is it attractive? Does it have a pleasing design?

This state of affairs gives art a high commercial value. Manufacturers have redesigned not only their products but also the containers and wrappings in which they are sold, because good design has a selling value. Whether it be mouse trap or locomotive, the design must be right and the display well planned. Buttons and automobiles, salads and kitchen stoves, padlocks and pearl necklaces—all must be set forth for customers in the most attractive manner if they are to compete with the wares of the dealer next door.

Because of this emphasis on design, your knowledge of art principles has money value. The business world often pays fancy prices for good art ideas. If you spend enough time and effort on art, you may develop into a professional designer who does the really skilled and creative work upon which manufacturers and dealers depend for the artistic quality of the goods they produce and distribute.

If you have not the talent or inclination for using art in a professional way, still you can apply its principles in almost any job you undertake, though it is merely arranging canned corn on the shelf in a grocery store. Most sales are achieved today, at least partly, by visual effects. If your work is not directly concerned with either manufacturing or selling, you can still find many ways of using everything you know about good design. Engineer, doctor, nurse, plumber, bank clerk, and stenographer—all have daily need for the fundamental principles of art.

Because of the high value placed on good design in the modern world, a word of warning may be in order. Do not get the idea that appearance is everything. The world still looks for quality behind the attractive surface. A lawn mower, beautifully streamlined, which fails to cut grass efficiently, will not meet selling competition very long. Functional design is not truly functional unless it lives up to its name.

As with products, so with services. A trained nurse who looks attractive and can arrange flowers artistically may pride herself that she is applying art principles in her profession. But if she fails in carrying out the doctor's orders or neglects her patient during a crisis in pneumonia, it would be better if she had no notion of art.

In some fields, notably that of advertising, design has been so highly emphasized that the world is beginning to grow skeptical. Now and then one hears two old proverbs quoted: "Beauty is but skin deep," and "Handsome is as handsome does."

As you take your place in the workaday world, make up your mind to use your knowledge of art honestly. Selling inferior products at the price of quality goods, even though it succeeds and makes you money, is not art; it is deceit. Art is honest. Violation of its sound principles produces only pseudo-art. Because some people have misused art in the past, the word "artful" now has the derogatory meaning of tricky. The world does not need more "artful dodgers," but it always needs more real artists.

1. Modern Merchandise

Turning Out Attractive Products

In your first job you may not have the privilege of designing anything more important than pages of typewriting, salads in a restaurant, or flower beds in the yards which you care for along the street. But even in these small matters

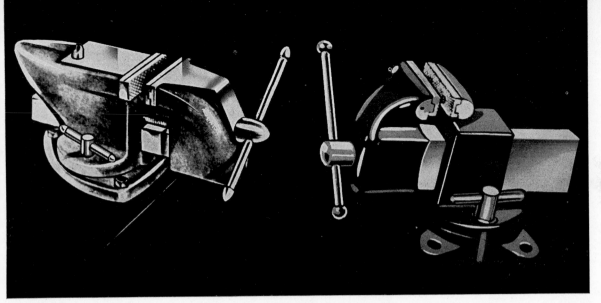

RE-DESIGNED AND OLD STYLE VISE

(Photographs by courtesy of Bureau of Design, Montgomery Ward & Co.)

RE-DESIGNED AND OLD STYLE SAW

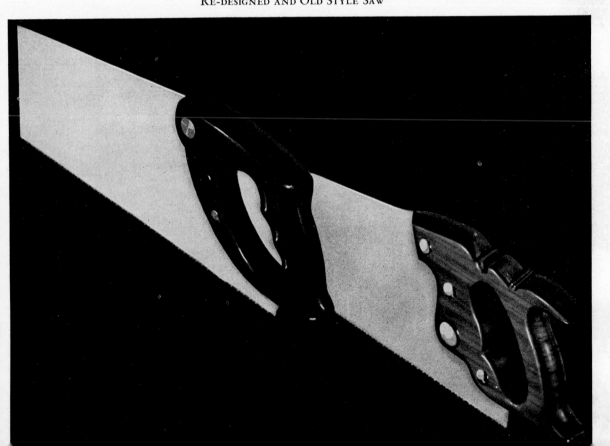

OLD STYLE COFFEE POT

OLD STYLE KETTLE

OLD STYLE SCALE

RE-DESIGNED COFFEE POT

RE-DESIGNED KETTLE

RE-DESIGNED SCALE

(Photographs by courtesy of Bureau of Design, Montgomery Ward & Co.)

NEW AND OLD STOVE

you can use the principles of good design, and you can be constantly learning more about art problems by observing the things around you.

Design is the organization of masses, shapes, or forms. These forms are determined by the uses to which they are to be put. Their arrangement in relation to each other is brought about by their efficiency in use. Any article

Can you design a better mousetrap?

is well designed when it is well proportioned and efficient, and when its shape clearly tells its function. The master designer arranges his working units and determines his proportions so that the parts work better and also look better. This is functional design.

Has the soda fountain where you work a functional design, or is it merely modernistic? The term "modernistic" has been used for such a variety of wild patterns without relationship to use that it is already in disrepute as a descriptive word. "Modern" is a better word to use, but since it changes for each new phase or fashion it is more accurate to designate the present trend in art by the word "functional."

Handmade versus machine made products. Handmade articles are often delightful because they suggest something of the artisan who made them. They have an individuality and personality that few machine-made objects have. Handwork is expensive, however, and runs up the price of goods so that few people today can afford handmade objects.

When the use of machinery first became widespread during the early days of the Industrial Revolution, the machine was not well understood. At first, it was used to make products in imitation of the handcrafts. It was set to turning out enormous amounts of jigsaw scroll work in imitation of hand carving, as well as many kinds of monstrosities in imitation of wrought iron. The early designers even went so far as purposely to put imperfections into their products so that they would look as though they were handmade. Today we see the falseness of this use of the machine. We realize that the machine can produce works of art if its possibilities are respected.

After all, it is just as honorable to produce a beautiful product with one tool as it is with another. There is very little pure handwork in existence in the world. Nearly everything that is made is made with some kinds of tools. We ordinarily speak of an object as handmade when the tools used to make it are crude and simple, and as machine-made when the tools are more complex. A competent designer can rise to the highest levels of artistic performance in working with the machine. Good designing is good thinking, and is not the product of crudeness of tools or methods. Machine-made and handmade products each have their place.

Delicate hand embroidery is charming on a baby's bonnet and suitable because children are precious to us. On the other hand, machine-made paper doilies are more suitable than fine handmade ones for use on tables where lunch is served rapidly and inexpensively. Yet for the handwork the only tool was a needle; for the paper doilies it was a complicated machine.

New materials. The development of new ways of using iron, steel, chromium, glass, cork, rubber, wood, and paper has opened up new avenues for the designing of new products. Aluminum has advantages over wood or cloth for window shades, since it is not only good looking but also resists heat and sunshine. New types of plastic materials, made from such humble things as soy beans, are well suited to functional design, whether the product be a bathroom floor or a bottle top.

When these new-type materials are used the wise designer takes full advantage of their textures or surface qualities, and lets them show for what they are instead of trying to cover them up by the application of some design of flowers or foreign materials. His rule is: let wood be wood, and let bakelite be bakelite. He does not try to paint glass to make it an imitation of mahogany.

If you have ambitions as a designer, hold up your artistic head, and face the world squarely. Take full credit for your achievements with new materials instead of acting ashamed as if you thought they were feeble imitations of the real thing. Metal beds that are painted to look like wood, and composition fountain pens grained to look like marble are both as false as a ceiling which is painted to represent carving.

Problems and activities. (1) While you wait for your ice cream or cool drink at the soda fountain, watch the boy who prepares it, and decide whether he is a real artist or just a "soda jerker." (2) Examine several machine-made or handmade articles in your home, and decide which ones are truly functional in design. (3) Arrange for each student to bring to the class some article with exceptionally good design, show it to the class, and explain wherein it represents good design. (4) Bring to the class something which you yourself have made, show it to your classmates, and get their reactions to your ability as a designer. (5) Show the class or tell them about some particularly bad piece of designing in manufactured goods, and indicate what mistake was made by its producers.

2. FOR ALL TO SEE

Displaying Merchandise for Sale

When you go window shopping in leisurely fashion, or when you are hurriedly searching counters and showcases for some article you need in just the right color, do you sometimes want to rearrange the merchandise? Perhaps you have seen a window with goods excellent in quality but so badly displayed that you were almost tempted to break the glass and set to work creating order out of the chaos. Have you been shopping at Christmas time when so much merchandise was on display that your eyes and your mind grew weary and you could not choose what to buy? It is well to remember all experiences of this sort if you are ever given the opportunity of arranging anything for sale. Whether it is cauliflower and carrots in the vegetable market or handbags and handkerchiefs in the department store, the principles of design should govern the display.

Backgrounds. Display space, whether it be a window, a showcase, or a floor section, is expensive and must be planned to get the best results. This space must be adaptable to various types of displays from day to day or week to week. Soft grayish colors are inconspicuous, are always in good taste, and still yield the right of way to the display which is set up against them. Strong intensities and light colors are more consistently gay and pleasant than the heavy ones. The floor should usually be darker than the walls of the display case to give a feeling of solidity. In high show windows, however, a gradually darkening effect on the walls as you go from the bottom to the top may be used to increase interest and add variety. In any case, the background for your exhibits should be simple and unified and appropriate for the display of merchandise. A conspicuous elaborateness of texture, pattern, or color will distract the customer's eye from the leading characters to the stage scenery and thus will actually waste money for the firm. The background should not contain anything that will steal attention away from the merchandise display.

A single theme. One point at a time is all that can be successfully put over to your prospective customer. In choosing merchandise for display, it is necessary first to decide upon the main message you wish to present and then bend every effort to driving home that message. Everything in the display should help to build up the main theme. If you run a three-ring circus with many events clamoring at the same time for your customer's attention, it will be impossible for him to concentrate on any one, and he will simply go away confused.

To fill or not to fill. Even when your display of merchandise is built around a single selling idea, it may still be too crowded. Of course, it is also possible that it may contain too little. A single apple in a grocery window, for instance, does not have as much drawing power as would the world's most famous diamond placed in a jeweler's window on black velvet surrounded by mirrors. A good working principle is that the greater the value of each article displayed, the fewer pieces of merchandise necessary for a complete display. The customers are likely to judge the value according to the square footage accorded to the article in the exhibit.

Organizing a display. If you must show a large number of articles at once, it is possible to arrange them in a number of small groups carefully chosen as to size and shape, then to arrange these groups in relation to each other so that one dominating group holds the center of the stage and is surrounded by

PIANO WINDOW DISPLAY

Can you create a window display that will draw customers from across the street?

(*Photographs by courtesy of Barker Brothers, Los Angeles*)

RECORD WINDOW DISPLAY

CHRISTMAS PRESENT WINDOW DISPLAY

How should a window display differ from a showcase display?

(*Photographs by courtesy of Barker Brothers, Los Angeles*)

GLASS CASE LINEN DISPLAY

several smaller and supporting groups. Thus you have order and organization instead of confusion.

The vegetable stand, the grocery, the drug store, and the five-and-ten-cent store have the double job of presenting a great deal of merchandise and at the same time avoiding a cluttered appearance. If you work in one of these places,

Is there any room for art in displaying groceries?

can you do your part to emphasize main features and subordinate others so that an impression of a main center of interest is created?

Winning attention. The job of your display is to seize the attention of the passer-by, focus his interest on the objects shown, and hold him on the spot until he has found something he wishes to buy. A chaos of unrelated objects confuses and tires him. Unless he comes to the store in the first place with the definite purpose of finding some article, he will probably turn away bewildered and unsold. Strong contrasts in dark and light or in hue are necessary in the central objects in order to draw the customer to your display. When he is thus interested in your goods, he will take time to examine the articles which are of less importance and which are less strongly contrasted with the background. In this way, by sequence of interest in the customer's mind, each article develops its own selling appeal and also prepares the customer for the next articles which are closely related to it in the display.

Sizes and shapes. Variety of size but repetition of shape helps to create a rhythmic display in which the eye passes easily from part to part. Too great a variety of shapes causes confusion because the mind is forced to tie together the unrelated contours. A variation of sizes, however, is less monotonous than a repetition of the same size. If the eye is carried through a sequence from small to large, as in the case of round perfume bottles, one feels a distinct pleasure in the repetition of contour and also a pleasant sense of change from the differences in size.

When sizes cannot be varied, different colors may be massed in small, medium, and large groups. The object which you wish to make the center of interest, if it has enough contrast in color, value, or texture, may be small in relation to those around it, or it may be given importance by being larger than any other object in the window. Circular forms may be contrasted with angular ones in order to bring them more sharply to notice, and in order to add strength to the total composition. A more complex form may be set off by plain space or by simple shapes subordinated to it, but too many complex forms interfere with each other, just as orchids do if they are fitted into a closely massed bunch.

Colors and textures. Strong contrasts of color help to create a center of interest in your merchandise display, while close relationships of color and texture are necessary in the subordinated areas in order to keep them from stealing the show. You can build up a center of interest by contrasting warm colors with cool ones, light values with dark, and full saturations with weak tints. Glass, metal, and shiny textures combine well with each other and contrast most sharply with rough or velvety, light-absorbing textures. The same principle applies to textures as to color, namely, that contrast should be used in order to focus the customer's eye on dominant interests and harmonies should be used in the less important areas.

Problems and activities. (1) Go on a window shopping trip and evaluate several displays in terms of principles given in this section. (2) Go inside a grocery or vegetable store, note how the merchandise is arranged and exhibited, and decide what you could do to improve it if you worked there. (3) Spend some time in several five-and-ten-cent stores, drug stores, or automobile accessory stores, note how the design of exhibits has been worked out in relation to the problem of crowding, and see how well the confused or miscellaneous impression has been avoided. (4) Tell the class about unusually good or unusually bad merchandise exhibits you have seen, and point out the specific causes of the good or bad effects.

3. WITH A SHINGLE OUTSIDE

Setting Up a Place of Business

It may be a long time before you will "hang out a shingle" marking your own office or place of business. Perhaps you have no ambition to do just that in the world; but whether you work by yourself or for others, there will be times when you must exercise choices and make decisions about the general appearance, both exterior and interior, of the place where you work. No business establishment is better looking than it is made by the combined art standards of its owner and his employees.

There is a general feeling in the world, in spite of experiences to the contrary, that a place of business which looks prosperous is prosperous. Certainly premises with a run-down look are no asset to a business; they are a definite handicap. If the place is ugly, drab, gloomy, or dirty, it is not likely to attract customers or clients.

In what ways can you help to make and keep your place of business looking its best? In the first place, you can develop some standards in the matter.

Cleanliness. Dirty corners and dusty equipment not only harbor germs but also suggest to the public that the firm is inefficient, lazy, and inconsiderate. Some kinds of work create more dirt and disorder than others, but this is no excuse for perpetual confusion and layers of grime. A shoe-repair shop cannot and should not look like a jewelry store, but it can be reasonably clean and orderly. It is part of the job of any employee to avoid making unnecessary litter and to clear up any that is unavoidable. Those who do the actual job of cleaning will usually do better work if they feel that their efforts are appreciated and reinforced by the other workers.

Light and air. Good air and satisfactory light are essential to both good workmanship and good salesmanship. If you forget to raise the blinds or to open the windows, you may not notice the dark and dreary dullness, or the foulness of

How could you help Mr. Smith to prosper?

the air after you have put up with it for a few hours, but customers coming in from the bright, fresh outdoors will quickly get the impression of a "stuffy old dump" and they will not give your merchandise half the consideration it may deserve.

A good front. Tearing off the old façade and replacing it with a new one is a popular way of giving a business a fresh start. But too many people make the mistake of thinking that the front is bad merely because it is old and will be perfect merely because it is new. The front should, of course, be related

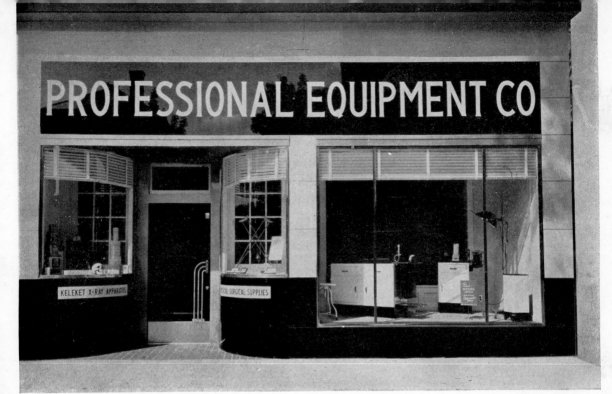

How many things should a store front tell the public?

LAMP FLOOR DISPLAY

What makes a display of merchandise attractive?
(*Photographs by courtesy of Barker Brothers, Los Angeles*)

CHINA FLOOR DISPLAY

to the entire building and to the business transacted behind it. Many business streets in our towns and cities have been ruined by the addition of "modernistic" windows and entrances to the first floor without corresponding changes above. Chromium and expanses of plate glass at the street level do not combine well with ornate stone or wooden cornices and tall narrow windows in the upper stories. Neither does bright red or yellow paint improve the front of a dignified old building. A front which imitates a lighthouse, a windmill, a shoe, or a tree may attract attention, but not all the attention will be favorable.

Large window space is desirable for many businesses today, and the plain horizontal lines of modern architecture, along with improvements in the manufacture of glass, make expansive windows possible. A front which is not extreme in style can be so designed as to harmonize with an old building.

The interior. When the outside is so appropriately designed as to get customers in through the door, the inside should not disappoint them. One of the greatest needs inside the building is light. Side walls usually have to be without any windows because of the block formation of places of business, but the front can be planned to let in as much light as possible, and the interior can be arranged to make the most of that light. Clear sparkling glass will let in much sunshine, and well-designed artificial lighting will be worth what it costs and more. If it is your duty to choose between a twenty-five and a sixty-watt globe to replace a burned out one, put in the sixty-watt globe, and brighten up the business.

Business equipment and furnishings. Compact arrangement and design are essentials of all equipment used in a place of business. No superfluous decoration is permissible. As any piece of business equipment or apparatus gets more and more complicated, there are more parts to be adjusted; they take up space and are a visual load as well as a mechanical load. Any isolated gadgets, uncovered pipes, bumps, or hollows should be organized into a simple well-proportioned form and the whole incased in a smooth surfaced jacket from which all dirt collecting corners are eliminated. If your equipment consists of a number of irregular and ugly-looking articles, try to simplify them or jacket them or enclose them in a hood or closet so that the whole achieves a streamlined effect.

225

Office atmosphere. Dark offices with heavy carved furniture, elaborate gilt-framed pictures, and plush curtains are, of course, out-of-date. Light colorful interiors express the spirit of modern business, which aims at streamlined efficiency. But most offices are neither antique and dignified nor fresh and modern; they are just offices. They could be made attractive in a businesslike way. The rectangular shapes of desks, tables, bookcases, and filing cabinets should repeat the horizontal and perpendicular lines of the room and should be so arranged as to emphasize the most important object and to subordinate the others. Curves and diagonal lines should be used sparingly, since the mood of an office is one of stability rather than of excitement. Every object in the office should fill a necessary purpose, and nothing should be allowed to remain unless it can pass this test.

As a beginning worker you will probably not be consulted about the office arrangement, but you can keep every part over which you have control clean and orderly. Whether you are office boy or stenographer, if you use some ingenuity, you may find ways of improving the place. In case the building itself, the entrance, the stairs or elevator, and the corridors are drab and dark, you might find some way of introducing light and color and simple decorations into your reception room. High, dark wood wainscoting absorbs the light. Perhaps you could gain permission to paint it the same light color as the walls. A change as simple as that might impress the whole office force with the need for redesigning the entire place.

Delivery trucks. The delivery truck or car is really a part of the sales force of any business. A nondescript truck with hit-or-miss printing all over it is a poor salesman. Customers unconsciously assume that the goods are of the same quality as the vehicle in which they are delivered. Therefore, a neat trim delivery truck and driver are essential to any business which undertakes deliveries of goods.

Violent colors and extreme designs are out of place on any vehicle, especially a service one. Cool, grayed colors are much better. They imply dignified service and reliable completion of contracts. Dark reds, blues, and greens may be combined with grays, tans, creams, or white in developing a suitable design for the delivery truck.

Conservatism should also control the placing of the firm name or slogan upon the car. It is poor taste to print the name and the business policy of the firm in big bold letters all over the side. If the surface is lacquered in one color, the firm name may be easily read and noticed even though small. The very restraint of the design will attract glances if the proportions of each part are satisfying. The shape of a delivery truck suggests the use of horizontal lines, though vertical ones may be used occasionally to oppose them. Diagonals and curves should be used sparingly, and such curves as are used should be those already established in the design of the car.

Problems and activities. (1) Take a walk up and down several business streets looking for business fronts that embody good and poor designs according to standards presented in this section. (2) Pick out a single business establishment to adopt, just as if you were going to work there. Check it over carefully and list the things which you could do to improve the looks of the place if you were one of its employees. (3) Go through the interiors of several different stores, garages, service stations, or other business establishments, and afterwards make a list of the principal kinds of ugliness you saw that could be corrected without undue time and expense. (4) Observe several concerns which combine business with work, such as restaurants, cleaning establishments, and service stations, and see if you can find ways of covering and streamlining the ugly equipment used in these businesses. (5) Go through the halls of several office buildings just as if you were picking an office in which to set up your business or profession, and decide what features you would like to change in these buildings. (6) Stand on the street corner for ten minutes watching commercial vehicles go by, and make note of the changes you would make in the designs of those vehicles if you owned them.

4. TELLING THE WORLD

Advertising Your Business

Advertising, as you know, has become a business in itself. Since the introduction of radio broadcasting, it makes large use of auditory appeal supplementing the older forms of visual appeal. As an artist interested in the use of form, line, color, and space, you are concerned chiefly with the visual aspects of advertising. One important thing to remember is that nobody deliberately starts out to read your advertising. You have to demand and get attention before you have a chance to convey your message. This is a problem to be solved best by forceful simplicity. No reader allots very much time to reading a single advertisement. Your message must therefore be decisive and short or it will not get over.

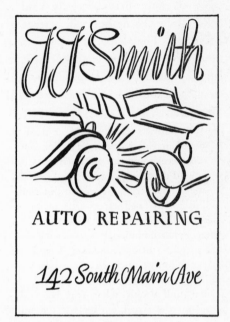

What do these advertisements lack as attention getters?

Billboards. If you put up a big sign by the side of the road, customers see it briefly in passing. It either impresses them favorably or leaves them with a desire to ask the chamber of commerce to have such blots removed from the landscape. Your billboard must be striking if it is to carry weight. Strong contrasts of dark and light and strong contrasts of color are necessary. Such eye-compelling contrasts must be well-designed. Spacing and balance are of great importance. Since the passer-by has time to read very little, words must be few and their lettering must be forceful.

Street signs. Signs over the store front or on doors and windows giving the firm name and the kind of business are not always regarded as advertising, but they are, of course, a part of business publicity. Probably no phase of advertising today so badly needs the services of good designers. Many of our business streets are a nightmare of signs both by day and by night. Each place of business, trying to outdo its neighbor and catch the public eye, adds another sign, larger or brighter in color. The result is confusion and discord but very little real publicity.

When you search on such a street for an office or shop that you want to visit, what signs really catch your eye? Are they the largest ones, those in brightest colors, or those repeated several times in various sizes, colors, and kinds of print? Among all the shouting, screaming signs, does your eye often come to rest on a simple well-designed firm name above the door or on the window?

The sign or signs (and there should not be a half dozen on one store front) giving the name and business should suit the kind of business and also the façade on which they are placed. Contrast in color or value may be used, but it should be remembered that too much use of contrast merely defeats its own ends just as do too many exclamation points. Keep in mind a fundamental principle of design: patterns show up best against plain surfaces. Letters and words form patterns. In order to be seen they need blank space around them. If all the business firms in a block would co-operate in carrying out this principle, they would be amazed at the improvement in publicity for all of them as well as in the looks of the street.

Posters. For posters and cards in the corner of a store, in the window, or in stations and streetcars, decide on the important thing to emphasize and build the design around that. Usually the message must carry for a considerable distance to people who may have poor vision. Color contrast is not so essential as on the large billboard, but value contrast is. Dark is more easily seen against light and light against dark. Striking colors may be used if the theme permits, but subdued colors are more appropriate if the merchandise is delicate. What you have learned in making school posters should be of service in this kind of advertising. Remember that there must be adequate blank space to form a background for the design, and the parts of the design—the print and the decorative symbols—must create a unified whole.

WORK

Newscuts. Magazine and newspaper advertising is a highly specialized problem, all the more so since color has entered the field. If you are faced with the job of planning such advertising, consult authoritative books and persons. There is space here for only a few words of advice. Remember that in the newspaper you have to rely on black, gray, and white instead of color. Your layout must harmonize with the uniform gray of the news page but must have white space surrounding the message in order that the gray and black values will contrast and will focus the eye. If your newscuts are so lacking in dark-and-light contrast that they do not attract readers, you lose money and nobody else gains anything.

Business stationery. The business letterhead is more important than many people realize. Without stopping to analyze our reactions, most of us form rather definite prejudices for or against a business from the kind of stationery it uses. An overpowering mass of uninteresting type and symbols repels anyone with an instinct for balance and proportion. The entire sheet of stationery should be a balanced arrangement of dark lettering against light paper, and the trademark or other insignia should be a unified part of the design as a whole. The letterhead must be planned with the typed letter in mind. Typed or written paragraphs form dark rectangles which should be more or less centered on the page. Light margins frame the letter and help prevent a cluttered or crowded effect. These margins may vary in width but should always be in scale with each other. That is, one margin should not be very narrow and another excessively wide.

The printed matter at the top should be neither too dark and heavy on the page nor too light and delicate, unless the business, for some special reason, requires a dainty effect. All except the very essential information should be eliminated because photographs and excessive amounts of lettering make a top-heavy beginning and ruin the chances of a balanced whole.

Trademarks often form an effective part of a letterhead, particularly if they are well-designed and composed of symbols which really convey the message of the business. You will do well to consult an expert printer regarding the type faces most suitable for the kind of effect you desire.

Problems and activities. (1) Analyze and evaluate the next billboards you see along the highway in terms of proportion, balance, and contrast. (2) Study and compare several business blocks for the general effect of the street signs. Try to determine what kinds of signs really attract the eye and why they do so. Draw up a set of rules about street signs which, if adopted by a merchants' association or chamber of commerce, would improve the streets of your town and also give everyone better publicity. (3) Analyze several streetcar cards or posters used in stores or elsewhere and decide which ones are good and which bad in design. (4) Make a rough sketch of a poster you would develop to tell customers about a super-bargain in one special item, making your own choice of the item. (5) Make a second sketch which you would use to call attention to a very different type of merchandise, and point out how and why it differs from the first. (6) Let each class member bring one or more business letterheads to class for a comparative study and evaluation of their designs. (7) Draft the design of a letter-head you would use if you were opening a small business in ladies' hats or men's furnishings. (8) Bring several newspaper advertisements to class, and evaluate the design of their cuts and lettering.

5. Man to Man

Selling Your Wares

In a sense all workers are salesmen. Each one is offering to the world either things or services, ideas, talents, or skills. If what you have to offer is genuine, you will usually find a demand for it, though the price the world is willing to pay may not be what you desire. Sometimes the value of what you sell and the demand for it can be increased by better salesmanship on your part.

Selling has been variously described as an art and a science. Probably it comes nearer to being a skill, and like all skills it can be learned partly through instruction and partly through practice. There are various ways in which a knowledge of art principles can be helpful. They can guide the salesman in making the best appearance possible and in displaying merchandise. A thorough understanding of design is essential in selling such things as clothes and household goods, because many customers rely on the salesman for advice. Can you tell the difference between real art and pseudo-art in the goods which you offer? Can you win and deserve the confidence of your customer in your advice concerning lines, colors, and textures? Do you practice what you know of the fundamental principles of art when you try to sell your services, your skill, or your ideas?

Personal appearance. Whatever you may be selling, your own appearance is a factor in your success. Pride, gladness at being alive, and desire to serve are wholesome emotions which have a direct effect on your appearance. Pride will cause you to spend a little extra energy on that necessary good grooming. It will compel you to stand with your head erect. It will help you to disregard

Can you radiate efficiency and expertness?

those things that are petty and small and to concentrate on the worthwhile problems in life. Gladness at being alive is a good tonic. It helps you to pull your dragging muscles upward. A desire to serve makes you forget yourself and overcome that awkwardness that grows out of self-consciousness.

Appropriate clothes. The costume for each job is determined by the job to be done. It may be overalls, a business suit, or a soft silk dress. Tailored clothes are not the only correct business dress. If they are really becoming, they are desirable because they give a businesslike and efficient air. Wear less severe lines and textures, however, if you are one of those to whom severity is not becoming. The chapters devoted to dress in an earlier part of this book will help you in planning suitable costumes for business or professional life.

USING ART PRINCIPLES IN THE WORKADAY WORLD

Selling particular kinds of merchandise. The art principles involved in selling are universal, but their applications and illustrations vary according to the kind of merchandise. A few examples may help you in applying your knowledge of art in your own particular field.

If you are selling foods, you want to use art as a means of whetting appetites. The butcher, the grocer, the baker, and the candymaker appeal to the senses in every way possible. Delectable odors are allowed to ooze out into the room or the street. The sense of touch is appealed to by the display of polished clean apples or velvety peaches. Sometimes tempting bits are offered for you to taste, such as a crisp, crunchy cookie or a new kind of pickle. Fruits and vegetables and baked goods are usually attractive in color, and the good salesman often makes use of color in the packing to make each food look its very best.

When food is being sold in a restaurant or hotel, the problems of making the foods attractive and making the environment pleasant are combined. Cheerfulness and spic-and-span cleanliness should rule the place. There should be not the least suspicion of grease or dirt in a single part of the establishment. The kitchen should be as clean as every other spot. Hard textures, such as metals, enamels, highly polished woods, and tightly woven fabrics help to suggest cleanliness and wholesomeness. Crevices, moldings, superfluous decorations, dust catchers, and unnecessary irregularities in the dining room should be eliminated. But in stripping away nonessentials be careful not to create a cold, severe, uninviting room. Highly polished surfaces, metal, and glass may cause a glare which is trying to both eyes and nerves. Wise use of textures and colors can give softness and warmth.

The effect of intimacy may be obtained by establishing each table or group of tables as a unit in the whole scheme. High-backed benches, panels, or low partitions may be used to divide part of a very large room into separate booths which give partial privacy to the diners. If possible, the ceiling and walls should be treated acoustically to soften the noise which is inevitable in a crowded dining room.

When you sell clothing or personal adornments, needless to say, you should know good design in clothing. You should practice the principles in your own attire and should master them so thoroughly that you can be a skillful counselor to customers who depend on you for advice and guidance.

Likewise when you sell home furnishings, it is important to know the principles of design in the home. Indeed, you should go a great deal farther and master finer shades and distinctions of the designer's art than have been presented in this book. Again you must be able to practice those principles in arranging your furniture displays and exhibits, and you need to be a skillful and tactful counselor and teacher of the customers whom you serve.

If you sell personal services instead of concrete merchandise—for instance, if you work in a beauty parlor or barber shop—you will need to specialize in those phases of design which are peculiar to your business. Some of these businesses have grown from very small beginnings to colossal proportions because the operators not only had a deft hand in doing the work but a sense of design by means of which they gave glamour to their customers. If you want to succeed in such a business by simple, straightforward, excellent service, your design should suggest efficiency through white or gray or cream enamel, mirrors, chromium plate, spic-and-span cleanliness, and polish. These, plus strong contrasts with dark or intense colors, create an atmosphere which suggests careful workmanship. If you want to add glamour, then adopt smooth rich textures, subdued tones, close harmonies, sophisticated lines, graceful forms, and the feeling of luxury which is compatible with glamour in service. The feeling of smoothness, pliability, and ease is gained through careful transitions between harsh contrast lines, forms, colors, and textures.

If you are selling automobiles, motorcycles, boats, and world-travel tours, you will have to understand the relation of the visual design of your articles to the purposes which these articles serve in travel. Power-driven vehicles are designed for beauty, speed, safety, and comfort, and you must understand how the lines involved in them are functionally related to the uses and purposes of the articles sold. Your salesroom, show windows, and advertising matter should embody modern principles of design, and you should be able to explain and demonstrate these principles to the customer. To a certain extent, travel is a luxury article, sold to people who can afford to pay well for it. Some of these people want transportation, not only as a means of getting somewhere, but also as a means of expressing their personalities. Business in this field is highly competitive, and a small difference of design may make a big difference of dollars.

Problems and activities. (1) Recall a salesperson who waited on you at the last store where you shopped, and decide what was exceptionally good or not so good about his or her personal appearance as a support for a selling career. (2) Tell the class about some case in which a salesman was very successful in his business because he was a good judge of art and design. (3) Tell the class about an unfortunate example in which the salesman's lack of artistic judgment hindered his success in waiting on customers. (4) Tell the class what kind of selling you hope to do, and get suggestions on what art abilities you should develop for your special work.

Part V
SUMMARY

XI. The Round-up

Summarizing art elements and principles

A round-up is as necessary in a textbook as on a ranch. However well the year's work may have been done in regard to each detail, there is need at the end for a big, general summary. In this way you have the chance to organize for future use all the practical concrete material you have learned in earlier chapters. If you have not mastered the material, this summary will suggest sections in which you need more study.

So far you have been learning how to do many specific things in the field of art. You have studied art in clothing, in the home, in your school, and in business. These are real problems which you must face and solve. In each problem that you have studied and completed you have increased your ability to recognize and use harmonious colors and pleasing shapes. Now it is time to begin thinking about some of the general principles that apply to all fields of art.

In chemistry we find scientists working with elements, such as hydrogen and oxygen. All our foods and articles of everyday use are compounds of these elements. In art we find a similar situation. There are elements which the artist uses: line, form, dark and light, color, and texture. They are called *art elements*.

These art elements are not combined haphazardly, but are used according to general principles which man has discovered. Some of the more important *art principles* are: visual satisfaction, originality, unity, rhythm, balance, harmony, and fitness. In the following section these *art elements* and *art principles* will be discussed separately so that each can be studied carefully. As you read, think how you can apply the information to the real problems of art in daily living.

239

SUMMARY

1. ART ELEMENTS

Line, Form, Dark and Light, Color, and Texture

As we define and explain the principal elements which the artist uses, let us not forget that these elements are always used in combination with one another. No one of them is used by itself.

Line

The outline of an object is one kind of line; it is also called the *contour* or *silhouette*. Another kind of line is the one which gives the direction of an object.

What feeling do you get from horizontal lines?

For example, a man standing up gives a vertical line, a running man gives a diagonal line, and a sleeping man gives a horizontal line. The line feeling in a work of art may be caused by single lines, or by the spine, or central line, of an object or group of objects. The spine, or central line, is that which seems to run through the middle of the object.

Line, consequently, does two things. It gives the boundaries of objects, and

240

it creates a feeling, or mood. In many creations one line direction dominates. This line direction may be vertical, horizontal, or diagonal. The dominating line, or the one that sets the mood, must be more important or stronger than any other line. *Subordinate lines* may directly oppose the main line direction. This means that shorter lines may cut directly across the path of the dominant line in order to stop it from carrying the eye out of the composition.

What is the difference between the effects of verticals and diagonals?

What is the effect of diagonals?

When tall or vertical lines are stressed, we feel a sense of uplift, spirituality, or grandeur, as when we gaze upon a mountain peak reaching into the upper atmosphere, a slender pine growing upward to the light, or a cathedral spire symbolizing man's quest for Heaven and spiritual values. Thus, vertical lines in nature suggest a certain "stable instability," an ambitious striving for perfection, a defiance of gravity.

SUMMARY

Horizontal lines give the feeling of strength, solidity, or repose. Some examples are a person resting in bed, a huge forest giant blown over and resting solidly on the earth, a concrete floor that could not be moved even by an earthquake, or the surface of a body of water that has found its level. These are all in marked contrast with the instability of upright objects or objects in a leaning or falling position. Horizontal lines thus represent equilibrium, or the most stable position which objects can take to counteract gravity or the forces of nature. They are truly lines of security.

Can you distinguish the difference between the effects of diagonal and horizontal lines?

Diagonal lines create a feeling of unrest, action, or vitality, as when a runner leans forward in the course of the race, or when powerful horses stretch forward to pull the heavy load, or when a falling tree leans over in the course of its earthward plunge. Diagonal lines thus create an effect of movement, and set up a tension which can only be relieved by some sort of action or countereffort.

The mood of line is caused by the type of line as well as by its direction. Long, smooth curves are graceful and give a feeling of ease; short, choppy curves are lively. Angles call the eye quickly from point to point and create spirited movement. In contrast, straight lines that recall the upright posture of man give a sense of uplift. Those lines that repeat the horizontals of the horizon give a sense of calmness and peacefulness.

Form

Form means shape, volume, or mass. It may be two-dimensional and flat, like a piece of paper, or three-dimensional and have depth in addition to height and width, like a box. The proportions of forms are important in determining how

What is the emotional effect of curved lines?

people react to works of art, and it will be worth our while to think a little about what makes pleasing forms.

Proportion of forms. Although two-dimensional forms have only height and width, these two measurements should be carefully related to each other. By this we mean that the height and width should be so planned that the form is satisfying in its proportions, or that its height is in pleasing relation to its width. If both height and width are equal, we get a square or a circle. This is called a one-to-one relation. If the height is twice the width, we get a one-to-two relation. This is often uninteresting because the eye can measure it too easily. One-to-three and one-to-four ratios are sometimes thought to be uninteresting for this same reason. More interesting ratios are two-to-three, three-to-five, five-to-seven, and other more complex ones.

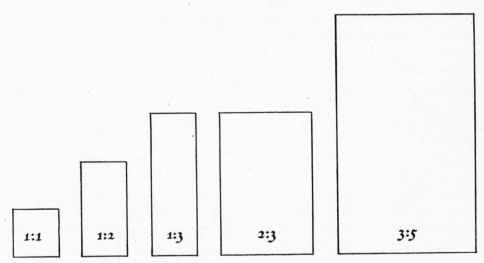

Which ratios of length to width do you find most satisfying?

There are, however, no laws or rules which will always give pleasant proportions. The use to which the form is to be put, the color and the texture, the material from which it is made, and many other factors make each problem in proportion something which must be studied. The best way to learn more about pleasing proportions is to try them for yourself, and see by actual experimentation which you like best.

The significance of form. We respond emotionally to forms, just as we do to lines, because forms make us think of objects we have seen. Tall forms give us an upward-reaching feeling, while low wide ones give a sense of peace and rest. Curved forms seem smooth-flowing. Angular forms may be powerful and poised if the horizontals and perpendiculars are felt; or they may be dynamic if the diagonals are felt more strongly. Straight surfaces are often contrasted with curves, and curves with angles, to give added interest.

In such ways as these, forms carry a message from the artist to you. They reveal the emotional accompaniment of his idea. In some of El Greco's paintings you will see vigorous, flame-like forms which convey the painter's religious feelings. In Grant Wood's paintings, on the other hand, you will find rounded forms and horizontals which express the feeling of the landscape in the mid-western United States. Each artist uses those forms which will tell you how he feels and what he is trying to express. This is true not only of paintings, but of sculpture, architecture and the industrial arts as well. As you walk along the street, notice the buildings you pass. What do their forms express? Are they lively and up-reaching, or solid and stable?

Geometric and irregular forms. Squares, rectangles, triangles, and circles are two-dimensional geometric forms. That is, these are the forms which are made with a ruler and a compass, and are the chief forms studied in geometry. Cubes, spheres, cones, and pyramids are three-dimensional geometric forms. Irregular forms are those which do not fall into any of these geometric patterns, but have shapes such as we find in leaves, stones, and other natural objects. The geometric forms are more easily combined in a design because they are simple and have much in common with one another. The irregular forms are more complicated but may be more interesting.

Dark and Light

Dark and light is another way of describing values of colors. The value of a color means its lightness or darkness. For example, red may be very dark, as maroon, or very light, as pink. The dark value is often referred to as a *low* value and the light as a *high* value.

Dark-and-light pattern. Dark and light often refers to the pattern of darks and lights throughout a work of art. Contrasts of value create interest and attract attention. If you study paintings, you will find that the greatest value contrasts are usually near the center. The same is true in advertisements, or well-arranged display windows. This type of contrast should be reserved for the places on which you intend to center interest, because when very light colors are placed next to very dark ones they attract the eye. More closely related values should be used for subordinate areas where too much attention is not wanted.

Significance of the dark-and-light pattern. Excitement or animation is suggested by strong dark-and-light contrasts, while quiet, rest, and peace are suggested by closely related values. This may be due to the fact that man reacts to change in his surroundings, but may remain inactive when everything around him remains in a stationary condition. For example, a sentry in a fortress tower is called into action when dots appear on the horizon. Similarly,

How can you best use dark and light to get attention?

when you walk along the street, you are likely to turn your head if you see a moving shadow in the edge of your vision.

The painter uses these observations to bring about certain reactions to what he has done. If he wishes to express peace and security, the dark-and-light pattern is harmonious, with few if any sharp changes. If he wishes to give a stimulating or exciting impression, he uses strong contrasts. This is equally true in arranging store windows. Which type of value pattern should you suggest for an automobile display window?

Light values are said to be high in *key*. When an artist works in a high key, he transmits a light feeling as of a bright sunlit day. The effect is joyous and gay.

Dark values are said to be low in *key*. They are somber or quieting like the shadows of evening. These uses of dark and light in order to create mood are significant in all creative work today.

Color hue

Color has three main properties or characteristics: hue, value, and intensity.

Hue is the characteristic we usually associate with the name of the color, as red, orange, yellow, green, blue, violet, or any intermediate step or steps between two of these. Hue is that property of color which is dependent upon the wave length of light. The white light of the sun contains all colors or hues. When sunlight falls on a surface, all, or part, or very little of the light is absorbed. That which is not absorbed is reflected. If all the white light is reflected, the surface naturally appears to be white. If nearly all of the white light is absorbed, the surface appears to be black. If any part is absorbed, the rest is reflected and registers in the eye as a hue.

What, then, happens when we see a piece of cloth as red? This means that all of the light rays of the sun except red are absorbed, and the red rays are reflected to the eye. If we see a green piece of cloth, only the green rays are reflected. In this way we get the full range of color vision.

Hues are not sharply divided from each other but form a continuous range from that with the longest wave length, red, to the shortest, violet. If we start somewhere between these extremes, for example, with green, we pass to yellow-green, yellow, yellow-orange, orange, red-orange, red, red-violet, violet, blue-violet, blue, blue-green, and return to green. Between these color names are many others.

The color circle. Since we may start at any point in the range of colors and return to it, the hues, arranged in their order, are best shown in the form of a circle. This is called the color circle.

Warm and cool colors. Warm colors are those in which red or yellow hues predominate. In other words, they are the colors that have the longest wave lengths, reaching down to the infra-red or heat waves. These are probably called warm because red and yellow through long experience have come to be associated with fire, flame, or glowing "red-hot" objects.

The blues and their neighboring hues are thought of as cool because long experience has led us to associate them with the sky, deep water, ice, and other cool or cold objects which more often reflect these shorter wave lengths of light. The ability to distinguish warm from cool colors is indispensable in creating color combinations. It is more than a mere learning of some new names. It enables you to choose colors that will arouse in others the sensations of warmth or coolness which you wish them to feel.

Contrasting hues. Hues which are opposite each other on the color circle are strongly contrasting. That is, green contrasts with red-violet and red. Yellow contrasts with violet-blue. Red contrasts with green and green-blue. Cool colors contrast with warm ones. When contrasting colors are used, one color should dominate in amount and the other color should be used in smaller areas.

Sequence of hues. Colors in which one hue dominates are closely related. Yellow-green, green-yellow, yellow, yellow-orange, and orange form a sequence of closely related hues because they all contain yellow. Orange, red-orange, red, red-violet, and violet all contain red. They form a sequence as they progress from orange to violet. Violet-blue, blue, blue-green, green, and yellow-green form a sequence of colors in which blue is felt. Such color sequences result in very pleasant, harmonious color schemes.

Color value

Value, sometimes called *brilliance* or *luminosity*, is the second property of color. It means the degree of lightness of the color, in terms of the total amount of light reflected. Value may be measured in terms of candle power, or the "number of light rays per square inch." Any substance which absorbs most of the light that strikes it, and therefore reflects only a small number of light rays, is said to be low in value, whether the rays reflected are of red, green, or any other hue.

Total black is the lowest possible value, because it is the total absorption of all light, or the reflection of no rays at all. But it is possible to have very low values of all the colors if the amount of light reflection is properly controlled. For example, the hue yellow such as in lemons or canaries is ordinarily thought of as a very light or high-value color. However, if yellow is placed in a room where only a very dim light shines on it, the value will drop very low. When the illumination drops to zero by your turning off the electricity completely, the yellow color becomes black, the absence of all light. Just before the illumina-

248

tion reaches the zero point, however, the yellow color has an extremely low value because very little light falls upon it to reflect.

Purple is usually thought of as being lower in value than yellow, or as being a "darker" hue than yellow. Yet a purple spotlight on a white screen may have higher value than a yellow spotlight if it is made by a more powerful electric bulb. In other words, a strong candle power of purple achieves higher value, luminosity, or brilliance, than a weak candle power of yellow does.

We have illustrated value in terms of light; let us now think of it in terms of pigments. A pigment, or dye, absorbs some of the light rays. A red pigment stops the rays of light that would cause the other hues and reflects only the red rays. Thus, when a piece of white cloth is dyed red, its total light-reflecting ability is reduced by the amount of the non-red light that is absorbed by the pigment, and its value is thus decreased.

Value may be illustrated further by an experiment in dyeing three pieces of cloth, one originally white, one gray, and one black. (These differ in their light-reflecting ability, the black absorbing practically all the light.) Dip the three into a red dye for the same amount of time. Red pigment is deposited on each. The three resulting pieces of cloth will differ in value, with the originally white cloth as the highest. (Intensities will differ also, but ignore this for the moment.) The white cloth will reflect all of the light that falls on it, except what the red pigment absorbs, and thus will give off a rather high total "candle-power" of light. The black cloth, if absolutely black, would absorb all the light rays, including the red ones, and thus have zero luminosity. But since absolute blackness is seldom achieved with dyes, and since the red pigment is deposited over the black, some small amount of light will be reflected, and there will be a very dark, or low, value of red.

Contrasting values. Very dark values and very light values, when used together, are contrasting. Contrasting values attract the eye and should be used in large amounts only in areas to which you wish to call attention. When contrasting values are used together, either light values or dark values should dominate in amount.

Closely related values. All dark values are closely related. All medium values are also close in relationship, as are all light values. Unity is promoted by the use of closely related values. Contrasts should be used only in carefully planned areas.

Sequence of values. Values that form a gradual progression from light to dark are in sequence. A sequence of values carries the eye through a composition and aids rhythm.

Color intensity

Intensity, also called *purity* or *saturation*, is the third property of color. (The word *chroma* is sometimes used to express the same idea.) It is the ratio of the amount of the hue to the amount of white light or of light from the opposite side of the color circle that is mixed with it. It is determined by the amount of the pigment, or dye, or light-reflecting substance, on the surface of the material.

For example, dip three pieces of white cloth into a red dye, but for *unequal* lengths of time. The piece that is removed quickly will absorb very little of the dye, and will therefore have a weak intensity, or low saturation, of red. The small amount of red pigment will absorb all but the red rays where it is deposited, but will not shut out all of the white light because it is not deposited in a sufficiently thick layer on the surface of the cloth. This combination of much white light with a little red results in a *tint* of red, called pink. This tint is really a high value of red. The piece of cloth that stays in the dye solution for the longest period of time will become fully saturated. It will receive a very large quantity of the pigment, and will have a strong, rich, or pure intensity of red. If we compare these two pieces of cloth, it is apparent that the richer one is more intense than the other. Another way of saying this is that one has more red in it. It is more fully saturated, and, consequently, more intense.

Neutralizing as a method of reducing intensity. Intensity may be reduced by the addition of color from the opposite side of the color circle. If you mix a full saturation of red pigment with the right amount of its opposite, green, you have a clash in which each pigment absorbs its opposite and there is no chroma, or distinctive hue, left. The result is some value of white light, or gray.

This *graying* of the color is accomplished by *neutralization* of hues, rather than by adding or taking away white light. "Graying" is used in this book to mean reducing the purity or intensity of a hue by the addition of its opposite on the color circle. Doing so is likely to influence the value also, but not in a direct proportion, nor in the same direction for all hues. Thus graying a violet hue by adding its opposite, yellow, may actually raise the value of the original violet, because yellow is a high-value hue.

Relation of value to intensity. The difference between value and intensity is this: value refers to the lightness or darkness of a color while intensity refers to the purity and saturation of a color. A green carpet, for example, may be either light green or dark green. This is value. The carpet may also be a bright, vivid green or a dull, neutral green. This is intensity.

The difference may be illustrated by an experiment which you can perform in class. Select two samples each of white, gray, and black cloth, identical except in value. Pin them together in two bunches so that each bunch has one piece of white, one of gray, and one of black. Dip the first bunch in some dye for just a moment. Dip the second bunch in for a much longer time.

All the pieces of cloth will be of the same hue because they were all dipped in the same color of dye. If the dye is green, all the pieces will be green. In the "brief-exposure" bunch you will have three different values of green. The white will come out a high value, the gray a middle value, and the black a very low value.

Now compare the white in the "brief-exposure" bunch with the white from the bunch which was in the dye longer. The second will be a richer, more saturated color. It will be "more green." This is intensity. (It will also be darker in value, but disregard that for the moment.)

Contrasting intensities. What happens when you put a piece of gray-green (low intensity green) near a piece of brilliant green (high intensity green)? You will probably find that the gray-green looks faded, muddy, or washed-out. This is because of the contrast of intensities. The brightness of the one makes the other seem very weak. Generally, this effect is not pleasant.

Contrasts in intensities are more effective if the hues are also different. For example, the gray-green might be effective near a brilliant red-orange. Can you imagine red-orange lilies in a gray-green vase? In such a combination both colors would look interesting.

Sequence of intensities. Instead of strongly contrasting intensities, it is often more desirable to have related or harmonious intensities of colors. It would be possible to arrange a series of greens from very weak through medium weak, weak, medium strong, strong, and very strong. In other words, we could have a series of colors beginning with one which is almost gray and ending with one which is bright green.

It is often more interesting, though, to change the hue slightly as the intensity is changed. For instance, in a sequence of greens from neutral green to a more pure intense green the hue may also change from a blue-green to green or to yellow-green.

Texture

Texture is the *visual* or *tactile* quality of *surfaces*. The visual aspect of a surface is that which we see, while the tactile aspect of a surface is that which we feel. Opaqueness, translucence, and transparency are visual aspects. Opaque

Texture: How could you improve these bowl and flower combinations?

surfaces are those through which we cannot see. Translucent surfaces we can see into, but not through; transparent material we can see through. Shiny materials contrast with those which are lusterless. Tactile aspects we can feel as well as see. The cold of glass and metal differs tactually from the warmth of wood. Roughness and smoothness are two tactile opposites. These textural or surface differences allow for the greatest opportunities in the design field today.

SUMMARIZING ART ELEMENTS AND PRINCIPLES

The value of tactile awareness in design. People like to feel things. The sensation of touch satisfies their curiosity in regard to surfaces. The touch, or tactile, sensation may be pleasant or unpleasant in varying degrees, and a knowledge of pleasant tactile sensations enables a designer to create articles of lasting pleasantness. Objects which people do not have to feel may be harsh and rough, but chairs, clothes, and other things which must be felt should be pleasant to touch.

Texture as pattern. In contemporary art of all sorts, textures play an important role. In many modern paintings surfaces are purposely made rough to add interest. Today's furniture is upholstered with textiles which you enjoy feeling. Interesting texture has in large part taken the place of applied ornament and design.

Problems and activities. (1) Using objects in the classroom, point out the art elements that have been discussed in this part of the chapter. (2) Contrast the meaning of line, form, and dark and light as they are revealed by an ink bottle; a chair; a door. Clarify your explanations by use of actual objects before your eyes. (3) Using several colored objects, such as books, sweaters, or paints, demonstrate to your classmates your understanding of the difference between hue, value, and intensity of color. (4) Using garments worn by class members, arrange a sequence of hues; of values; of intensities. See how nearly your classmates agree with your idea of what is a good sequence. (5) Make up a graded sequence of textures that would harmonize, and another sequence that would contrast with the first.

2. PRINCIPLES

Developing Your Art Judgment

Whether you are judging a costume, a room arrangement, an exhibit, a poster, a building, a carving, a painting, or a flower arrangement, you combine your ability to feel and your ability to think. In judging your own creative work while it is in process, you do the same thing. You put shapes, lines, and colors together as you feel that they should be; then you analyze them, or think them through, to see if they are chosen and combined in the best way possible. The questions that you ask are these: Is the result *visually satisfying*? Is it *original*? Does it have *unity, rhythm,* and *balance*? Is it *harmonious*, not discordant? Is it *suited* to its purpose? These words are keys to the great art principles that aid you in analyzing any work of art. Each will be considered briefly in the following pages.

Visual satisfaction

Visual satisfaction to most people means beauty. If they find a thing visually satisfying, they say, "That is beautiful." In judging a work of art, however, you would seldom question, "Is that beautiful?" You would be more apt to say, "Does it satisfy me?" If it does, and if you are interested in analysis, you try to determine why it is pleasing. If it is displeasing, you try to discover the cause of your dissatisfaction in order to remedy it. The satisfaction you feel depends on the artist's choice and use of line, form, dark and light, color, and texture.

A design that is visually dissatisfying makes you feel confused or unhappy. For example, an overhead electric-light fixture that is not obviously fastened

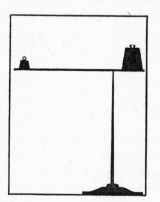

Why are these designs not visually satisfying?

to the ceiling by a sufficiently strong chain or other support will make you want to get out of the room before the expected crash occurs. Similarly, a chair which looks top-heavy or clumsy does not invite you to sit in it. A room in which the furniture is placed at many angles brings about a sense of disorder and discomfort. These are examples of poor design.

A good design, in contrast, makes you feel comfortable. It is easy to look at and easy to understand. It does not puzzle you, nor does it trouble you. You feel that all the parts are well-organized, and that each is in its proper place. You feel that someone has really given the object sufficient thought to make it visually satisfying.

Originality

Originality, or an expression of the artist's personality, is essential to every work of art. Imitation of the work of another artist or of an object in nature is not art production; it is merely an example of skill. An artist is one who creates with art elements. Copying or imitation is never creation. Neither is it creative to work according to another person's dictation. To be original you must learn to handle your medium so that it communicates what you want to express. Creative work is original. The following are some essentials of originality:

Visualization. Before an artist begins to work with his hands, he usually has at least a fairly good idea of what he wants to do. He seldom knows exactly what his painting, or chair, or window display will look like, but he knows in part how he wants it to look. From that point on he works by the trial and success method. If lines or colors seem right, he leaves them. If they do not seem right, he changes them. He works in this way until the project is finished.

Distortion. A painter or sculptor invariably exaggerates or distorts natural objects in his art work. He does this to make his meaning clearer. If a twisted tree at timberline expresses his idea and feeling, he will make it more twisted and wind-whipped than it really is. He may find it necessary to alter the color. The same thing is true of pictures of people. Every great artist exaggerates and distorts what he is painting or carving to make his message clear.

Simplification. Elimination or simplification of unimportant details is as necessary as exaggeration. To make important things most important, and to take out everything which does not contribute to the theme, is the work of the creator.

Style. The artist who is original in his way of working possesses style. He uses his imagination and thinks through the problem in his own way. He lets his feeling and his knowledge guide him, and he expresses himself according to his own feelings. The result is his own particular style. Often the style is so different from that of any of his predecessors that it is not understood by those who see his work. An open mind and a willingness to learn from the artist are necessary to the student. The more unusual the artist's way of seeing, the more he will add to your ability to see, if you come to understand him. Original expression on the part of the artist extends the understanding of all those who are willing to learn from him.

Unity

Unity means the "holding-togetherness" of a work of art. The spectator receives the impression of a single, self-contained work. This unity is dependent upon all subordinate parts being tied to a main area or idea. There must be a single impression communicated by the centering of interest on a dominant theme, area, or object. All other interests should be subordinated but related to the dominant interest. This oneness, or unity, is accomplished by having one main idea or object from which everything else grows.

Unity by means of theme. A single theme may be used as the unifying power of any work of art. It is necessary to decide on the idea to be presented and then use those shapes and colors which will strengthen the main theme by repetition or contrast. Those things which distract are eliminated. This kind of unity was discussed under the problems of arranging an exhibit in a school display case; it applies to all kinds of art.

Unity by means of attention value. In many unified works of art there is a center of interest. When interest is centered, it is the same as saying that your attention has been claimed. You want to look at that part of the object more than at the other parts. There are many ways to build a center of interest. One is to have several lines meet at a point, just as highways meet at an important intersection. A large shape also is likely to attract attenion. An unusual shape will do the same thing. Contrasts of all sorts are valuable in making centers of interest. Contrast of value, hue, or intensity in colors, contrasts of textures, and contrasts of patterned and unpatterned areas are effective.

Unity by means of line direction. Interest centers wherever two lines cross at an acute angle. The eyes also tend to follow any collection of many lines which converge or come together as if they were roads leading to a city. The crossing and converging of lines, then, should be reserved for definite areas that you wish to be most important, and in a lesser degree for subordinate centers of interest.

Can you tell why one of these notebook covers has unity and the other has not?

Unity by choice of forms and sizes. Unusual shapes show up against simple ones. Large shapes also seem more important than small ones. These are by no means unbreakable rules for obtaining dominance and subordination, but are often helpful when used together with convergence of lines and contrast of colors and values.

Unity by means of dark-and-light treatment. Contrasts of dark and light show up against a background of closely related values. Light values against

257

dark attract the eye. Dark values stand out against light values. If these value contrasts are used indiscriminately, the result is disorderly and confusing. If they are used to build up most important areas, and in lesser degrees to accent subordinate centers of interest, a single impression is achieved.

Unity by use of hues. Any work of art should give a dominant color impression. A use of all the colors in the rainbow in equal amounts would result in confusion. A oneness is obtained by an all-pervading feeling of green, green-yellow, yellow, orange, red, violet, blue, or any other color. This color may vary slightly in hue, and may include a considerable range of values and intensities. Centers of interest may be in contrasting hues; but a room, a picture, a stage setting, or a costume should make you remember one color.

Unity by use of intensities. As there should be one color felt throughout a work of art, there should also be one intensity feeling. The general effect may be one of full saturation, medium intensities, or grayedness. Contrasts of intensity are used for centers of interest, but the mood throughout should be vivid and rich, or neutral, or subdued and quiet.

Unity by means of texture. It is difficult to give a verbal definition of unity of texture. Many experiments are being made in order to ascertain satisfying combinations of materials. We do know that there must be a likeness of feeling. That is, soft, smooth, and fine things belong together; harsh, rough, and sturdy things are also compatible. A mixture of incompatible textures gives a broken-up, disjointed feeling.

Unity by use of patterns and plain areas. Centers of interest and subordinate accents are most easily seen when placed against unpatterned or plain areas. Pattern, or variations of lines, forms, tones, and colors, may be used for emphasis, while plain or unbroken areas may be used around them to set them off.

By these various means, attention is called first to the most important part of the work of art. Attention is then drawn in succession to each other part in the order of importance and then back to the center. Emphasis of important parts, with subordination of less important ones, brings about unity.

Rhythm

Rhythm is pulsating movement. It is the kind of movement that is continuous and smooth, yet is not monotonously uniform. The flow of blood in your arteries is rhythmic. It flows continuously, but the rate of flow varies with the pulse beat. Likewise, walking and dancing are rhythmic, because each involves an on-going movement which is interestingly broken by a regularly recurring step or beat. Dancing usually involves a more complex rhythm than walk-

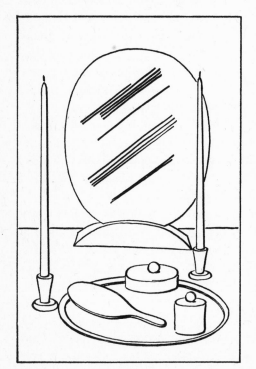

Can you explain what produces good or bad rhythm in these groups of objects?

ing, and may be much more interesting on that account. Rhythm in art is quite comparable to rhythm in walking or dancing. In a work of art rhythm is the movement which is felt by the spectator. The eye is carried through the composition in a series of regular steps by means of lines, forms, values, hues, and intensities.

In order that this measured movement may be regular and smooth, not jerky, the progression is dependent upon rhythmic sequences in sizes and upon rhythmic sequences or gradations in hues, values, and intensities. The direction in which the eye is carried through the composition is dependent not only upon the direction of lines or contours of forms but also upon the progression created by sequences and gradations.

Rhythm through line direction. The eye travels along center lines and edges of forms as it journeys through a composition. The direction of these lines must carry the interest through but always hold it within the work of art. As these lines cross other lines, there may be pulses, or beats, in the rhythm; but the movement is unified because of the on-going character of the lines that determine the movement.

Rhythm through progression of sizes. The eye is carried easily from large to medium to small, or from small to medium to large. For smooth and rhythmic movement there should be a measured change in sizes of forms within the work of art. This carries the eye more easily, just as a progression of strides in dancing makes the process of dancing rhythmic instead of irregular. Irregular transitions in sizes in a work of art might force the eye to "limp" through it.

Rhythm through dark and light. As value contrasts catch the attention, the eye moves from the most striking of these contrasts to less dominant ones in turn. The progression between contrasts is made more easily if there is a regular gradation from the darkest to the lightest values. Strong contrasts come forward, while closely related values recede. Strong tonal contrasts attract the eye to the center of interest, while sequences in value attract it to subordinate interests and back again to the center of interest where it should rest easily. Very irregular gradations of dark and light cause a jerky progression, again comparable to a limp in walking, and are rated as bad rythmic design.

Rhythm through sequence of hues. As you have learned, reds and yellows advance, while colors containing blue recede. Progression from warm colors to cool colors creates a receding movement, and this progression backward will take place with an even or uneven rhythm according to the intervals between steps in terms of distance on the color circle. If transitions from one color to the next in the line of the eye's progress are uneven or irregular, there will be a disconcerting interruption of rhythm as the eye "stumbles" from color to color in its movement through the series.

SUMMARIZING ART ELEMENTS AND PRINCIPLES

Rhythm through sequence of intensities. Fully saturated colors advance, while grayed or weak colors recede. In creating a rhythm through intensities it is always well to change the hue with each change in intensity. In other words, a sequence in intensities is more pleasing if it is also a sequence in closely related hues.

Rhythm through placing of interests. People, animals, flowers, and other objects are interesting because of what we know of them. The arrangement of these interests assists rhythm, as our eyes are attracted to them in the center of interest, or to each of them in turn as they are arranged as subordinate interests.

Rhythm by means of textures. Opaque texture advances, while transparent texture recedes. Polished opaque surfaces advance before unpolished opaque surfaces. Broken surfaces with variations of dark and light by means of shadow or pattern come forward, while smooth unpolished surfaces recede. Movement through an arrangement or composition may be further aided by the use of variation in these textures. Contrast in texture will attract the eye to centers of interest, while sequences in texture will carry the eye through subordinate areas and back to the main center of interest.

Transitions or gradations of texture may be as monotonously uniform as the steps of a person in walking, and thus create a simple texture rhythm. Or they may be varied in some more complex pattern so that the texture rhythm is as interesting as the rhythm of the dance.

As you come to understand rhythm in works of art, you find that there are many different means for directing the eye and the muscular reactions, and that each of the elements (line, color, texture, etc.) can be used to create either simple or complex patterns of rhythmic movement. Furthermore, several such media may be combined to create a symphony of rhythmic movement, each one supporting the others in an effort to get the same effect.

Balance

Balance is desirable in works of art because a sensation of unbalance is physically and mentally distressing to the spectator. This is probably due to the fact that we have all had the experience of falling as a result of losing our

SUMMARY

balance. Unbalance in art communicates to us the sensation of losing our own balance. In order to keep our equilibrium we know that we must balance a heavy weight squarely in the center, must carry equal weights on both sides, or must counteract a heavy weight on one side by lighter weights at a greater distance on the other, or by compensating tensions of other kinds. Weights and tensions then, are the stuff by which balance is maintained.

Balance by means of weights. A physical sensation of lightness is communicated by colors which are light in value, or pale and weak in intensity. Small objects seem lighter than large ones if the values and intensities are equal. The reverse of this is also true. Dark areas seem to be heavy. Very dark areas seem heavier than medium ones. Pure, strong colors, especially those in the dark range, communicate the sensation of greater heaviness than medium strong, weak, or grayed hues. Large objects seem heavier than small ones of the same values and intensities. These weights must be balanced in any work of art so that equilibrium is established.

Balance of tensions. Tensions mean pulls or strains, as opposed to dead weight. A rope which pulls you creates a tension, whereas a stone in your hand is a dead weight. These tensions may be caused by lines or forms. Tensions are set up by the feeling of pull or strain between weights. In a painting, balance may also be established from front to back as large objects, dark values, warm colors, and strong colors pull forward, while small objects, light values, cool and grayed colors push into the distance.

Balance of equal weights. If two identical candlesticks are placed equidistant from a center line on a mantel, that balance is symmetrical. Symmetry, or likeness of two sides, has been created. If a plate or tray is added in the center, the balance is still symmetrical, because a half of the plate belongs to each side of the arrangement. A placing of equal weights on two sides of a center is the easiest type of balance to create and to understand. For this reason symmetrical balance is often less interesting than arrangements that are a little more subtle.

Balance of unequal weights. "Asymmetrical" or "occult" balance means the balancing of unequal weights. In creating this type of equilibrium we think of a seesaw, or teeter-totter, with a larger person on one end than on the other.

Large forms, strong dark-and-light contrast, and large areas of saturated color should be moved in toward the center of the seesaw. Small forms, medium dark-and-light contrasts, smaller areas of saturated color, or larger areas of grayed color may balance their more dominating associates if moved farther away from the center of the seesaw. This type of balance must be created by

Which of these patterns is balanced symmetrically? Which asymmetrically? Which not at all?

"feel," or a sensitivity to visual weights. These weights must be arranged and rearranged until the artist feels that his work is in equilibrium.

Harmony

Harmony is created by an orderly or logical arrangement of the elements of a work of art. A lack of harmony is more noticeable than its presence, because without harmony there is confusion, which is always distressingly noticeable. Harmony and unity have much in common, since they are dependent upon a close relationship of lines, shapes, and sizes of forms, values, hues, intensities, and textures. Harmony is the "belonging-togetherness" of art elements. Most works of art must also have some contrast to give the necessary verve and sparkle.

Line and shape harmony. A repetition of lines and shapes creates harmony. Lines which repeat each other give a feeling of order, as does also a similarity

What produces or spoils harmony in each of these combinations?

of shapes. This similarity should not be carried to the point of monotony, but variety should be used only as a means of centering attention upon closely related harmonies.

Size harmony. Size harmony is brought about by a measured progression of sizes rather than by likeness in sizes, for like sizes are deadly monotonous. In a measured progression of sizes the change should be one of gradual growth from small to large. This way of creating size harmony also produces rhythm.

SUMMARIZING ART ELEMENTS AND PRINCIPLES

Value harmony. Closely related values, or those of about the same darkness or lightness, are harmonious. The largest areas of a work of art should be closely related in value. Strong contrasts of value, as you have learned, should be reserved for dominant and subordinate centers of interest.

Color harmony. In any color, except white, black, and neutral gray, one hue dominates. If these colors are neutral or grayed, they easily harmonize. As they become increasingly strong in intensity or saturation, they are more difficult to combine. The three hues which are most easily felt in any color are blue, red, and yellow.

A color harmony is most easily created by: (1) choosing cool or bluish colors, (2) choosing warm colors in which yellow is felt, or (3) choosing warm colors in the red range. This does not mean that these colors are blue, yellow, or red, but only that the color vibrations of blue, yellow, or red are visibly present. If the color harmony created throughout a work of art is cool, it may be offset by dominant and subordinate centers of interest of contrasting warm colors. If the color harmony is warm, emphasis on interest areas may be obtained by contrasting cool colors. The unity of the work of art is dependent upon the balance of the warm and cool, or the pure and grayed areas, respectively.

Harmony of textures. Similarity of textures brings about harmony. Brick, oak, and heavy linen have much in common. Fine serge and smooth linen go well together. Silver and polished glass are satisfying companions. Textures should be tested together for similarity in feeling before they are combined. Delicacy and preciousness go with each other but not with coarseness and sturdiness. There should be enough variation in textures to create a contrast of surfaces and prevent a monotonous similarity, but they should communicate a feeling of belonging together.

Fitness

Fitness means suitability. A silk dress trimmed with lace is not beautiful on a golf course, because it is not suitable to the requirements of the sport. A delicate antique chair in an athlete's lounging room is not suitable. Any work of art in order to be enjoyed should be suitable or appropriate in a given situation for a particular need. The material used in it must be suited to the purpose.

SUMMARY

Integrity in the choice and use of materials is also necessary in the creation of a work of art. Taking it for granted that art is not something to be stored in museums, but rather something with which to be surrounded in our daily lives, we say that art should help us to live more easily and more pleasantly. If art is to be manifest in a home, that home must be organically sound; that is, planned for living, not just "surface-pretty." An object of use should have its form suited to its function. It should work more smoothly because of its better

When is an article
properly fitted for its
function?

chosen forms and materials. This implies the elimination of those parts which do not work toward the betterment of the whole. By the same token, simplicity rather than ornateness usually characterizes the work of art.

Problems and activities. (1) Study one wall of your classroom, considering the blackboard or window space as a design, and decide whether it gives you visual satisfaction. Compare your decision with those of others, and in doing so make clear your understanding of the term "visual satisfaction." (2) Pick up six or eight different books, and rate them as to originality of cover designs or of title pages. Make a similar ranking of other objects as to originality until you and your classmates agree on what constitutes true originality of design. Is originality effective if other art principles are violated? (3) Pick out the factors by which unity is achieved in each of several different classroom objects. (4) Analyze several neckties as to the methods by which rhythm was achieved by their designers. (5) Using dresses or fashion plates for demonstration, point out specific ways by which each of the main devices for achieving balance was employed. Do the same for architectural features of the school or neighborhood. (6) Pick out as many examples of good harmony as you can within the four walls of your classroom, and explain how each was achieved. Do the same for several cases of lack of harmony. (7) Report several cases from your experience which would illustrate examples of lack of fitness, as defined here. (8) As a final summary of all your thinking in this course, write one hundred words on the subject, "Form Follows Function."

Index

Accessories for costumes, 33-37
Advertising, 227-231
Appearance of your home, 94-99
Appropriateness of costume, 19-21
Arranging flowers and art objects, 172-177
Art elements, 240-253
Articles of costume, specific, 22-39
Art, in education, 181-211; in industry, 215-235
Art objects, 172-177
Art principles, 253-267

Balance, 261-263; in costume design, 25-26
Banquets and parties at school, 189-193
Bathroom design, 112-115
Bedroom, 106-108
Body shape, 40-61
Bowls, vases, and flowers, 172-177
Breakfast room, 126-129
Buildings and school grounds, 193-198
Business building fronts, 223-227
Business promotion and advertising, 227-231

Camouflaging, facial defects, 55-59; figure defects, 51-55
Carnivals and school parties, 189-193
Carpets, 156-159
Classrooms, 198-204
Cleanliness of costume, 14-17
Color harmony for costumes, 62-85
Color hue, 247-248
Color intensity, 250-252
Color, of eyes, 70-71; of hair, 67-69

Color scheme, total, 64-67
Color value, 248-250
Commercial art, 215-235
Cool color types, 77-79
"Copycat" home design, 99-104
Costume accessories, 33-37
Costume as a whole, 9-21
Curtains and draperies, 164-167

Daily written work, 204-211
Dark and light, 245-246
Defects of figure, 51-55
Design, of manufactured goods, 216-219; of suit or dress, 23-27; of your home as a whole, 94-99
Dining room, 122-126
Display of merchandise, 219-223
Dramatics, 185-189
Draperies, 164-167
Dress or suit design, 23-27

Elements of art, 239-267
Ensemble, 9-21
Entertainments and parties at school, 189-193
Eye color, 70-71

Face painting, 37-39
Facial defects, 55-59
Fat persons, 41-46
Figure defects, 51-55
Fitness, 265-267
Floor coverings, 156-159

Florid complexion, 73-74
Flowers, 172-177
Food and parties at school, 189-193
Footwear, 27-29
Form, 243-245
Form and figure of body, 40-61
Fronts of business buildings, 223-227
Frozen North color types, 77-79
Functional design of merchandise, 216-219
Functional home design, 99-104
Furnishing the home, 144-177
Furniture, choosing and placing, 159-164;
    modern, 153-156; period, 144-153

Gray-haired persons, 83-85
Grounds and school buildings, 193-198
Guest room, 109-112

Hair color, 67-69
Halls, 141-142
Halls and school buildings, 193-198
Hanging pictures, 167-172
Hangings, 164-167
Harmony, 263-265; of costume colors, 62-85;
    of costume parts, 17-19
Hats, 29-33
Heavy persons, 41-46
Height, minimizing, 48-51
Home furnishings, 144-177
Homestead as a whole, 89-104
Hue, 247-248

Inappropriate costume, 19-21
Industrial art, 215-235
Intensity of color, 250-252
Intermediate color types, 82-83

Kitchen, 129-132

Laboratories and classrooms, 198-204
Landscaping your home, 94-99
Learning techniques in art, 1-5
Light and dark, 245-246

Line, 240-243
Lipstick and rouge, 37-39
Living room, 115-122

Maintenance of clothes, 14-17
Make-up, 37-39
Manuscript and notebooks, 204-211
Men's hats, 29-33
Merchandise design, 216-219
Merchandise display, 219-223
Mirrors, 164-167
Mixed color types, 82-83
Modern furniture, 153-156

Nail polish, 37-39
Neatness and cleanliness, 14-17
Neighborhood for your home, 91-94
Normal figure, costume for, 59-61
Normal skin color, 74-75
Notebooks and manuscript, 204-211

Originality, 255-256
Ornamental art objects, 172-177
Overweight persons, 41-46

Papers and written assignments, 204-211
Patterned accessories, 33-37
Perfect figure, costume for, 59-61
Period furniture, 144-153
Personality and dress, 10-14
Personality in salesmanship, 231-235
Pictures, 167-172
Playroom, 135-138
Plays and dramatics, 185-189
Poster making, 181-184
Principles of art, 239-267
Puppet shows, 185-189

Recreation room, 135-138
Red complexion, 73-74
Rhythm, 258-261
Rooms of the house, 105-143
Rouge and lipstick, 37-39

Rugs, 156-159
Rumpus room, 135-138

Sallow complexion, 71-73
Satisfaction, visual, 254-255
School art, 181-211
School, buildings and grounds, 193-198; par-
    ties, 189-193; posters, 181-184; written
    work, 204-211
Selling, 231-235
Setting for your home, 94-99
Shape and size of body, 40-61
Shoes, 27-29
Short persons, 48-51
Showing merchandise for sale, 219-223
Silver-haired persons, 83-85
Site for your home, 91-94
Size and shape of body, 40-61
Slender persons, 46-48
Southern Sun complexions, 79-82
Specific articles of clothing, 22-39
Specific rooms in the house, 105-143
Stage and theatre design, 185-189
Storage rooms, 142-143
Store fronts, 223-227
Stout persons, 41-46
Study methods in art, 1-5
Study room design, 132-135
Suitability of costume, 19-21
Suit or dress design, 23-27

Summary, 239-267
239-267
Sun room,
Sun-tanned

Tall persons, 4
Tanned skin, 7
Techniques for
Texture, 252-253
Theatrical art, 185-
Thin persons, 46-48
Total color scheme,
Total costume, 9-21

Underweight persons, 4
Unity, 256-258
Upkeep of clothes, 14-17

Value of colors, 248-250
Vases and bowls, 172-177
Visual satisfaction, 254-255
Vocational art, 215-235

Warm color types, 79-82
White-haired persons, 83-85
Window draperies, 164-167
Women's hats, 29-33
Work rooms, 142-143
Written work, 204-211

Yellow complexion, 71-73